MARITIME TRADERS IN
THE ANCIENT GREEK WORLD

This is the first full work since Hasebroek's *Trade and Politics in the Ancient World* to deal directly with the place of maritime traders in ancient Greece. Its main assumption is that traders' juridical, economic, political, and unofficial standing can only be viewed correctly through the lens of the polis framework. It argues that those engaging in interregional trade with classical Athens were mainly poor and foreign (hence politically inert at Athens). Moreover, Athens, as well as other classical Greek poleis, resorted to limited measures, well short of war or other modes of economic imperialism, to attract them. However, at least in the minds of individual Athenians, considerations of traders' indispensability to Athens displaced what otherwise would have been low estimations of their social status.

C. M. REED is William States Lee Professor of History at Queens College, Charlotte, North Carolina.

MARITIME TRADERS IN THE ANCIENT GREEK WORLD

C. M. REED

William S. Lee Professor of History
Queens College,
Charlotte, North Carolina

CAMBRIDGE
UNIVERSITY PRESS

PUBLISHED BY THE PRESS SYNDICATE OF THE UNIVERSITY OF CAMBRIDGE
The Pitt Building, Trumpington Street, Cambridge, United Kingdom

CAMBRIDGE UNIVERSITY PRESS
The Edinburgh Building, Cambridge, CB2 2RU, UK
40 West 20th Street, New York, NY 10011–4211, USA
477 Williamstown Road, Port Melbourne, VIC 3207, Australia
Ruiz de Alarcón 13, 28014 Madrid, Spain
Dock House, The Waterfront, Cape Town 8001, South Africa

http://www.cambridge.org

First published 2003
Reprinted 2004

Printed in the United Kingdom at the University Press, Cambridge

Typeface Adobe Garamond 11/12.5 pt.   *System* LATEX 2ε   [TB]

A catalogue record for this book is available from the British Library

ISBN 0 521 26848 6 hardback

To Jean

Contents

Acknowledgments

For their tutelage in the use of ancient evidence I am much indebted to Alec McGeachy at Davidson College, Minor Markle at the University of Virginia, and at Oxford John Davies and above all the late Geoffrey de Ste. Croix.

Readers know de Ste. Croix as a spirited, controversial, left-of-center Greek historian who produced empirical and theoretical studies of great scope and distinction. He was also the ideal thesis advisor – unfailingly kind, patient, and indefatigable. So extensive was his influence on the present work that I am tempted to list him as a partner in it, if that did not also implicate him in subsequent mistakes of fact or interpretation on my part. My wife and I are especially grateful to him and his wife Margaret for their hospitality while we were in England.

This work also profited greatly from a year's fellowship at the Center for Hellenic Studies and a later summer there. I am most grateful to Deborah Boedeker and Kurt Raaflaub for their hospitality on subsequent visits.

Michel Austin, Paul Cartledge, John Davies, and David Harvey offered very helpful detailed advice on the contents in their thesis form. My thanks to David as well for recently mentioning another maritime trader, Theogenes, who in Eupolis' *Demos* is said to own more than one merchant vessel (*PCG* F 99.5–70); the reference arrived too late to be included in the text. Pauline Hire, Peter Krentz, Michael Sharp, Kurt Raaflaub, and Linda Woodward saved me from many errors by their comments on the book's later drafts.

For various kindness in connection with this work I also thank my daughter Laura Reed and friends Bob Knott, Charles McAllister, Fred Stanback, and Ran Turner.

This book is dedicated to my wife, without whose love and labor it never would have been finished.

Abbreviations

ANCIENT AUTHORS

The names and works of ancient authors are abbreviated as in the third edition of the *Oxford Classical Dictionary* (hereafter *OCD*[3]) with the following exceptions:

Andok.	Andokides
D.	Demosthenes
Isok.	Isokrates
Lykourg.	Lykourgos
X.	Xenophon

Where hellenized Greek names might be unrecognizable to non-specialists (Kypros for Cyprus) or monstrous (Peiraieus for Piraeus), I use the more familiar form.

MODERN WORKS

For periodicals I use the abbreviations in *L'Année Philologique*. The following modern works are abbreviated.

Arnaoutoglou	I. Arnaoutoglou, ed. and trans., *Ancient Greek Laws: A Sourcebook* (London and New York 1998)
Fornara	C. W. Fornara, ed. and trans. *Archaic Times to the End of the Peloponnesian War: Translated Documents of Greece and Rome* i (Cambridge 1977)
Harding	P. Harding, ed. and trans., *From the End of the Peloponnesian War to the Battle of Ipsus: Translated Documents of Greece and Rome* ii (Cambridge 1985)
Hornblower and Greenstock	S. Hornblower and M. C. Greenstock, eds. and trans., *The Athenian Empire*, 3rd ed. (London 1983)

Michel	C. Michel, *Recueil d'inscriptions grecques* (Paris 1900–27)
ML	R. Meiggs and D. Lewis, *A Selection of Greek Historical Inscriptions to the End of the Fifth Century B.C.*, rev. ed. (Oxford 1988)
Pleket	H. W. Pleket, ed., *Epigraphica II: Texts on the Social History of the Greek World* (Leiden 1969)
Pouilloux	J. Pouilloux, ed. and trans., *Choix d'inscriptions grecques: Textes, traductions, et notes* (Paris 1960)
Rhodes	P. J. Rhodes, ed. and trans., *Greek Historical Inscriptions 359–323 B.C.*, 2nd ed. (London 1986)
Schwenk	C. J. Schwenk, *Athens in the Age of Alexander: The Dated Laws & Decrees of the 'Lykourgan Era' 338–322 B.C.* (Chicago 1985)
Tod	M. N. Tod, *Historical Inscriptions* ii (Oxford 1948)

References to Greek terms

Summary definitions in English are followed by references to fuller ones other than those of LSJ.

asylia: Freedom from seizure of one's goods (*OCD*³ 199)
ateleia: Immunity from public burdens (Harding 178)
dikai emporikai: Law cases involving maritime traders (Cartledge *et al.* [1990: 223–4])
eisphora: Special tax on property (Cartledge *et al.* [1990: 223], Harding 179, *OCD*³ 514, J. A. C. T. [1984: 364]
emporion: Trading place (*OCD*³ 524)
enktesis: Privilege of possession of land, granted to a non-citizen (Cartledge *et al.* [1990: 224], Harding 180, *OCD*³ 525)
euergesia: Public benefaction (s.v. "euergetism" *OCD*³ 566)
ges enktesis: s.v *enktesis* above
metoikos: Resident non-citizen (Cartledge *et al.* [1990: 231], Harding 181, *OCD*³ 969, J. A. C. T. [1984: 367])
metoikon: Annual metic tax (same references as above item *metoikos*)
nautodikai: Athenian overseers of trials involving sea travelers (*OCD*³ 1029–30)
polemarchos, polemarkhos: Athenian overseer of trials of certain foreigners (Cartledge *et al.* [1990: s. v. *arkhon* 217–18], Harding 181–2, *OCD*³ 1203, J. A. C. T. [1984: s.v. *arkhon* 362)
proxenos: Citizen appointed in his own polis to look after affairs of another polis (Harding 182, *OCD*³ 1268, J. A. C. T. [1984: 370])
proxenia: The privilege of being a *proxenos* (same references as above item *proxenos*)
sitophylakes: Athenian overseers of grain sales (*OCD*³ 1414)
xenos, (pl.) *xenoi*: Foreigner(s) (Cartledge *et al.* [1990: 240], J. A. C. T [1984: 373])

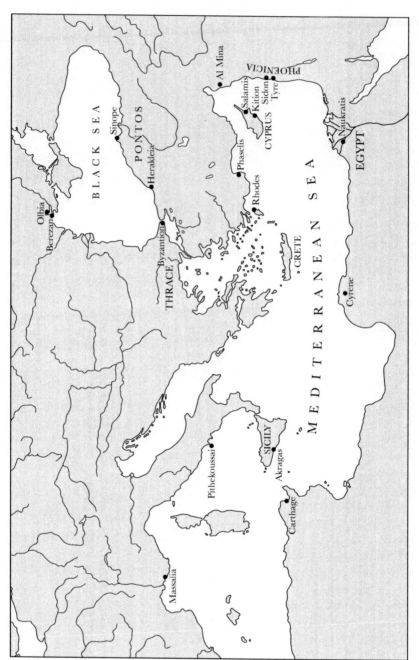

Map 1

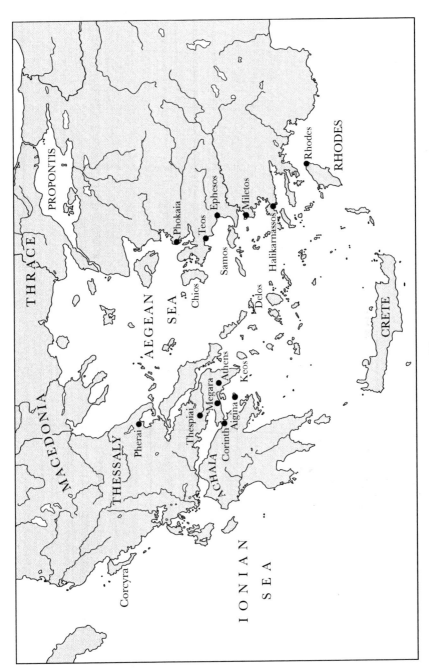

Map 2

Introduction

The law respecting sufficiency of evidence ought to be the same for ancient times as for modern ... [yet] our stock of information respecting the ancient world still remains lamentably inadequate to the demands of an enlightened curiosity. We possess only what has drifted ashore from the wreck of a stranded vessel... The question of credibility is perpetually obtruding itself... [with the result that] expressions of qualified and hesitating affirmation are repeated until the reader is sickened.   Grote (1888: v–vi)

For the past decade I have worked at an American private liberal arts college whose small size obliges faculty to teach outside their specialties. Until recently, due partly to the press of administrative duties, I taught my specialty (ancient Greek history) only once every two years, yet as the resident economic historian I teach the "History of Capitalism" to M.B.A. candidates every semester, either in the evenings or on the weekends. Then in 1993, when no replacement could be found immediately for a departed social theory instructor, I volunteered to fill in and have been teaching it annually ever since.

One possible effect of teaching such different subjects outside one's own specialty is that in each one manages to learn just enough to be dangerous, yet in fact their effect on my view of the present subject has been chastening in two important respects.

First, teaching the History of Capitalism course reminds me constantly of how *very little* evidence there is for the place of maritime traders in the ancient world.[1] Imagine the mass of documents Alfred Chandler, the founder of the new subject of business (as distinct from economic) history, ploughed through to write his path-breaking books on the rise

---

[1] Cartledge (1998: 7–8) repeats this point, made as well by Grote in the opening quotation of this Introduction.

of the modern corporation and its managers.[2] Nor do we lack for a trove of evidence on merchants from the pre-modern era. Consider the large body of evidence unearthed by S. D. Goitein on the Cairo Geniza community of Jewish maritime traders in the tenth through the thirteenth centuries A.D., from which emerged his masterful six-volume account, followed by another devoted to a translation of the merchants' correspondence.[3]

Compare that with what we know of maritime traders in ancient Greece. The surviving evidence is not only meager but also markedly unrepresentative.[4] Most of our information comes from a series of forensic speeches delivered in fourth-century Athens, itself so singular among classical Greek poleis. Beginning there and working backwards, one must be careful not to generalize from Athens to elsewhere. Already by the fifth century the evidence runs out, leaving the historian at sea with his traders. I hope the failure to say anything new or bold about the archaic period will be attributed to a reluctance to generalize unduly from the few flawed bits of evidence rather than from a lack of imagination.

Teaching modern social theory has been chastening in another respect. Above all it has revealed the perils of misusing "ideal type" concepts. Ideal type constructs such as "administered trade" or "consumer city" play a vital role as components of new conceptual "maps" that, imposed on old terrain, transform its topography.[5] But when employed in questions aimed at eliciting empirically testable responses, ideal type concepts distort by implying uniformities or differences that do not exist. Was the "administered trade" of the mercantilist-minded early modern French state anything like the trade "administered" by classical Athens as described in Chapter 5 below?

---

[2] His principal books are *Strategy and Structure: Chapters in the History of the Industrial Enterprise* (1962); *The Visible Hand: The Managerial Revolution in American Business* (1977), which received a Pulitzer Prize; *Scale and Scope: The Dynamics of Industrial Capitalism* (1990). Chandler's work represents a crucial intellectual benchmark ancient economic historians should be more familiar with, for reasons given in the Conclusion. For a survey of his career and a complete bibliography of his publications to 1987, see McGraw (1988: 1–21 and 505–17).

[3] Goitein (1968–93). The first two volumes (on *Economic Foundations* and *Community*) are most relevant for the study of these merchants' activity and place in society. See also Goitein (1973).

[4] For example I can locate no mention of *any* Rhodian *emporos* or *nauklēros*, unnamed or named, for the classical period. On Rhodes as a center of trading activity in the pre-hellenistic fourth century, see further Ch. 3 and the references in nn.27–8 of Ch. 3.

[5] Max Weber employed ideal type concepts to rewrite the conceptual map of Greco-Roman socioeconomic life, although most ancient historians took little notice for decades. It in no way slights Moses Finley's achievement to say that he spent much of his career transforming into full-scale studies Weber's gnomic utterances in (1976: 727–814 = 1212–1372 in the Roth-Wittich two-volume translation [Berkeley 1978]).

Clearly not. *Must* ancient Rome be either a "consumer" or a "producer" city?[6]

I can recall a time when practitioners of ancient Greco-Roman history never realized that their historical "cameras" even *contained* a "lens," so that "the evidence spoke for itself." Now, as if to atone for such an antediluvian point of view, some ancient Greek specialists devote much effort to lens-polishing rather than to looking *through* the lens at the historical reality beyond.[7] To do the latter well we obviously cannot fall back on the "common sense" invoked by vulgar empiricists of an earlier era; in order to achieve empirical "bite," our principal questions[8] must employ adequate concepts at a level of generality somewhat lower than that of the ideal type variety, concepts that do justice to the complexities of whatever historical issue we study.

The principal question of this study: What was the place, in the states they came from but mainly in the poleis they traded with, of those who engaged in inter-regional exchanges of goods with the poleis of classical and archaic Greece? Chapters 1–6 are devoted to the classical period; Chapter 7, to the archaic. Chapters 1 and 2 ask who maritime traders were, what they carried, and how important was long-range commerce in comparison with other modes of exchange. Chapters 3–6, the heart of the book, ask about traders' juridical place (citizens or non-citizens in the poleis with which they traded); their level of wealth relative to others; how they were officially dealt with in the poleis with which they traded; and, finally, their "social status" and its role in unofficial, individual Athenian evaluations. Chapter 7 inquires into the proportions of various modes of archaic exchange and the personnel involved. The Conclusion is an over-brief attempt to ask why the merchant's place in classical Greece differs so much from the place of his various counterparts in contemporary America.

This is not a novel, so its end can be revealed at the outset. I argue that those trading at classical Athens were mainly poor and foreign (hence politically inert), and that Greek poleis resorted to persistent yet limited measures, well short of war and lesser varieties of economic imperialism, to attract them; I argue, finally, that, in the minds of individual Athenians

---

[6] See, e.g., Parkins (1997); Whittaker (1990: 110–18). See also Whittaker (1995), Shipton (1997: 397–400), and the later references in n.7.

[7] E.g., von Reden (1995a). She multiplies distinctions beyond my comprehension. On the other hand my understanding of the relevant theoretical issues was enhanced by briefer expositions directly related to the topic of this book. I forego excellent older examples and recommend only the best of the recent lot, in order of appearance: Hopkins (1983), Morris (1994), Meikle (1995), Cartledge (1998), Davies (1998), and Morris (1999).

[8] On the neglected role of questions in intellectual inquiry of all sorts, see Collingwood (1939: 29–43).

at least, considerations of traders' indispensability to their city's welfare displaced what otherwise would have been low estimations of their social status.

On the subject of traders and trade in the archaic period, I merely refine what I wrote earlier[9] and update the bibliography. The brief Conclusion expands to the broadest possible perspective, charting the most crucial stages in the remarkable transformation in the place of merchants from ancient Greece to the present.

Given the principal question asked, my answer is "substantivist" to the core.[10] But I feel no obligation to defend that perspective with the theoretical luxuriance of a Sitta von Reden[11] or the fervor of a Paul Millett or Wesley Thompson.[12] The arguments herein in fact stand to be judged in light of important empirical studies offered by those – such as Edward Cohen and Thomas Figueira – whose non-substantivist perspective generated different questions on related topics.[13]

The rest of this Introduction is devoted to points of procedure and organization. *All* Greek terms and passages in this volume are translated into English, but in reproducing the original Greek I have resorted to two scripts – either the Greek transliterated into English or the ancient Greek, depending on the nature of the passage. When Greekless readers encounter transliterated Greek that is not preceded or followed by a translation, they should consult the sections at the front of this book entitled "Abbreviations" and "References to Greek Terms." If a Greek passage includes variations on the Greek terms defined in the aforementioned section or in the text, I use transliterated Greek there as well, on the principle that, in the same way children learn new words, the Greekless reader profits from recognizing the letters of a word he or she imperfectly comprehends. For all other Greek terms I use ancient Greek script, accompanied by an English translation. I apologize to purists for such an awkward compromise but am committed to accommodating the increasing number of Greekless students who opt for

---

[9] Reed (1984).

[10] Cartledge (1998: 6) on the substantivist-formalist distinction: "For the formalists, the ancient economy was a functionally segregated and independently instituted sphere of activity with its own profit-maximizing, want-satisfying logic and rationality, less 'developed' no doubt than any modern economy but nevertheless recognizably similar in kind. Substantivists, on the other hand, hold that the ancient economy was not merely less developed but socially embedded and politically overdetermined and so – by the standards of neoclassical economics – conspicuously conventional, irrational and status-ridden." See also Morris (1994: 352–5 and 1999: xii–xiii); Davies (1998: 233 and 236 n.20); and Cartledge (1998: 6–7).

[11] See n.7 above.

[12] Millett (esp. 15–18, 163–6, 312 ["La lutte continue."]); Thompson (1978 and 1982).

[13] Cohen (1992), as well as Cohen (1993); Figueira (1998).

upper-level courses in ancient Greek history, especially given the increased interest in socio-economic topics.

I treat 323 B.C. as the terminal date neither because of political changes nor because of any subsequent transformation in the place of traders, but rather because the nature of our evidence changes drastically. Chapter 7 on the archaic period is of necessity speculative, but there and elsewhere I have not felt obliged to mention all the speculations of others. A mainly destructive treatment, intent on cataloguing the follies that have plagued studies of traders and trade over the past century, would have been more than twice as long as this work.

Finally, the reader should be alerted to five other features. First, the Catalogue (Appendix 4) is a prosopographical warehouse of particulars about traders in the classical period; it excludes groups of *emporoi* about whom little or nothing is known individually. Second, neither the Catalogue nor Appendix 2 on traders' states of origin pretends to be representative. Third, anxious to avoid the charge of "flawed cliometrics,"[14] I never offer various tabulations from the Catalogue as conclusive; they always are provided in tandem with other considerations. Fourth, slave, fleet, and army traders as well as trade are discussed at 20–5 below and included in Appendix 1; otherwise they are excluded from Chapters 1–6 and the Catalogue. Fifth, Chapter 7 discusses the archaic references to all the above categories – individuals about whom something is known, groups of traders, and slave/fleet/army traders.

[14] So named by Cohen (1992: 170–83); see also Cohen (1990b).

CHAPTER I

Coming to terms

INTRODUCTION

This chapter addresses several questions. In the Greek world of the classical period what sorts of people engaged in inter-regional trade? Was there a clear division of labor, whereby some earned most of their living from long-distance trade and still others engaged in it as a sideline activity?

I argue that in the classical period there was a clear division of labor. One group, composed of those called *emporoi* and *nauklēroi*, derived most of their livelihood from inter-regional trade. (These two words are commonly and somewhat misleadingly rendered in English as "traders" and "shipowners"; in his 1935 article[1] Finley [333–6] rightly pointed out that *nauklēroi* may have regularly engaged in *emporia* themselves.) The second group consists of various sorts of people who engaged in *emporia* from time to time but who did not rely on it for most of their livelihood.

That in brief is the general picture. Can we be more specific? Yes and no. On the one hand we can mention other traits that usually seem to characterize those called *emporoi* or *nauklēroi*. On the other, as Finley (1935: 320–2, 333–6) showed, the ways in which these words were actually used prevent us from claiming that, because someone is called an *emporos*, then by definition he must have made a career of wholesale trade in goods, carried by him on someone else's ship, that were owned but not produced by him. Again and again in the ancient sources appear people called *emporoi* who fail to meet one or another of these criteria. But even if we abandon any pretense to lexicographical exactitude, it nonetheless remains important to ask what those called *emporoi* normally had in common, what those called *nauklēroi* normally had in common, and what *emporoi and nauklēroi* normally had in common. This chapter takes up where Finley left off,

---

[1] This article, published by Moses Finley at age twenty-three, was only his second on the ancient Greco-Roman world. There followed a hiatus of almost two decades before he next published on an ancient topic. See further Shaw and Saller in Finley (1981: ix–xxvi and 312).

adding or clarifying a number of crucial distinctions he either omitted or failed to discuss adequately. The first section deals with *emporoi*; the second, with *nauklēroi*; and the third with yet others who engaged in *emporia*.

EMPOROI

The traits that *emporoi* almost without exception appear to share I term "primary characteristics." "Secondary characteristics" apply to *emporoi* in the majority of cases. Primary and secondary characteristics differ only in the number of exceptions tolerated. There can be very few exceptions to a primary characteristic; there can be more to a secondary characteristic, but one still must be able to say that "usually" or "normally" the secondary characteristic applies. Beyond both primary and secondary characteristics are of course yet other features shared by many *emporoi*, but these need no special designation.

I argue that *emporoi* shared two primary characteristics. If we exclude army and slave traders, then virtually without exception those called *emporoi*:

1 ***Carried on interstate trade.*** Hasebroek (1933: 1–3) correctly insisted that this feature is what basically distinguished *emporoi* from *kapēloi* (retail sellers). Finley (1935: 333 and 328 n.37) claims one exception to this rule, "one instance where the *emporoi* were also shopkeepers in the Agora," but this exception is at best a very tenuous inference from Thuc. 3.74.2, in which a fire set to houses around the *agora* of Corcyra destroyed many goods belonging to *emporoi*.[2]

2 ***Relied for much (or probably most) of their livelihood on interstate trade.*** This primary characteristic, to which I find no recorded exception, is a neglected but extremely important one, for it not only serves to distinguish *emporoi* from all sorts of other people engaging in *emporia*, on whom see 13–14 below; it also points to the only sense in which *emporoi* had a "profession" – a word that, at least when applied to *emporoi*, has created a certain amount of confusion.[3] The *Oxford English Dictionary* defines "profession" in its most general sense as "any calling or occupation by which one habitually earns his living." But even in this broadest sense "profession" fails to encompass what *emporoi* did for a living. Sailing

---

[2] Cf. McKechnie (1989: 194 n.24).

[3] I do not claim that reflections on language can either "solve" or "dissolve" the question of whether there was a "merchant class" in ancient Greece. That is a sociological question, the answer to which depends on one's notion of "class." But the various notions cannot even be properly discussed in their ancient Greek context until certain prior clarifications are made.

conditions[4] forced most *emporoi* to limit their trade by sea to half a year or less. Since most *emporoi* were not wealthy,[5] most of them probably found it necessary to continue working in the off season as well. Our ignorance of the sort of work *emporoi* did outside the sailing season in no way alters the ironic result – that for half the year or more most *emporoi* probably did not earn their living by the activities that prompt us to call them *emporoi*. Still, they clearly must have earned a very important part of their livelihood by sea trade, else they would have chosen a less risky[6] line of work and remained ashore year-round.

There is no firm way to distinguish the following secondary characteristics from the primary ones just mentioned. In the face of source limitations one is obliged to speculate, relying more on general considerations than on specific evidence. I argue that (again, with the exception of army and slave traders) those called *emporoi usually* or *normally*:

1 **Traveled by sea.** The geography of the Greek world guaranteed that long-distance trade would normally be by sea.[7] At the same time Xenophon's claim that "Athens receives much merchandise by way of land"[8] disqualifies trading by sea as a primary characteristic of *emporoi*, although one wonders with Gauthier[9] just how important was the land trade to and

---

[4] On the dates of the sailing season see Casson (1971: 270–3 and nn.1–5). *Emporoi* could continue sailing between Rhodes and Egypt year-round ([D.] 56.30), but the northern grain and timber routes used by most of the *emporoi* trading with Athens, for instance, were closed for more than half the year.

[5] As I argue in Ch. 4.

[6] For references to the threat of seas, wars, and pirates to *emporoi* and *nauklēroi* in the classical period, see esp. the following: Plut. *Cim.* 8.3–4; Thuc. 2.67.4; X. *Hell.* 5.1.21; Andok. 1.137–8; [Lys.] 19.50; 22.14; Isok. 18.61; Ephoros *FGrH* 70 F 27; D. 8.25; [D.] 12.5; D. 19.286; [D.] 34.8–10; D. 35.31–3; 37.54; [D.] 52.4–5. Middle and New Comedies also stress the dangers of sea trading: Alexis *CAF* F 76 = *PCG* F 76; Diphilos *CAF* F 43 = *PCG* F 42.10–14; Men. *Pk.* 808–10 (OCT); fr. 59 (OCT). The titles of three plays (one of them from Old Comedy) include the word *nauagos* ("shipwreck"): Ar. *CAF* F 266 = *PCG* F 277 (*Dionysos Nauagos*); Ephippos *CAF* F 14 = *PCG* F 14 (*Nauagos*); Paramonos *CAF* (*Nauagos Choregon*) = *PCG* (*Nauagos*). On the threat of piracy, see further n.41 of Ch. 5.

[7] Finley (1935: 328 n.37) cites X. *Eq. mag.* 4.7 to show that, although *emporoi* carried on interstate trade, it was "by no means necessarily by sea." Since *Eq. mag.* says only that all poleis welcome those who import things, it is hardly worth citing in this connection. To Finley's list (1935: 328 n.36) of sources confirming that *emporoi* normally engaged in travel by sea should be added Philo Judaeus' description (*De opificio mundi* 147) of the *emporos* (among others) as *enudros* (a "water creature"). Lib. 18.82–3 in particular confirms the superiority of water over land transport for bulky articles like grain. See more generally Burford (1960).

[8] X. *Vect.* 1.7: καὶ κατὰ γῆν δὲ πολλὰ δέχεται ἐμπορία. Following Gauthier (1976: 51) and others, I prefer the neuter plural *emporia* to the dative singular. Finley (1935: 332) wrongly criticizes Hasebroek and Knorringa for failing to pay adequate attention to trade on land by *emporoi*. Hasebroek (1928: 2–3) not only acknowledges such activity; he also puts it in its proper perspective. And no scholar has more to say than does Knorringa (1926: 22, 42–3, 55, 63), albeit in his unsystematic way, on land trade by *emporoi* as the exception to sea trade.

[9] Gauthier (1976: 51). On Thuc. 7.28.1, which mentions overland trade between Euboia and Attica by the Oropos–Dekeleia route, see Westlake (1948).

from Athens. Finley (1935: 328 n.37) lists other references to land trade and traders but omits the following:

a Pl. *Plt.* 289e: someone characterizes *emporoi* (among others) as "traveling from city to city both by sea and by land."

b Diod. Sic. 11.56.3: Themistokles in 471/0 B.C. meets two Lynkestians (nos. 45 and 46 in the Catalogue) who are said to be "engaged in trade and . . . therefore familiar with the roads."

2 **Traveled in someone else's ship.** This applies to virtually all of those who share the secondary characteristic of travelling by sea.[10] Therein surely lies the basis for the phrase found throughout both the literary and inscriptional evidence – *hoi emporoi kai hoi nauklēroi*. And, if a shipowner engages in *emporia*, our sources distinguish between his *nauklēria* (shipowning) and *emporia* (trading).[11]

Why? It cannot be that *nauklēroi* do not do what *emporoi* do, which amounts to depending on interstate trade for much of one's livelihood. For, as has been mentioned earlier and will be explored at 12–13, that description applies to many shipowners as well. It must be that *emporoi* do not do what *nauklēroi* distinctively do; and that, as 12–13 shows, can only be shipowning.[12]

3 **Owned the goods they traded in.** Only two recorded cases possibly qualify as exceptions. One is that of Timosthenes (no. 24), who may be the agent of Phormion II (no. 23).[13] The other is that glaring exception to so many rules, the slave agent Lampis II (no. 13). His owner, Dion, may also have owned the goods Lampis II carried and traded in (on which see item 2 of no. 13). Whether many seagoing agents carried the goods of others depends on the level of business organization in classical Greece. At 36–40 below I argue that the rudimentary level of business organization precluded enterprises run by wealthy entrepreneurs who dispatched agents to do their trading.

4 **Did not produce the goods they traded in.** No doubt throughout the classical period many farmers and craftsmen continued to follow an older

---

[10] Finley (1935: 333–4 and 329 n.43) claims that "some *emporoi* unquestionably did own vessels," but both the cases he cites are questionable: τὰ πλοῖα τὰ αὑτῶν in D. 8.25 and τὰ πλοῖα τὰ αὑτῶν τὰς τῶν ἄλλων ἐμπόρων ναῦς in Isok. 17.57 might simply be telescoped versions of "the ships on which they sailed and carried their goods . . ."

[11] For example Andok. 1.137 and *IG* i³ 133 (after 434/3).

[12] Why, then, one might ask, if the activities of a *nauklēros* so often include *emporia* and not vice versa, did the Athenians in an honorary decree (*IG* ii² 360) choose *emporos* (the word with fewer connotations) to describe Herakleides of Salamis in Cyprus (no. 60), who is almost certainly a *nauklēros*? (See further item 2 of no. 60.) At 51–3 below I argue that this very revealing abnormality can be explained only by its appearance in an *official* setting, where it further confirms what we already knew about attitudes of the Athenian polis towards foreign *emporoi* and *nauklēroi*.

[13] On Timosthenes see further item 3 of no. 23, and no. 24 *in toto*.

pattern of trade, hawking their goods along the coast in small vessels, as Hyperbolos,[14] the Athenian abused as a lampmaker who entered politics, may have done. Were these called *emporoi*? They never are in the surviving evidence,[15] and there is a good reason why. Such people were viewed by contemporaries as deriving most of their income from farming or from lampmaking and so were called[16] "farmers" (γεωργοί) or "lampdealers" (λυχνοπώλαι) despite taking to sea to sell their goods. This is not to say that an *emporos* could not have produced things in the off-season that he peddled on the first leg of his sea travels. But my guess is that such a person was termed an *emporos* if he derived most of his livelihood from trade in goods he did *not* produce, such as timber or grain from the northern Aegean or Black Sea areas.

I claim further that two other characteristics of *emporoi* are not primary or secondary characteristics, since too many exceptions exist to the rule that *emporoi*:

1 **Remained emporoi year-in, year-out.** The *Oxford English Dictionary* defines "profession" in part as something one "habitually" does for a living. Our evidence seldom reveals whether an *emporos* or a *nauklēros* continues to go to sea year after year; we usually see the *emporoi* and *nauklēroi* in the Catalogue at only one point in their lives, but the following exceptions are instructive:

   a An unnamed retired *emporos* (no. 8) says he engaged in foreign trade "for a long time." ([D.] 33.4).

   b Nikoboulos (no. 22) mentions his career in what may be sea-trading (D. 37.54), and other passages (D. 37.6, 10, 15, 25) suggest that he has not yet retired. On him see further Millett (1991: 193–6).

   c Pyron of Pherai (no. 42) is described by Isokrates (17.20) as one who "was accustomed to sail to Pontos." Nothing more is known of Pyron, who possibly qualifies as a long-term *emporos* on the strength of this passage alone.

---

[14] Aristophanes *(Eq.* 1315) alludes to Hyperbolos' sailing in a σκάφη to hawk the lamps he made. We will find no solid information in a passage compounding comic sarcasm with the ambiguity of σκάφη (on which see Ehrenberg [1974: 125]). Even in its seaworthy sense σκάφη ("skiff") refers to a vessel too small for coastal trade (Casson 1971: 329–31 and 335–8). For further references in the plays and scholia to Hyperbolos' lampmaking, see *PA* 13910; on Hyperbolos' background and career see further Davies (1971) no. 13910 and Connor (1971: 152–5).

[15] Neither of the exceptions listed by Finley in (1935) 336 n.67 refers to *emporoi* who produced the goods they traded in: Heraclides 60 (fr. 611 Rose) refers to a γεωργός ("farmer") who sells his own products, while Pl. *Grg.* 517d in fact distinguishes the suppliers (*emporos* and *kapelos*) from the maker (*demiourgos*) of goods.

[16] Normally in the classical period producers who sold their own goods are identified by their craft or by the goods themselves and not by the blanket term, *autopoles*. Finley (1935: 336) rightly notes the rarity of that word, in spite of Heichelheim's claim to the contrary (Heichelheim 1964: II 54). See also Finley (1935: 336 n.68).

d The unnamed Athenian in *P Oxy.* 2538 probably spent more than a few years as an *emporos*: see his son's description of the father's occupation in item 2 of no. 61.

e Lykon of Achaia (no. 47), as he is first described in [D.] 52.3, sounds very like a long-term *emporos*.

These examples[17] together with the very nature of an *emporos'* work suggest that many may have remained *emporoi* year after year. It would take more than a season to establish a reputation as someone a bottomry lender could rely on;[18] it would take time to understand the ins and outs of bottomry contracts themselves[19] and to learn with which ship captains to risk one's life at sea. It would also take time to make helpful contacts in, for example, Pontos, and to learn how to decipher the many rumors heard there and elsewhere about where one could get the best price for one's cargo.[20] Here the exceptions threaten to prove the rule: we know of only two people in the entire Catalogue who for certain did *not* remain *emporoi* or *nauklēroi* for most of their lives. Yet Leokrates[21] probably remained an *emporos* for some five years, and Andokides[22] probably engaged in *nauklēria* and *emporia* for even longer.

Many, then, continued to work as *emporoi* year-in and year-out. Does long-term trading therefore qualify as a primary or as a secondary characteristic of *emporoi*? Probably neither: enough people *may* have been short-term *emporoi* to disqualify year-in and year-out trading as even a secondary characteristic.

One further point: confusion surrounds not only the sense in which *emporoi* constitute a "profession," but also the sense in which they were "specialized." In one respect of course they were: most of our evidence concerns *emporoi* who traded above all in grain.[23] But an *emporos* regularly

---

[17] All the preceding examples refer to *emporoi*, but certain *naukleroi* too engaged in trade for more than a single year and probably for even longer. The *naukleros* Herakleides of Salamis (no. 60) traded actively for at least the period 330/29–328/7 B.C. (see item 2 of no. 60). The speaker in [D.] 56 accuses the *naukleros* Dionysodoros (no. 33) and his partner the *naukleros* Parmeniskos of reaping the profit from an unpaid loan for yet a second year ([D.] 56.4, 16, 45). The speaker clearly has in mind further loans rather than further *emporia* or *naukleria*, but Parmeniskos at least ([D.] 56.29–30) continued to trade throughout these two years.

[18] See [D.] 34.30.

[19] Hasebroek (1928: 10–11, 21, 89–90) thought most *emporoi* illiterate; he is proved wrong by Harvey (1964). This appears in a revised and expanded version as Section 9 of Harvey (1966); cf. Lombardo (1988: 181–7) and esp. W. V. Harris (1989). On the use by Greek merchants of writing in the archaic period, see Coldstream (1977: 299–301) and W. V. Harris (1996). The lead tablets found at Berezan (Chadwick [1973]) and Pech Maho (Chadwick [1990]) are further evidence of merchants' literacy, *if* the inscribers were in fact *emporoi*.

[20] See X. *Oec.* 20.27–8; [D.] 34.36–7, [D.] 56.8–10, 25; Lykourg. *Leoc.* 14–15, 18–19; [Lys.] 22.14.

[21] No. 40; see esp. item 2.　　[22] No. 41; see esp. item 2.

[23] On the importance of the trade in grain with classical Greece, see 15–26 below.

returning from Pontos to Athens with grain might just as regularly take with him on the outward trip a variety of goods for sale. And after returning to Athens with the grain, he might use his profits to buy still other goods that he transported to another polis and sold there. Circumstances might further prompt the *emporos* who regularly sold grain at Athens to forsake both the grain *and* Athens, if he could get a better price for other goods elsewhere.[24]

2 **Sold to retailers.** *Emporoi* normally may have sold their grain to retailers at poleis like Athens, but they regularly may have used the profits from the sale of grain to buy in Athens other goods that they carried home and sold directly to consumers in the off-season.[25]

Having disqualified these last two criteria as primary *or* secondary characteristics of *emporoi*, we are left with the original six. So, if we exclude army and slave *emporoi*, then for the classical period at any rate we can say that the word *emporoi* in its commercial sense refers to those who relied on interstate trade for much or probably most of their livelihood, normally trading in goods, carried by them in someone else's ship, that were owned but not produced by them.[26]

NAUKLĒROI

The word *nauklēros*, at least in its commercial sense,[27] has a single primary characteristic to which I find no exceptions: it refers to one who was the owner of a seagoing merchantman.[28]

---

[24] See further Hasebroek's excellent comments (1928: 83–4) and the references in n.20 above.

[25] The ancient authors show as much interest in *emporoi* after they deliver the grain and leave Athens as do Hollywood directors in minor actors who leave the set: both *emporoi* and actors vanish abruptly from sight and mind. Finley (1935: 336 n.66) found what he thought were four references to retail trading by *emporoi*, but two of these (Thuc. 3.74.2 and *GDI* iv 875 n.52) are questionable.

[26] Cf. Finley (1935: 335–6, esp. his items 3–4, 6–8). For the most recent treatment of the term *emporos*, see Vélissaropoulos (1980: 35–7).

[27] In n.64 (1935: 335) Finley lists a number of cases in which the word *nauklēros* and its cognates are used to refer metaphorically to something other than shipowning. These cases he calls "the only exceptions" to the non-metaphorical, commercial use. In fact in at least six other instances these words do not refer to shipowning: Aesch. *Sept.* 652, where *nauklērein* means "to steer" or "to guide"; *nauklēria* means something like "means of transport" in Eur. *Hel.* 1519, and "crossing" (or "sailing" or "voyage") in *Hel.* 1589 and *Alc.* 256; a *nauklēros* drives a chariot in Eur. *Hipp.* 1224; the only example from prose works is well away from shipowning but perhaps retains an element of "commerce": in Isae. 6.19 a woman *nauklērei* ("manages") a brothel. (To put it more accurately, she manages a tenement house in which prostitutes are lodged.)

[28] See Casson (1971: 314–15) and Vélissaropoulos (1980: 48–9) for sensible remarks. On 77–86 Vélissaropoulos discusses the principal roles and their titles among the crew of a merchant vessel. Finley (1935: 335) agrees that the work *nauklēros* has "a definite and exclusive meaning, namely shipowner. But even here there are variations within that meaning." Finley's word "variation" nicely

Was year-in, year-out *nauklēria* (shipowning) a primary or a secondary characteristic of *naoklēroi*? Given his investment in a ship, one usually remained a *naoklēros* for more than a trading season or two, unless pirates, storms, or wars deprived him of it within that time.[29] Katzev (1972: 52) notes that the fourth-century Kyrenia merchant vessel that he uncovered in 1968/9 was at least eighty years old when she sank; it therefore *might* have stayed in the same family through three generations of *naoklēroi*. Long-term shipowning therefore probably qualifies as at least a secondary characteristic of *naoklēroi*. More uncertain is whether *emporia*, long- or short-term, also qualifies as a primary or a secondary characteristic of *naoklēroi*. The sparse evidence is unhelpful: only ten[30] *naoklēroi* in the Catalogue are said to engage in trade, and even fewer (five)[31] are said to borrow on bottomry; but many others may have done both, and of no *naoklēros* in the Catalogue can we say with certainty that he did not trade.[32] The stringent standards for primary characteristics probably disqualify the practice of *emporia* as a primary characteristic of *naoklēroi*. Rather than quibble over whether it constitutes even a secondary characteristic, we should attend instead to the vital point (vital at least for historical if not for terminological purposes) that in the classical period *naoklēroi* undoubtedly carried on *emporia* more regularly than did any other group of people except *emporoi*.

THOSE OTHER THAN *EMPOROI* AND *NAUKLĒROI*

Five categories of people other than *emporoi* or *naoklēroi* also engaged in *emporia*:[33]

suits the puzzling case of the slave agent Lampis II (no. 13), who is repeatedly (item 2 of no. 13) called the *naoklēros* of a ship he may or may not own. Casson (1971: 316 n.70) thinks Hegestratos (no. 5) both the owner and captain of his vessel: "In Demosthenes 32, a rascally *naoklēros*, caught redhanded attempting barratry, is drowned, and his equally rascally associate then tries to talk the *proreus* [first mate] and sailors (32.7) into abandoning ship. No captain is mentioned, which seems to suggest that the drowned man had commanded his own vessel…"

[29] See n.6 above for examples of *naoklēroi* and *emporoi* who lose lives, ships, or other property to pirates, storms, or wars.

[30] Possibly no. 5 (D. 32.2, 12, 14–15); no. 13 [D.] 34.36–7); no. 21 (D. 35.52–3, 55); possibly no. 23 ([D.] 49.31, on which see also item 3 of no. 23 and 36–7; nos. 33 and 34 (see item 2 of no. 33); no. 41 (see item 2); no. 47 (lines 14–16 of *IG* i³ 174); no. 48 (lines 15–21 of *IG* ii³ 98 [ML no. 80 = Fornara no. 149]); no. 60 (see item 2).

[31] Possibly no. 5 (D. 32.2, 12, 14–15); no. 18 (D. 35.33); probably no. 21 (D. 35.52–3, 55, on which see also n.35 in the Catalogue); nos. 33 and 34 ([D.] 56.3–6).

[32] In the second section of Ch. 2 I claim that at least three *naoklēroi* – Lampis I (no. 2), Dion (no. 13), and Phormion II (no. 23) – probably did not go to sea with their ships, but that in no way precludes their engaging in trade through agents. There is no evidence that either Lampis I or Dion did so, and the evidence for Phormion's involvement in *emporia* is both meager and ambiguous. (On Phormion's *emporia* see esp. item 3 of no. 23 and 36–7.)

[33] This list extends and corrects Hasebroek's (1928: 13–15), which is full of errors.

1 ***Those who import goods for their domestic and/or business use:*** Diodotos' family imported grain from the Thracian Chersonese for its own consumption;[34] a farmer in Theodosia imported saltfish from Pantikapaion for his farm-workers (D. 35.32, 34); and Demosthenes accuses Meidias of importing fences, cattle, and door posts for domestic use, as well as pit-props for the silver mines he leased (D. 21.167 and schol.).

On occasion these goods may have been imported duty-free or as outright gifts. The Erythraians for instance (*Syll.*[3] no. 126) grant the Athenian general Conon duty-free imports and exports (surely for his private use), while in other grants the duty-free clause explicitly applies to goods "for his own acquisition" or "for his own household."[35] To Conon's son Timotheos goes a gift of timber from Amyntas, King of Macedonia;[36] and Demosthenes is alleged to have received a gift of 1,000 *medimnoi* of wheat a year as a bribe from the rulers of the Bosporan state (Din. 1.43).

2 ***Those who finance a trip abroad by taking with them a shipload or more of goods.*** Examples include: (a) the son of the prominent Bosporan Sopaios, who sent the youth abroad with money and two shiploads of grain (Isok. 17.3–4).[37] (b) Another young man from Pontos who financed *his* trip to Athens with a shipload of saltfish (Diog. Laert. 6.9). (c) The philosopher Plato, who is said to have paid for his stay in Egypt by selling olive oil (Plut. *Sol.* 2.8).

3 ***Soldiers who engage in emporia on military expeditions.*** Thucydides (6.31.5) mentions that soldiers as well as merchants took goods for barter and sale on the Sicilian expedition.[38]

4 ***Pirates who engage in emporia by transporting and selling the goods or people they capture.***[39]

5 ***Farmers or craftsmen who engage in emporia by traveling*** in order to sell elsewhere the goods they themselves grew or made. (In this chapter see further 9–10 and nn.14–16.)

---

[34] [Lys.] 32.15. Cf. X. *Oec.* 9.3.

[35] Fourth century B.C.: *Syll.*[3] nos. 278, 332, and Michel no. 321; third and second centuries B.C.: *Syll.*[3] no. 941 and Michel no. 332. See also Theophr. *Char.* 23.4 and Hopper (1979: 114).

[36] [D.] 49.26, 28–30, 33–40, 60–6. See further Millett (1991: 208, 210–12, 217); Cohen (1992: esp. 36–7); Trevett (1992: 93–6).

[37] On this venture see further Millett (1991: 208, 210–12, 217) and Cohen (1992: esp. 38–40, 116–19). On the rhetorical strategy behind the speech itself, see Morris (1994: 360).

[38] See also Thuc. 7.13.2; Arist. *Eth. Nic.* 1160a 14–18.

[39] See for example [D.] 52.5; 53.6 (together with Pritchett [1991: 248–9, 254–5]); Andok. 1.137–8; Tod no. 170. For a more comprehensive set of references to piracy, see n.41 of Ch. 5.

CHAPTER 2

Classical modes and patterns of exchange

INTRODUCTION

Having come to terms with the words *emporos* and *nauklēros* in Chapter 1, I ask in this chapter about the principal items carried by maritime traders and how vital these were to the Greek poleis with which they traded. These queries entail four more particular questions: How much of the inter-regional exchange of goods in the classical period was by commerce as distinct from other means of exchange? What proportion of this long-distance trade was in the hands of those, described in Chapter 1, who made it their primary occupation? Even if quantification remains impossible, can we say anything meaningful about the number of maritime traders? And what was the level of demand for the principal commodities traders transported to Greek poleis? A great need on a large scale for imports of certain items might bear directly on the place of traders in the poleis of classical Greece – the subject of Chapters 3–6 and the heart of this book.

Implicit in that last sentence is an important working assumption: since this is a monograph on traders, not on trade, I take up trade only inasmuch as it illumines the place of traders. No attempt is made here to provide an exhaustive account of the modes and patterns of exchange in classical Greece. I do not offer, in other words, as a companion to the Catalogue of Traders, a Catalogue of Trade, wherein I extensively chart the passage of wares, detail finds of artifacts, or reflect at length on their places of production or destination.

Most of the evidence available for answering the four questions raised above relates to classical Athens, although a bit survives for other poleis. So, as elsewhere in Chapters 1–6, the principal focus is on Athens. I first examine the trade in grain, then the trade in timber for warships, and finally both the slave trade and slave traders, coupled with the traders who accompanied armies and fleets. So little is known about this ensemble of slave or army or fleet traders that I go ahead and ask of them here the questions reserved for Chapters 3–6 below about traders in grain, timber, and other commodities.

THE TRADE IN GRAIN

Scholars agree that both the volume[1] and variety[2] of goods flowing into fifth-century Athens increased in direct proportion to her increase in power. They also agree that classical Athens' demand for one item exceeded that for all others. Both Athens' laws governing trade and the honors she awarded non-Athenians for supplying goods point to an overriding preoccupation with her grain supply.[3] Almost all the *emporoi* and *nauklēroi* mentioned in the Catalogue were involved in the grain trade at some stage,[4] and several source passages[5] suggest that *emporoi* normally were assumed to be traders in grain. We know that other classical poleis depended on external sources of grain,[6] but the scale of Athens' dependence, whatever the date of its origin, probably remained uniquely large throughout much of the classical period.[7]

---

[1] On "the general trend throughout much of classical antiquity towards the production of larger surplus" see Hopkins (1983: xiv–xxi). On growth at Athens: Morris (1994: 364–5).

[2] On the variety see X. [*Ath. pol.*] 2.7–11; Thuc. 2.38.2; Hermippos *CAF* F 63 = *PCG* F 63; Ar. *Holkades CAF* F 400–29 = *PCG* F 415–43; Isok. 4.42: X. *Vect.* 1.6–7; 3.1–2. For speculation about how far down the economic scale the access to such imported goods extended, see Braund (1994), Foxhall (1998: 305–6), and Davidson (1997: esp. 227–46).

[3] On the supply of grain to classical Athens see Gernet (1909) and Hopper (1979: 71–92), both largely superseded by the excellent overview in Austin (1994: 558–64), supplemented by Jameson (1983) and Osborne (1987: 97–104).

[4] See also D. 18.87; 20.31.   [5] X. *Oec.* 20.27; DK ii 90 [*Dissoi logoi*].

[6] For the fifth century see esp. Hdt. 7.147.2, evidence that as early as the Persian Wars grain was shipped from the Pontos to Aigina and the Peloponnese; also *ATL* 11 D 21, lines 3–4; *ATL* 11 D 4, lines 34ff; Thuc. 3.86.4 (grain to the Peloponnese from Sicily). Grain to numerous poleis in the fourth: Tod no. 196 = Rhodes no. 20 = Harding no. 116 and the discussion in Hopper (1979: 83–5), Kingsley (1986: 165–77), and Brun (1993: 185–96); Tod no. 163 (over 100,000 *medimnoi* of grain from Pontos to Mytilene, *c.* 350 B.C.). We hear of Aegean-wide shortages in the late 360s ([D.] 50.6), in 357/6 (D. 20.31–3), and in Alexander's time ([D.] 56.7–10, [Arist.] *Oec.* 2.2.33), on which see esp. Camp (1982) and Garnsey (1988: 154–62).

[7] Pritchett (1991: 466–7), speaking of Athens' dependence on imported grain: "The grain trade came nearest in importance and general functions to the part played in our modern city life by the big public utilities companies." See nn.12–18 below for the principal references. Even Garnsey, who downplays and downdates grain imports to Athens, estimates that "Athens in the fourth century had to find grain for perhaps one half of its resident population from outside Attica . . . in a normal year" (1998: 194, 198). On the scale of the grain trade with Athens in the fourth century see further Whitby (1998) and the following source references: D. 20.31–2; Philoch. *FGrH* 328 F 162 (230 ships), to be compared with Theopomp. *FGrH* 115 F 292 (180 ships); *IG* ii² 1613, line 302; Tod no. 196 = Rhodes no. 20 = Harding no. 116; cf. D. 18.87; 20.31. On Athens' grain shortages between 338/7 and 323/2 see esp. Garnsey (1988: 154–64).

Where did classical Athens and other Aegean poleis look for grain? To eastern sources, principally Egypt but Cyprus and Kyrene as well;[8] to Sicily and south Italy in the west;[9] and to the most important sources by far, those to the north, principally Pontos but Thrace as well.[10] Casson[11] sketches sailing conditions along the three routes and Davies[12] the flow of various goods in triangle patterns along each route, culminating in the arrival of grain at Athens. No reader interested in an overall pattern of the flow of goods and itineraries of traders should miss Lionel Casson's lucid, synoptic account in Chapter 9 of his *Ancient Mariners* (1991).

When did imports of grain become necessary for Athens? Until the mid-1980s most scholars believed that the need originated in the archaic period. But in 1985 Peter Garnsey's disagreement[13] provoked a debate in what remains "one of the fastest moving areas of ancient historical studies," so that "no statement can have long term validity."[14] Garnsey's new theses were twofold: he wanted to date the need at Athens for external grain to the post-Persian Wars period and to downplay the amount imported thereafter,

---

[8] For evidence of grain shipments from Egypt to Greece in the fifth century see Bacchyl. fr. 20B lines 14–16 (Snell–Maehler) *apud* Ath. 2.39 e–f; Philoch. *FGrH* 328 F 119 and Plut. *Per.* 37.4; Thuc. 8.35.2–3;? 4.53.3. In the fourth: possibly *IG* ii² 206; *IG* ii² 283; Lykourg. *Leoc.* 18–19; [D.] 56 *passim* (the best source for trade in grain with Egypt); see further Roebuck (1950). Evidence for grain from Cyprus to Greece can be found in Andok. 2.20 (fifth century) and in *IG* ii² 407 and *IG* ii² 360 (fourth). From Kyrene in the fifth, possibly Thuc. 4.53.3; in the fourth, possibly *IG* ii² 176 and Tod no. 196 = Rhodes no. 20 = Harding no. 116. (This last document is evidence of a *gift* of grain, not trade therein.)

[9] In the fifth century grain arrived in Greece from Sicily (Hdt. 7.158.4; Thuc. 3.86.4), but apart from a questionable reference in a Sophoklean fragment (*TrGF* IV F 600 = Plin. *HN* 18.65), there is no evidence that grain came to Athens from Sicily or south Italy until the second half of the fourth century (see D. 32.4, 9, 21, 23, 26; also [D.] 56.9; *IG* ii² 408). See further Fantasia (1993) on grain for Greece from Sicily. See also no. 55 in the Catalogue, Sopatros of Akragas, who is honored *c.* 331–324 B.C. by Athens for importing unspecified goods, probably grain, since this is a period of grain shortage at Athens.

[10] From Thrace: X. *Hell.* 5.4.56 and 6.1.11. For evidence of grain shipments from the Black Sea area to Greece in the fifth century, see Hdt. 7.147.2; *ATL* II D 21, lines 3–4; *ATL* II D 4, lines 34 ff. = ML no. 65 = Hornblower and Greenstock no. 159 = Fornara no. 128; Thuc. 3.2.2; X. *Hell.* 1.1.35. In the fourth: Isok. 17 *passim*, esp. sect. 57; D. 20 *passim*; *Syll.*³ no. 212; D. 17.20; 18.87; 20.32–3; [D.] 50.4–6, 17–19.

[11] Casson (1994a: 519–26).

[12] Davies (1993: 224–5 and 1998: 229 n.6). See also Isager and Hansen (1975: 19–29).

[13] Garnsey's "Grain for Athens," rp. in Garnsey with an important addendum (1998: 195–200). His comments in Garnsey (1988: 110–13) are largely devoted to arguing that "a regular grain trade [for Athens] with the northern Black Sea or with Egypt in the archaic period is a figment of the imagination" (113); cf. esp. Keen (1993).

[14] The quote is by Davies (1992: 301), who provides a brief summary (300–1) and a full bibliography (301 n.53) of the older view, together with a bibliography (301 n.54) of the newer view through 1991, to which should be added Garnsey and Morris (1989), Garnsey (1992, rp. 1998), Gill (1994: 102), Arafat and Morgan (1994: 129), Tsetskhladze (1994: 124), and Foxhall (1998: 301–2). See nn.15–20 for other relevant references.

right through the rest of the fifth century and the fourth. By 1998 he could claim support from a number of experts who had wrought a revolution in the study of Greek patterns of land use.[15] Their evidence, argued Garnsey, supported a higher grain yield for classical Athens than previously estimated, although Garnsey recently acknowledged that, compared with patterns of Roman land use, Athens' relatively small scale "reduces the plausibility of any model of the grain supply of Attica";[16] and Morris compounds doubt by noting that "relatively minor changes to the numbers [in these land-use studies] totally transform the models."[17]

This debate about the use of Attic land has been combined with disagreements about the size of Athens' population in the fifth and fourth centuries.[18] In the face of continued opposition[19] Garnsey acknowledges that

Existing source references and probabilistic assumptions concerning the crucial variables of population size and grain yields create margins of error too wide to make possible anything other than very crude estimates of the average level of Athenian self-sufficiency in a given period.[20]

We must fall back on general considerations. From the second quarter of the fifth century onwards the growth of Athens' power brought a corresponding growth in wealth, which in turn paid for slaves, attracted metics, and thus increased the need for imported grain, especially from Pontos. In Chapter 1 I mentioned several features of the grain trade that might prompt people to engage in it over an extended time. Here one can add another reason: Athens' annually recurring reliance on outside sources of grain promised steady work for those willing to make the long and dangerous voyage to distant ports, particularly Pontos, from which Greek poleis in the Aegean basin mainly secured their grain.

Roughly how many maritime traders might bring grain to classical Athens or other points around the Aegean? We know some of the variables involved – the single trip possible per season to Pontos,[21] the one- or two-person scale of trading enterprises,[22] and the small carrying capacity

---

[15] Davies (1992: 301) nicely categorizes the various issues raised by these scholars and supplies a bibliography (n.54). Garnsey (1998: 195–200) updates the bibliography and comments further.

[16] Garnsey (1988: 200).   [17] Morris (1994: 361).

[18] For bibliography and the most recent exchange, see Garnsey (1988: 197–8) and Whitby (1998: 109–14).

[19] See esp. Keen (1993) on the archaic period and fifth century and Whitby (1998) on the fourth. In his "Addendum" Garnsey (1998: 195–200) comments on both pieces. See also Pritchett (1991: 465–72) for further criticisms of the minimalist view of Athenian grain imports.

[20] Garnsey (1998: 200).   [21] As Casson (1994a: 521) points out.

[22] On the size and organization of maritime trading enterprises, see further 36–40 and Appendix 2.

of each merchant vessel – small, that is, compared to the size of some hellenistic merchant vessels.[23] The most contested variable is the volume of grain imported by Greek poleis, but no one doubts that the total imported by all classical poleis was enormous by Greek standards, in the many hundreds of thousands of *medimnoi*. The upshot is clear, even if the arithmetic remains impossible: in the classical period the grain trade offered work for large numbers of maritime traders; and the need for grain at Athens, and probably elsewhere too, became acute enough to make these traders indispensable.

THE TIMBER TRADE

By the classical period central and southern Greek poleis were not blessed with supplies of wood sufficient for their needs, so they were forced to seek it elsewhere. Classical Athens imported wood for temple fittings, housing, furniture, and fuel, but we are more interested in the wooden walls vital for her military prowess.[24]

If with Haas[25] we assume that before Themistokles Athenian timber resources already were small and a trireme fleet unlikely, and with Amit[26] that Athens from 480 to 410 B.C. maintained at least 200 warships, then we can agree with Borza[27] that imperial Athens' fifth-century need for imported ship timber was "huge" and even larger in the fourth century, if one exempts the first thirty years thereof. "From the early 350s to 323/2 the net number of serviceable warship hulls was considerably greater than 250 and perhaps not much less than 380."[28]

Like grain, timber too had to be imported long-distance in merchant ships to classical Athens, where the warships were built. The major Athenian

---

[23] "The freighters that brought grain to Athens or were the standard carriers for overseas transport of wine and oil were ... capable of holding 100 to 150 tons on the average, while vessels capable of hauling 250 or more were not uncommon" (Casson 1991: 114). For more detail see Casson (1971: 182–4 and 1994b: 101–26), as well as Wallinga (1964: 1–40) and Stronk (1992–3: 129–31). The fourth-century Kyrenia and Porticello ships had far smaller capacities: the former, about 25 tons (Steffy 1987: 100); the latter, about 30 tons (Eiseman and Ridgway 1987: 108). On the other hand, Hadjidaki (1996: 588) estimates that the amphora-laden merchant vessel she excavated in the northern Aegean carried a cargo of approximately 126 metric tons.

[24] The *locus classicus* on timber and its uses in the Mediterranean ancient world remains Meiggs (1982).

[25] Haas (1985: 37–46), against Jordan (1975).

[26] Amit (1965: 18–26) for both fifth- and fourth-century tallies of warships.

[27] Borza (1987: 34). Borza estimates that, on the basis of Amit's ship tallies (n.26 above), Athens at any given time in the fifth century needed 300,000 oars alone!

[28] Gabrielsen (1994: 126–9 and notes). His upper amount correlates nicely with the number of slipways (372) for warships (94 of them also usable for commercial vessels) counted by Blackman (1982: 204–6). See also Amit (1965: 24–7). On Athens as a fourth-century naval power, see also Cawkwell (1984).

source of such wood was Macedonia,[29] where timber was a royal monopoly. (Fortunately for historians, certain Macedonian treaty arrangements with Greek poleis[30] or export rights granted private citizens[31] were officially or unofficially recorded and hence survive.) So when, in the reigns of Philip II and Alexander the Great, relations with Athens were strained or broken, other sources had to be found.[32] There was also an attendant need for other warship-related items, such as pitch.[33]

The concluding comments of 16–19 on grain apply to timber, too. For *any* Greek polis with pretensions to sea power[34] huge imports of ship timber were indispensable; and, given the amounts shipped together with the small size of the ships[35] and trading operations, the number of shippers involved must have been sizeable. (Unfortunately we catch a glimpse of only one *emporos* or *nauklēros* [no. 27 in the Catalogue] involved in the timber trade, and there the circumstances are not typical.)[36]

SLAVE, FLEET, AND ARMY TRADE AND TRADERS

This section resembles the preceding two in asking how extensive was the slave, fleet, and army trade in the classical Greek world and by whom such trade was conducted. It differs in also raising here questions about the place of slave, fleet, and army traders that I do not ask about other sorts of traders

[29] Meiggs (1982: 123–5); Borza (1987: 41–7). See also Borza's speculations (50–1) about how the Athenians paid for Macedonian timber. Evidence of timber to Athens from Macedonia in the fifth and fourth centuries: *IG* i³ 89, lines 55–61 = Hill (1951): B 66; Walbank (1978) no. 60 = a new fragment plus those reported by Schweigert (1938: 269–70) and Merritt (1945: 129–32), on which see further MacDonald (1981); *IG* i³ 117 = ML no. 91 = Fornara no. 161; *IG* ii² 102 = Tod no. 129 = Harding no. 43; Andok. 2.11; X. *Hell*. 6.1.11; D. 17.28; 19.114, 265; [D.] 49.26–30, 33–42, 59–61; *IG* ii² 1672; Theophr. *Char*. 23.4; Theophr. *Hist. pl*. 4.5.5; 5.8.

[30] See for example *IG* ii² 102 = Tod no. 129 = Harding no. 43, the text of a treaty between Amyntas III and Athens, usually dated to 375/4 or 373/2. On Athens' fifth-century relations with Macedonian rulers, see further *IG* i³ 61 = ML no. 65 = Fornara no. 128 (not for timber) and *IG* i³ 89, lines 55–61 = Hill (1951): B 66; *IG* i³ 117 = ML no. 91 = Fornara no. 161. Cf. Philoch. *FGrH* 328 F 119; Hdt. 7.158.4 (481 B.C.). Poleis other than Athens negotiated with Macedonia for timber: for two early fourth-century treaties between Amyntas III and the Chalcidians, see *Syll*.³ no. 135 = Tod no. 111 = Pouilloux no. 25 = Harding no. 21.

[31] For example, around 370 B.C. Amyntas III grants timber to the Athenian Timotheos, later sued for not repaying a loan the latter took out to pay the freight costs ([D.] 49.26–30). See D. 19.265 for another example.

[32] See Meiggs (1982: 125, 211, 351–4) for a list of those sources.

[33] The standard treatment of the trade in pitch is now Meiggs (1982: 467–71).

[34] The ancient sources report that Corinth was the first polis to build a large number of triremes (Thuc. 1.13.2; Diod. Sic. 14.42.3).

[35] Specialized ships for carrying timber did not appear until the period of the Roman empire, according to Meiggs (1982: 338). From the fifth century until then regular merchant ships sufficed.

[36] The unnamed *nauklēros* in [D.] 49 transports a load of timber (a gift from Amyntas to the Athenian, Timotheos) to Athens and there receives payment for the freight costs ([D.] 49.25–30, 33–41, 60–1).

until Chapters 3–6. The paucity of evidence for the slave, fleet, and army trade *and* traders[37] makes it more sensible to treat both in one place.

The phrase "army and fleet trade" applies to the provisioning of military forces on the move as well as to the transport and sale of booty in the wake of military action. Pritchett's encyclopedic accounts of both[38] reveal that we know more about the disposition of booty than about provisioning, and in particular more about *human* booty, which in short order brings us to the slave trade.[39] A glance at the category "nature and disposition of booty" in Pritchett's lengthy "tables of booty"[40] provides the best overview of the large scale of such commerce, whereas the brevity of his "traders in booty"[41] reveals how little we know about the merchants involved.[42]

Did most slaves arrive in the Aegean basin through war or trade? The distinction collapses when we realize that even slaves introduced into the Greek world through trade may have been taken by force by other non-Greeks. The question thus becomes, were most slaves in Greece obtained "externally" (largely by purchase from outside the Greek world or its fringes), or "internally" (largely by Greek military activity or piracy)?

Pritchett argues for the latter;[43] Finley, for the former.[44] Downplaying internal wars and especially piracy as sources of supply,[45] Finley argues that after *c.* 600 most slaves in Greece were non-Greeks from the Danubian basin, the Black Sea region, and barbarian Asia Minor;[46] he cites Byzantion and Ephesos as examples of major outlet marts.[47] More recently Garlan buttressed Finley's case with an argument from general considerations – the

[37] The evidence for slave traders in the Roman period is also scarce: Harris (1980) claims to assemble the known particulars in a mere two pages (130–1).

[38] On provisioning: Pritchett (1971: 30–52). On booty: Pritchett (1971: 53–84 and 1991: 68–202). See Wheeler's excellent recent review of Part V (1991) in (1992–3: 410–18). More of a loose catalogue of sources with commentary than a tightly-woven treatment, Pritchett's 1991 account of booty is more careful than Bravo's (1980), esp. Bravo's analysis (693–843) of Greek terms, which Pritchett (1991: 68–9) excoriates; cf. Gauthier's favorable review of Bravo in (1982).

[39] Finley's 1962 article (rp. 1981), remains the most sensible and balanced account of the trade in slaves with classical Greece. For a more comprehensive view, written for non-specialists, see also his excellent "Aulos Kapreilios Timotheos, Slave Trader," first published in *Horizon* and rp. in Finley (1977: 154–66).

[40] Pritchett (1991: 505–41).   [41] Pritchett (1991: 425–33).

[42] See also n.37 above.   [43] Pritchett (1971: 80–2).

[44] Finley (1977: 162–4); see also Davies (1984: 282) for careful comments about the slave trade in the hellenistic period.

[45] Finley (1981: 173–4). Wiedemann (1981: 106–21) translates ancient passages describing the sources of Greek and Roman slaves. The commerce in slaves on the one hand and war and piracy on the other were hardly mutually exclusive. Unransomed victims of war and piracy regularly were sold into slavery. On ransom or enslavement after capture in war, see Ducrey (1968: 74–91, 131–9, 238–45, 255–7) and esp. Pritchett (1991: 223–96). On piracy see the references in n.41 of Ch. 5.

[46] This is a main thesis of Finley (1981: 167–75 and 271–3).

[47] Finley (1981: 168), citing Herodotus 8.105 (Ephesos) and Strabo 4.38.1–4 (Byzantion).

only sort of support available, given the near-absence of source material. Citing the preponderance of non-Greek names among Greek slaves, Garlan thinks the Greek preference for barbarian slaves, coupled with an increasing reluctance to enslave Greeks, supports the thesis that most slaves in late archaic and classical Greece came from outside the Greek world through purchase at its edges.[48] He plausibly subsumes this trade in slaves under the growing volume of *all* commerce with the non-Greek world to the north in the same period, capping his argument by pointing out that classical chattel slavery flourished in precisely the poleis open to such commercial exchanges – Chios, Athens, Corinth, and Aigina.[49]

The Finley–Garlan thesis strikes me as more plausible for yet another general reason. Even the lowest recent estimates of slave numbers in fourth-century Athens leaves them in the tens of thousands.[50] Add to Athens the other poleis (mentioned above by Garlan) with reputedly large numbers of slaves, and it becomes more reasonable to think that Greeks would rely principally on long-distance "external" exchanges, simply because these provided a more reliably regular and larger supply than did more sporadic, haphazard means such as internal wars or piracy. Furthermore, in the fifth century imperial Athens was increasingly able to meet the costs for slaves thus supplied.

Switching now from trade to traders,[51] I discuss below their degree of specialization, place of origin, level of wealth, and official and unofficial attitudes towards them. Was the "external" slave trade with classical Greece largely in the hands of professionals? Generalizing from Rome outwards and backwards, Harris thinks not: "[One] reason why slave traders were so hard to track down is that a good proportion of the selling was done by people who had other occupations or traded in other commodities."[52]

---

[48] Garlan (1987: 13–15) in English; rp. (1989a: 83–4) in French.

[49] Garlan (1987: 18–20) in English = (1989a: 89–92) in French.

[50] Whitby (1998: 113) plausibly infers a minimum figure of 15,000–30,000 slaves from Garnsey (1988: 90) and Sallares (1991: 60) in 323/2, when the overall population of Attica was quite low.

[51] Almost without exception classical authors use the word *emporos* to refer to one who buys slaves from his procurer and transports them elsewhere for sale. There is a possible overlap in Aristophanes' *Plut.* 518–21 between such *emporoi* and those called *andrapodistai*, but Ehrenberg (1974: 119) may be wrong in reading the two terms as equivalent; the *emporos* mentioned there may be different from the local dealers called *andrapodistai*. Bolkestein (1958: 111) and Pritchett (1971: 81–2) think *andrapodokapelos* commonly meant "slave trader" or "slave merchant," but I can find no example from the classical period; in Lucian (*Ind.* 24), however, the word unmistakably refers to a local dealer. The word *somatemporos*, equated by Harpocration with *andrapodokapelos* (s.v. the latter), is even rarer and to my knowledge never used by an author of the classical period. On terminology see further Pritchett (1991: 425 n.625).

[52] W. V. Harris (1980: 129), cited by Bradley (1987: 46) and Braund and Tsetskhladze (1989: 115), who agree with Harris.

That doubtless rings true for the early archaic period, where aristocrats such as Odysseus combined raiding, trading, and estate management.[53] But in the classical period a case can be made for specialization, especially in the "external" slave trade. Athens obtained two vital items – grain and slaves – from the Black Sea region, but the grain trade was financed by bottomry loans, whereas the slave trade was not, so that normally the two would not overlap. I would opt further for slave traders "who had their personal connections and methods in the various regions outside the Greco-Roman world proper."[54] The logistics of, and time consumed by, such long-distance transfers called for men who made slave trading their principal occupation;[55] and the large, persistent demand for slaves in the poleis of classical Greece promised steady work for such traders.

Where were the "external" slave traders from? The Phoenicians, the foremost slave traders of the Levant,[56] also operated in the Greek world during the classical period.[57] Otherwise we have no evidence and must guess. Perhaps many slave traders were from cities located on the perimeter of the Greek world that served as points of outlet for slaves from beyond. Panionios of Chios might be one example;[58] from the Roman period another would be Aulos Kapreilios Timotheos,[59] whose tombstone was discovered at the site of ancient Amphipolis. Since some are said by Xenophon to become (among other things) slave traders because of poverty,[60] the backward and poorer parts of Greece may have produced *emporoi* dealing in slaves as well as other sorts of *emporoi*.

Specialization in the "internal" slave trade is less likely. Since military campaigns both required provisions and produced slaves, some of the merchants accompanying a fleet or army probably engaged in both sorts of trade: their means of transport for either was the most convenient available.

With almost no evidence we nonetheless can imagine that the sorts of traders accompanying armies might vary. The *emporoi* accompanying

---

[53] For a good overview of slavery in archaic Greece, including the slave trade, see Rihll (1996: esp. 96–101, 104–60), and (less relevant here) Rihll (1993).

[54] Finley's description (1977: 163).

[55] Herodotus (8.105) describes Panionios of Chios as a super-specialist, trading exclusively in eunuchs.

[56] See esp. Joel 3.6.

[57] I can find no explicit reference to Phoenicians trading in slaves with Greeks of the classical period. The *emporos* whom Antiphanes (*CAF* F 168 = *PCG* F 166) describes bringing two children from Syria for sale in Greece might be Phoenician. In the archaic period Phoenician slave traders were active in the Greek world (*Od.* 14.288–97; Hdt. 2.54), and we may assume that the same was true for the classical period. What the Sidonian *emporoi* who were granted privileges by Athens (Tod no. 139 = Harding no. 40) brought to Athens is not specified, but other such honors were granted to services connected with the grain trade, not with that in slaves. Some of the Phoenicians following Alexander's army *kat' emporian* may have been slave traders (Arr. *Anab.* 6.22.4).

[58] See n.55 above.   [59] On whom see Finley (1977).   [60] X. *Symp.* 4.36.

the Athenians and their allies to Sicily[61] may well have been drawn from those described in Chapter 1 – that international group of traders ready to go wherever and to trade in whatever brought the most profit. On the other hand an army may have depended partly upon traders from the area in which it operated, as Xenophon's soldiers did upon Sinopean and Herakleot *emporoi* during their march along the southern coast of the Black Sea.[62] Sometimes the difference between the army suppliers called *emporoi* and those called *kapeloi* must have been infinitesimal.[63]

The official attitude of the Greek poleis and of those within these poleis to those who supplied their fleets and armies is probably no different from state and individual attitudes discussed in Chapters 5 and 6 below. Just as the *emporoi* mentioned in 5 and 6 provided grain for citizens at home, so did army and fleet *emporoi* for citizens (and allies) on campaign. In all likelihood both the polis and its individual members welcomed such traders but confined any interest in them to the services provided. Cyrus in Xenophon's *Cyropaedia* therefore expresses very Greek sentiments when he welcomes the *emporoi* wishing to follow his army, offering loans to the respectably needy as well as gifts and honors to those who do their job well.[64]

This carefully focused interest in fleet and army *emporoi* is nonetheless an intense one. Not only on behalf of its citizen consumers at home does the polis forcefully intervene in trade; it does the same for its citizens and allies on campaign. Public officials appointed by the state regularly accompanied military expeditions to guarantee that provisions were provided.[65] The Athenian polis even requisitioned thirty foodbearing transports for the Sicilian expedition.[66] And after Arginusai not only the Spartan triremes but also the *emporoi* sailing with the Spartan fleet were ordered by the Spartan commander to sail to Chios.[67]

Adding substantially to his earlier account of booty (1971: 53–100), W. K. Pritchett in Part v of *The Greek State at War* documents how tightly Greek

---

[61] Thuc. 6.31.5; 7.24.2–3. Early in the war the Spartans, having captured at sea a number of *emporoi* supplying the Athenians and their allies, put them to death (Thuc. 2.67.4). Purchase from *emporoi* was only one of a number of ways campaigning fleets and armies secured their supplies. For a description of the various ways see Pritchett (1971: 41–9) and de Ste. Croix (1972: 399–400). The fullest fourth-century account of *emporoi* operating with an army is in [Arist.] *Oec.* 2.2.33. For a poignant account of their activity see X. *Ages*. 1.21. See further Pritchett's catalogue of passages (1991: 427–33) that refer to *emporoi* who followed armies in the classical period and beyond.

[62] X. *An.* 5.6.19–21.

[63] How different, in other words, were the *emporoi*, in X. *Cyr.* 6.2.38–9 from the *kapeloi* in *Cyr.* 4.5.42?

[64] X. *Cyr.* 6.2.38–9.

[65] Pritchett (1971) describes the officials and lays out the source references on 37–8.

[66] Thuc. 6.44.1; cf. 6.22.   [67] X. *Hell*. 1.6.37.

poleis also exercised control over war profits. Sparta appointed officials specifically responsible for the disposition of booty, which was sold in the field, the profits accruing to the polis (1991: 403–16). Athens too exerted strict official control over the disposal of booty, especially the sale of prisoners of war (1991: 416–25).

In Chapters 5 and 6 below I argue that state and individual preoccupation with τροφή ("food") prompted the Athenians to notice one thing only about those who shipped grain to Athens – the essential service to the polis that they provided. No evidence from the classical period shows Athens or any other Greek polis to be similarly preoccupied with either the slave trade or slave traders. In these circumstances something other than the service they provided may have drawn attention – a slave trader's foreign origin or relative poverty, for example. But if anything attracted notice it was probably the "commodity" in which he dealt. Xenophon and Aristophanes point to a stigma attached to slave dealing, probably on the local, retail level.[68] Otherwise we have no evidence for the classical Greek world. I suspect that the normal attitude throughout Greco-Roman antiquity was not so much disdain, as some scholars believe,[69] as indifference. Most Greeks probably cared as little about how slaves reached classical Greece in large numbers as do my American neighbors about how the more than 16,000 different items now in stock reach their local supermarket.[70]

CONCLUSION

Five conclusions emerge from this survey of the grain, timber, slave, fleet, and army trade.

1 Taken together these sorts of trade constitute the great majority of long-distance transfers in the classical period, so that most of the inter-regional movement of goods was by trade and not by other means.

2 The nature of the grain and timber trade dictated the sort of men who plied it – the *emporoi* and *nauklēroi* described in Chapter 1 who made

---

[68] X. *Symp.* 4.36 and Ar. *Plut.* 520–1; cf. Pl. *Resp.* 589e. We cannot be certain whether *andrapodizontai* in Xenophon and *andrapodiston* in Aristophanes refer to local slave retailers or the wholesaling *emporoi* who transport slaves. I opt for the former, the latter being out of sight and hence out of mind. Consider the parallel with tax collecting: most of the popular prejudice against tax collectors in Roman Judaea or early modern France focused on those at the local level, not on those who forwarded it.

[69] W. V. Harris (1980: 129) and Bradley (1987: 46) on Roman attitudes.

[70] A slave trader from the Roman period, Aulos Kapreilios Timotheos, was sufficiently pleased by his rise from slavery to dealing in slaves to identify himself as a slave trader on his imposing tombstone (Finley 1977). There (164–5) Finley also explains that Herodotus' condemnation (8.105) of the slave trader Panionios applied not to slave trading but rather to his trade in eunuchs.

such commerce their principal occupation. In the penultimate section of this chapter I also reviewed the singular role of slave traders.

3 The large scale of the demand by Greek poleis for grain, timber, and slaves (enormous by comparison with the tiny size of traders' operations), guaranteed work for quite large numbers of professional maritime traders, even if we cannot quantify further.

4 Chapter 5 deals with the high degree of state interference in the grain and timber trade, a boon to substantivists. But, *from the maritime trader's point of view* rather than that of the polis, his work was a series of risk-filled ventures in which market logic operated powerfully. Sheer economic rationality prompted him to take his goods to where he could get the biggest margin. No polis offered him the direct subsidies of the sort that American farmers receive from a capitalist state; no polis cushioned him financially in the wake of losses from an unprofitable or even disaster-filled venture, as do contemporary welfare states. The substantivist-formalist dichotomy does not serve us well here. And substantivists are obliged to acknowledge the significant, ever-increasing market element in the most crucial long-range exchanges in the classical Greek world – the commerce in grain, timber, and slaves.[71]

5 Finally, whatever the still-disputed date of its inception, classical Athens' need for grain and timber became sufficiently acute that, by the fourth century, shortages prompted substantial official responses. What were these? And how did such a large-scale dependence affect the unofficial attitudes of individual Athenians towards the maritime traders who brought the goods to Athens? These questions, after prefatory chapters on traders' "nationality" and level of wealth, are addressed in Chapters 5 and 6.

---

[71] For source references see n.20 of Ch. 1. Even Millett (1990), in a substantivist treatment of exchange at Athens, is prepared to acknowledge (191–4) the grain trade as one in which a rough-and-ready calculation of supply and demand prevailed. A central thesis of Scott Meikle's most helpful, recent book (1995: 5, 153) on Aristotle is that the latter "has a body of thought [principally *Eth. Nic.* 5.5 and *Pol.* 1. 8–10] directed specifically at analysing [the] . . . development [of the ever-increasing market element]."

The juridical place of maritime traders

Chapters 3–6 deal with the place of *emporoi* and *nauklēroi* both in the states they traded with and in the states they came from. Chapter 3 concerns the maritime trader's juridical place (whether citizen or foreigner where he traded); Chapter 4, his level of wealth relative to others in a polis; Chapter 5, the official polis attitude to traders; and Chapter 6, attitudes of citizens within the polis to traders.

Most of the evidence concerns those trading at Athens. Were they mainly Athenians? Since so much of our information dates from the fourth century, it is best to begin there and then consider separately the evidence from the fifth. The great majority of those trading with Athens in the fourth century appear to be non-Athenians:[1] Aeschines (1.40) casually refers to "the *emporoi* or other foreigners or citizens...";[2] and of the sixty-one fourth-century *emporoi* and/or *nauklēroi* in the Catalogue only twelve[3] are Athenians[4]

---

[1] Both Knorringa (1926: 80) and Cohen (1973: 118) think the reference in [Lys.] 22.17 to *emporoi* as "those who sail into [Athens]" supports the case for *emporoi* as foreigners. It does not: the speaker has in mind *emporoi* who bring grain; in order to get the grain Athenian *emporoi* too must go elsewhere and then "sail into" Athens.

[2] Finley (1935: 330 n.48) thinks the passage "is unique in the literature of the period and is undoubtedly to be explained by the use of *allos* to mean not 'other' but 'in addition', as in Plato, *Grg.* 473c–d, τῶν πολιτῶν καὶ τῶν ἄλλων ξένων..." I see no reason why ἄλλων should not be translated as "other"; hence, "As many of the *emporoi* or of the other foreigners or of our own citizens..." Cf. Arist. *Pol.* 1327a 11–31.

[3] Nos. 8 (E), 15 (prob. E), 16 (E), 22 (poss. E), 23 (N), 24 (poss. E), 25 (N), 31 (prob. E), 32 (prob. E), 35 (N), 36 (N), and 61 (E). I exclude nos. 40 (Leokrates) and 41 (Andokides), both of whom probably only traded while in exile, and both of whom in exile probably never traded at Athens (although Andokides did trade with Athenians on Samos [Andok. 2.11]). I also exclude no. 39 (Chairephilos), who probably had retired from trading by the time he was awarded Athenian citizenship. Erxleben (1974: 473, 477) finds twelve fourth-century Athenian *emporoi* and *nauklēroi*; Isager–Hansen (1975: 72) claim to have found twelve in the forensic speeches alone. See further Marianne Hansen's tabulations (1984: 72–3).

[4] It would be helpful to know how many non-Athenian fourth-century *emporoi* and/or *nauklēroi* actually traded at Athens, but this figure is impossible to determine. To say that a certain *emporos* did so or did not is too often pure guesswork, and we do not even know whether many *nauklēroi* in the Catalogue engaged in trade at all, much less at Athens. (See further 12–13 on the proportion of *nauklēroi* who also engaged in trade.)

trading with Athens.[5] Another revealing piece of evidence is more oblique: the speaker in [Lys.] 22 urges the jury (22.21) to "court" (χαριεῖσθε) the *emporoi* who trade with Athens by voting death for the grain dealers, the implication being that if the *emporoi* are not courted they might take their grain elsewhere. Since one of the Athenian maritime laws (*nomoi emporikoi*) forbade Athenian citizens and metics to carry grain elsewhere,[6] the speaker must be assuming that *emporoi* are non-citizen, even non-resident. Xenophon must assume the same when he mentions his plans (*Vect.* 3.1–5, 12–13) to attract more *emporoi* to Athens; the Athenian law just cited made non-Athenian, non-resident *emporoi* the only ones who needed persuading.

Of post World War II historians, Ehrenberg (1974: 140) most confidently believes that the *emporoi* trading at Athens were largely Athenians, yet the single piece of evidence he cites fails to support his case. From Isok. 17.57 Ehrenberg[7] concludes that "it was only to Athenian *emporoi* that the Bosporan kings gave permission to export corn from their country." The speaker in Isok. 17.57 actually says that in times of grain shortage his father and King Satyros "sent away empty the ships of other *emporoi* while granting to you [*humin*] export rights." Demosthenes shows that the word *humin* in this passage is not confined to Athenian citizens; he reminds an Athenian jury (20.31) that Satyros' successor Leukon has granted exemption from duty to "those carrying [grain] to Athens" and priority of lading to "those sailing to you."[8]

---

[5] Hasebroek claims that there were practically no Athenians among those trading at Athens (1933: 101; see also 22, 28, 96, 146–7, 171). The implausibility of this claim has already been suggested by Jones (1940: 91 and nn.73–6), Mossé (1962: 121–2), de Ste. Croix (1972: 265 n.58, 393–4), Isager–Hansen (1975: 71–2 and nn.74–8), and Whitehead (1977: 117, 123 n.38). D. 23.146 confirms that *some* Athenian citizens were *emporoi* in the fourth century.

[6] [D.] 34.37; D. 35.50; Lykourg. *Leoc.* 27. We do not know if this "emporic law" (*nomos emporikos*) was in effect at the time of the speech against the grain dealers (386 B.C.: Gernet and Bizos [1924: II 84 and n.I]). The need for such a law dates from early in the fourth century: "In the fifth century Athens was at the height of her power and in a position to intervene directly to safeguard her interests, whereas in the fourth century she was obliged to have recourse to indirect means, such as legislation" (Austin and Vidal–Naquet [1974: 116]). So the law in question might have existed by the date [Lys.] 22 was delivered. At least we have testimony to the early existence of officials associated with the *nomoi emporikoi*: the speaker in [Lys.] 22 refers to the *sitophylakes* (5, 8, 16), and an inscription dated 375/ 4 B.C. provides the earliest mention (lines 21–2, 41) of the "overseers of the import market" (*epimeletai tou emporiou*) (Stroud [1974: 158–9, 180–1]).

[7] 1974: 140 and n.4; see also 149 and 160.

[8] Even more recent books make Ehrenberg's mistake. Isager–Hansen (1975: 204) refer to those carrying grain to Athens as "Athenian merchants," and Hopper (1979: 84) refers to the ships in which the grain traveled as "Athenian vessels." At first glance Athenian citizens themselves appear to make the same mistake. In different speeches two Athenians (D. 35.50, Lykourg. *Leoc.* 27), citing the law that requires citizens and metics to bring grain only to Athens, use the same misleading words, "If any Athenian transports grain to any other place . . ." (ἐάν τις Ἀθηναίων ἄλλοσέ ποι σιτηγήσῃ). But

Virtual silence confronts anyone who turns to the fifth-century evidence. Erxleben (1974: 478 and 501) claims that well into the Periklean era trade at Athens was in the hands of poor Athenians, but he cites (478) only X. *Mem.* 3.7.6, which merely acknowledges[9] that *some* Athenian citizens may have been *emporoi*. Isokrates' reference (7.32–3, 44) to those bygone days when the benevolent rich citizens helped struggling poor citizens engage in *emporia* probably refers to no specific era, but might apply to the fifth century. We cannot know whether the *emporoi* trading with Athens before *c.* 375 B.C. were mainly Athenian or not, but doubtless more and more foreign *emporoi* began to visit Athens as she grew in power, wealth, and size between *c.* 475 B.C. and the Peloponnesian War.

The lack of evidence also thwarts any attempt to examine systematically the juridical status of traders in places other than Athens. There persists a tendency to think that an instance of inter-regional trade obviously important for a given polis by itself implies a decent proportion of influential citizen traders.[10] We have just seen that this was not the case at Athens, where most of the maritime traders appear to be non-Athenian. Athens is exceptional in so many respects, true, not least because it is far and away the best documented case, so that it is unrealistic to demand conclusive evidence that things were different elsewhere. Salmon speculates that "the proportion of Corinthians involved in the Corinthian trade was probably higher, even in the fourth century, than in the Athenian case," based in part on the high proportion of merchants' marks on Corinthian vases, but he acknowledges that the sample is small.[11]

On its face the study of vase graffiti promises to reveal more about the "nationality" of maritime traders, yet this has not proved the case to date. From such graffiti J. Elayi for example argues that merchants at Al Mina III (430–375 B.C.) were Phoenicians and not Greeks,[12] but Miller points out that these are probably the owners' and not the traders' inscriptions.[13]

in both cases the mistake is deliberate: both speakers tailor their version of the law to suit the case at hand, and in both cases the person whom they wish to identify as the culprit is an Athenian citizen. More puzzling is the appearance of "the Athenian *emporoi*" (*[hoi e]mporoi ho[i Athenaion*) in an inscription (*IG* ii² 416) honoring Praxiades of Kos. This restoration by Wilhelm would make the inscription read in part, "The Athenian *emporoi*, the *dēmos* of Samos, the other Athenians present, and the rest declare that Praxiades of Kos looks after the *emporoi* and *naukleroi* so that grain comes to the Athenian *dēmos* as abundantly as possible . . ." The puzzle is removed by adopting J. K. Davies' more plausible (unpublished) alternative: "the *emporoi* on hand" (*hoi e]mporoi ho[i parontes*).

9 As does Plut. *Per.* 12.6 and Thuc. 2.67.4.
10 See the discussion of books by Clavel Lévêque and Hodge in n.32 below.
11 Salmon (1984: 160–1); see also his cautious remarks on 147–54, 159–64, and 405–6.
12 Elayi (1987: esp. 256–8, 260). See also Elayi (1988: esp. 61–106).
13 Miller (1997: 86). See further the entire section entitled "*Emporoi* and *Naukleroi*: The Carriers of Trade Goods" (85–8).

Unfortunately, other prominent trading sites in the classical period, such as Chios and Samos, yield no information about who traded there or with whom the merchants from there traded.[14]

Appendix 1 provides an alphabetical list of all attested states of origin, both for individuals in the Catalogue and for groups such as Sidonian *emporoi*. Some of these states clearly produced more traders than others, but again it must be stressed that the nature of the evidence prevents Appendix 1 or the Catalogue from providing a representative cross-section.

Trade routes[15] offer one clue, although we must not assume that grain coming to Greece from another area was necessarily carried by traders from that area.[16] Athens for instance gave individual honors to *emporoi* and *nauklēroi* from on or near the vital eastern[17] and northern[18] grain routes, but one of those living on the eastern route engaged in the northern trade,[19] while another from the same eastern city may have been active on the western route to Sicily.[20] Athens also honored two men from Herakleia (presumably on the Black Sea) for importing wheat and barley from Sicily to Athens.[21]

Athens gave her only recorded blanket grants of privilege to *emporoi* and *nauklēroi* from on or near the eastern grain route. Probably in the early 360s Sidonian *emporoi* visiting Athens were excused from the obligations of metics, if they overstayed the time when a *xenos* was legally required to register as a *metoikos*.[22] In 333 B.C. *emporoi* from Kition (a Phoenician city on Cyprus) were granted the right to acquire land on which to build a

---

[14] On Samos see the careful account by Shipley (1987), who refuses to generalize from inadequate evidence, especially for the classical period. On Chios' commercial relations with other Greek poleis, see the overview by Sarikakis (1986).

[15] For a description of these routes, see the references in nn.11 and 12 of Ch. 2.

[16] See further de Ste. Croix (1972: 265–6).

[17] See in the Catalogue nos. 50, 51, 52, and 60. For eastern sources of grain for Greece, see further n.8 of Ch.2.

[18] For sources of grain on the northern route, see further n.10 of Ch. 2.

[19] Herakleides of Salamis (no. 60). For his activity in the Black Sea area see item 2 of no. 60. For sources of grain on the western route see further n.9 of Ch. 2.

[20] The Athenian decree (*IG* ii² 283) honors a possible *emporos* from Salamis in Cyprus (no. 50). He brought grain (and perhaps fish too) from Egypt (lines 2–3). He is nowhere said to have brought grain from Sicily, but it is recorded (lines 8–10) that he paid the ransom that obtained the release "from Sicily" of captive Athenians.

[21] In *IG* ii² 408 Memnon and someone else of Herakleia (nos. 53 and 54 of the Catalogue) are honored for delivering barley to Athens and selling both barley and "Sicilian wheat" (lines 12–14). Ziebarth (1896: 131) queried the largely restored *S[ikelikon]*, probably because he thought it unlikely that men from Herakleia in Pontos would trade with Sicily, but the references cited in the notes just preceding suggest that traveling thus far was not exceptional.

[22] *IG* ii² 141 = *Syll*.³ no. 185 = Tod no. 139 = Harding no. 40. See further Austin and Vidal-Naquet (1977: 273–4), and Whitehead (1977: 8–9, 14–15), and (on the decree's date) Moysey (1976). Appendix 1 provides references to other Phoenicians trading with classical Greece.

sanctuary of Aphrodite, "just as the Egyptians built a sanctuary of Isis."[23] (These Egyptians may well have been *emporoi*, too.) Such blanket grants to Phoenician and (perhaps) Egyptian *emporoi* may indicate that they appeared in relatively large numbers in fourth-century Athens.

On or near the eastern route lay Rhodes and Phaselis.[24] Doubtless Rhodes' importance as a center of commercial life predates the hellenistic period, when the amount of relevant evidence for Rhodes increases.[25] In 1980 Michael Walbank published the fragment of an Athenian inscription dated to 330–326 B.C. honoring Rhodians[26] for importing grain to Athens. If this date is correct, it constitutes the only mention of Rhodian traders from the classical period; but the stone cutters' script on the inscription prompted Tracy to move the date to the first half of the next century.[27]

So we remain without unambiguous references, specific or general, to Rhodian *emporoi* or *nauklēroi* in the classical period. Lykourgos refers (*Leoc.* 15–16) to late classical Rhodes as a place where *emporoi* who traverse the Greek world "stay" (ἐπιδημοῦσιν). They probably "stay" at Rhodes in the same sense that Phoenician *emporoi* living and retaining citizenship in Sidon are said to "stay for purposes of trade at Athens."[28] And the merchant vessels brought by Rhodian triremes into Rhodes immediately after Chaironeia belong not necessarily to Rhodians but to *emporoi* and *nauklēroi*, place of origin unspecified, en route to Athens (Lykourg. *Leoc.* 18).

Phaselite traders appear to play an important role in both fifth- and fourth-century trade with Athens;[29] the only Phaselite traders about whom

---

23 *IG* ii² 337+ = *Syll.*³ no. 280 = Tod no. 189 = Schwenk no. 27 = Rhodes no. 16 = Harding no. 111. See Austin and Vidal-Naquet (1977: 274–5), also Engen (1996: 61, 114–15, 432 nn.151–4). Simms (1989: 216–21) provides the historical context for the *enktesis* grants to both Kitians and Egyptians. See also Garland (1987: 101–11) on foreign cults in Piraeus.

24 Sailing conditions forced merchant ships returning from Egypt to Greece to sail north by northeast to Cyprus, then along the southern coast of Asia Minor, stopping at Rhodes ([D.] 56.9–10; cf. Lykourg. *Leoc.* 18; Thuc. 8.35.2–3). See further Casson's description of this route (1950): 43–56, esp. 43–8.

25 A Kyrene decree (*SEG* ix 2 = Tod no. 196 = Rhodes no. 20 = Harding no.116) reveals that in the Aegean-wide grain shortage of the 320s B.C., Rhodes received 30,000 *medimnoi* from Kyrene, compared with the following other amounts: Athens, 100,000; Olympias, 60,000; and 50,000 each to Argos, Larisa, Corinth, and Kleopatra. On this decree and its historical context see further Brun (1993: 185–96).

26 (1980): 251–5.

27 Tracy (1995: 35). Walbank in his *Hesperia* article (1980: 253) also posited an alternative, third-century date for the inscription. See further Engen (1996: 156–7 and 436 nn.224–8).

28 On the Sidonians see n.22 above, in particular lines 31–2 of Tod no. 139. On the verb ἐπιδημέω see further Whitehead (1977), esp. 10, 11 and n.36, 21 n.9. For other primary and secondary references pertaining to pre-hellenistic Rhodes and its commerce, see Berthold (1984: 47–50) and Gabrielsen (1997: 64–74).

29 I follow de Ste. Croix (1961: esp.100–8) in assuming that the Phaselis decree (*IG* i³ 10 = ML no. 31 = Fornara no. 68) offered Phaselites a speedier procedure before the Polemarch for resolving

something is known individually (nos. 19–21) are engaged in the fourth-century Pontic trade, but given Phaselis' location others were surely active on the eastern route as well, perhaps aboard the fifth-century merchant vessels sailing to Athens "from Phaselis and Phoenicia and that part of the mainland" (Thuc. 2.69.1).[30]

Some Greek states may have produced numerous traders for a combination of reasons: Chios, for example, because of its location and fine harbor;[31] Massalia,[32] because of its location and poor land; Aigina,[33] because of its paucity *and* barrenness of land as well as its location. Lack or barrenness of land might also have caused those places that reputedly produced many fishermen or pirates to produce *emporoi* as well; and *emporia* may have been the way still others escaped from the poverty and backwardness of inland areas.

legal disputes, probably including those arising out of bottomry loans. Nowhere in the decree are *emporoi* or *nauklēroi* explicitly mentioned; but, (if de Ste. Croix's above analysis is correct), the privilege offered by the decree might be aimed particularly at Phaselite traders, and thus might testify to their importance at Athens. (R. Seager [1966: 172–84] has challenged the above interpretation.) See further Thuc. 2.69.1, which as de Ste. Croix puts it (1961: 105 n.1) "provides evidence that *c.* 430 Phaselis was at least an important port of call for merchants trading with the Aegean, if not the actual home of such merchants." On Thuc. 2.69.1 see also the reference in n.30 below. As for the fourth century: D. 35 provides the Catalogue with nos. 19–21 from Phaselis and more importantly shows that in the 340s Phaselite traders were well known at Athens, although (as ML p. 31 point out) "the *ex parte* denunciations of their shiftiness and chicanery [in D. 35.1–2] need not perhaps be taken too seriously." Cf. de Ste. Croix (1961: 104 n.3).

[30] See further on this passage Hornblower (1991a: 355–6).

[31] Arist. *Pol.* 1291b 23–4. For reservations about whether those referred to here are actually *emporoi*, see Newman (1887b: 173).

[32] On Massalia's location, particularly as a Mediterranean outlet for tin from Britain, see Diod. Sic. 5.22.4; 5.38.5; Strabo 3.2.9; cf. Polyb. 3.41.4; Strabo. 4.2.1. On its poor land see Strabo 4.1.4–5. Massalia's government appears to have remained oligarchic from the archaic through the Roman periods (Arist. *Pol.* 1305b 3–10; 1321a 26–31; Strabo 4.1.5; Cic. *Flac.* 26.63; *Rep.* 1.27.43). Clavel-Lévêque claims that in the archaic period Massalia built up "un vaste empire commercial" (1977: 19). Here I want only to criticize her analysis of a constitutional change that she dates at the beginning of the classical period (118). Aristotle (*Pol.* 1321a 26–31) remarks that at Massalia some who had previously been outside the governing class were admitted to it. Clavel-Lévêque (116) assumes that before this reform the governing class was defined by "leur participation à l'*emporia*," and concludes (119) that the reform itself admitted to power those who were "à la fois *emporoi* et producteurs de céramique ou de vin." All of this must be regarded as unwarranted speculation, as is Hodge's recent claim (1998: 113) that "Massalia was a trading state . . . and in a trading state . . . the commercial interests must have been important enough to win some sort of recognition," although he acknowledges that "there is no sign of it [traders' political clout] here" (an ambiguous "here" that probably means "in the ancient evidence"). I much prefer Goudineau's more skeptical and plausible view that little is actually known about ancient Massaliot *trade* (1983: 76–86). About Massaliot *traders* we know even less: in particular, apart from nos. 4 and 5 in the Catalogue, we know nothing about the "nationality" of those responsible for the items going into or coming out of Massalia in the classical period. On Massaliot trade see further Arafat and Morgan (1994: 126–8) and the bibliography therein.

[33] Arist. *Pol.* 1291b 23–4. On the poverty of the soil: Strabo (8.6.16) citing Ephoros. On trade with Aigina in both the archaic and classical periods, see Figueira (1981: esp. 230–98); cf. de Ste. Croix (1972: 267 n.1).

That any Greek state banned its citizens from engaging in *emporia* seems unlikely. Xenophon (*Oec.* 4.3) says that certain states made it illegal for citizens to work at *banausikas technas* ("the menial trades"),[34] but elsewhere (*Lac.* 7.1) he clearly distinguishes the *technai* from maritime trading as well as from shipowning and farming. I can find only one instance in which the word *techne;* is associated with *emporia* or its cognates, and there (Pl. *Euthphr.* 14e) the word *techne* appears to mean the "way, manner, or means whereby a thing is gained, without any definite sense of art or craft" (LSJ).

The remarks of de Ste. Croix (1972: 266) serve nicely as a conclusion for this chapter:

The merchants who conducted the foreign trade of many individual Greek cities, then, were not only citizens and metics of these cities: many of them belonged to what we might almost call an "international merchant class" – men who traded from place to place, wherever they saw an opening, and did not concern themselves entirely (or even mainly perhaps) with the trade of the state in which they had citizenship or domicile.[35]

---

[34] Cf. Arist. *Pol.* 1278a 25–6.
[35] See also Austin's summary remarks (1994: 561) in what is to date the best overview of the grain trade in the classical Greek world.

CHAPTER 4

The level of wealth of maritime traders

INTRODUCTION

How wealthy, by comparison with those in the "upper class" of Greek *poleis*, were the *emporoi* and *nauklēroi* trading at Athens or elsewhere? By definition (see 12–13) a *nauklēros* not only owned a merchant ship, one of which brought forty minae when sold in the fourth century ([D.] 33.12); he may have normally owned a slave crew as well: "Demosthenes' matter-of-fact allusions [[D.] 33.8–10; 34.10] to seagoing freighters manned by slaves shows how common the practice must have been in the fourth century B.C." (Casson [1971: 328]). A single ship and slave crew would make a *nauklēros* moderately wealthy, but the term "wealthy" applied here to *nauklēroi* refers only to those who were more than moderately wealthy. The following *nauklēroi* in the Catalogue appear to fall into this latter category: Lampis I (no. 2), possibly Apollonides (no. 17), Phormion II (no. 23), probably Philippos (no. 25), Andokides (no. 41), and Herakleides (no. 60). Three of these – Lampis I, Phormion II, and (possibly) Andokides – are the only *nauklēroi* said to own more than one vessel.[1]

As for *emporoi*, Hasebroek cites [D.] 34.51 to support his claim that "merchants and shipowners...were invariably without any capital worth mentioning of their own."[2] In [D.] 34.51 a bottomry lender predictably claims that "the means for engaging in trade come not from those who

---

[1] Two of the exceptions, Lampis I and Phormion II, date from the fourth century. As for the fifth: in *IG* i² 128 (= *IG* i³ 130), dated by Lewis (1960: 190–4) to 432/1 B.C., *nauklēroi* are said to contribute to some sort of state levy, each of them paying a drachma on his ship [lines 4–5]; on these *nauklēroi* see further Lewis' extensive and attractive restorations in *IG* i³ 130 and the article cited above as well as my discussion of *IG* i³ 130 in Appendix 2. Isager–Hansen (1975: 74) think *IG* i³ 130 shows that "each *nauklēros* has only one ship," and lines 4–5 do suggest this, perhaps as the general rule to which there might be exceptions. Roughly a quarter of a century later appears one possible exception: Andokides (no. 41) mentions his "shipownings" (*nauklēriōn*: Andok. 1.137). See further item 2 of no. 41.

[2] Hasebroek twice on (1928: 7) (cf. [D.] 56.48). See also Hasebroek (1928: 8–21 [esp. 8–12], 38, 89, 96, and 101).

borrow but from those who lend; and no ship, no shipowner, and no passenger can put to sea without the help of the lenders." This passage in no way supports Hasebroek's claim.[3] Bottomry loans provided such good insurance that even some who were able to "put to sea without the help of the lenders" might choose not to.[4] If a ship carrying the grain bought with borrowed money did not arrive safely back at Athens, the borrower normally was not obliged to repay the lender. Wealthier *emporoi*, therefore, as well as poorer ones, probably resorted to bottomry loans simply for the protection they offered against the enormous risks involved in trading by sea.[5] Millett (1983: 44 and 188–9 n.22) downplays this "insurance" element, arguing that it "was an effect rather than a cause" of maritime lending. Such a scholarly quibble should not prevent us from believing that borrowers would be acutely aware that the terms of bottomry contracts[6] absolved them of the obligation to repay. Why else would Zenothemis and Hegestratos (nos. 4 and 5) try to scuttle their vessel at sea (in D. 32), or Artemon and Apollodoros (nos. 19 and 20) lie to their creditors (in D. 35)?

THE FOURTH-CENTURY EVIDENCE

Bottomry loans thus reveal nothing about maritime traders' relative level of wealth. We must look elsewhere, and again (as in Chapter 3) it is best to consider the fourth-century evidence separately from that of the fifth. The commercial activity of forty-five men listed as *emporoi* or *emporoi-or-nauklēroi* in the Catalogue probably fell in the fourth century. Sixteen[7] are not poor, but seven of the sixteen rank as only possible rather than definite or probable *emporoi* or *emporoi-or-nauklēroi*. These tabulations are

---

[3] Millett (1983: 44) acknowledges the threat to Hasebroek's claim: "If it is accepted that maritime credit was taken out purely as an insurance policy and not as a loan, it cannot be argued that traders were forced to borrow through poverty." Why "either or"? Why cannot loans both serve as insurance *and* provide the capital needed by poorer *emporoi*?

[4] For overviews of maritime loans in classical Greece, see the very brief *OCD*[3] entry and in more detail esp. de Ste. Croix (1974), as well as Amit (1965: 126–7), Vélissaropoulos (1980: 301–8), Millett (1991: 189–91), and Cohen (1992: 146–50, also his acute comments [46–60 and 1990a] on the landed/maritime classification of loans). For endorsements of the "insurance" function of maritime loans as risk absorbers, see Finley (1999: 141); de Ste. Croix (1974: 42–3); Casson (1991: 102–3); Cohen (1992: 140–6); and Todd (1993: 337–40).

[5] On the dangers of sea trade, see further n.6 of Ch. 1. On the perennial risks of long-distance sea trade in grain in particular, see Braudel's comments (1982: 457) on early modern Europe.

[6] The text of one bottomry contract survives, cited in [D.] 35.10–13. Casson (1991: 105–7) and Davies (1993: 222–5) provide translations.

[7] Nos. 1 (prob. E or N), 4 (poss. E), 8 (E), 9 (prob. E), 11 (E), 12 (E), 16 (E), 22 (poss. E), 29 (E), 39 (poss. E), 40 (prob. E), 42 (poss. E or N), 53 and 54 (poss. E), and 72 (poss. E or N). I exclude here anyone "probably not" either an *emporos* or an *emporos-or-nauklēros*.

meant to lay out the known particulars and cannot pretend to be conclusive, but further evidence also supports the case for the relative lack
of wealth on the part of *emporoi*: several fourth-century sources[8] confirm
that poverty drove people into *emporia*; other sources[9] group *emporoi* together with those who follow other modest pursuits.[10] And a disproportion-
ately large number of wealthier traders appear in the Demosthenic corpus,
since only wealthier ones could afford the services of Demosthenes and the
other orators. The tentative conclusion: most fourth-century *emporoi* were
poor, and even most *nauklēroi* fell somewhere below the upper echelon of
wealth.

THE ORGANIZATION OF EMPORIA

Before turning to the fifth-century evidence I want to use Phormion II
(no. 23) as the point of departure for discussing the way in which *emporia*
was organized. Almost all the evidence on this subject dates from the fourth
century rather than the fifth.

Phormion II owns merchant vessels but probably does not himself go to
sea.[11] For many in the Catalogue the evidence is missing, but apart from
Phormion II and perhaps two others (Lampis I [no. 2] and Dion [no. 13])
it appears that the other *nauklēroi* and *emporoi* regularly take to sea –
the *emporos* with his goods, the *nauklēros* aboard his own vessel, with
other goods in the hold that perhaps are his as well. How are we to regard the three most plausible exceptions to this rule? Are Dion, Lampis I,
and Phormion II shore-based magnates dispatching agents to trade on
their behalf? Dion we know only as the owner of a single slave (no. 13)
who combined trading, lending, and possibly ship-captaining.[12] Lampis I
is called "the largest shipowner in Greece," but we are never told of any

---

[8] The most reliable is X. *Vect.* 4.6. (In that passage the poor who turn to money lending [τοκισμούς]
engage in petty lending, not in bottomry lending.) See also Arist. *Pol.* 1320a 39 and Ael. *Ep.* 18.

[9] Ar. *Plut.* 904; Pl. *Leg.* 918d, 919d; Arist. *Pol.*1290b 38–1291a; perhaps X. *Mem.* 3.7.6 should also be
included, since the third book of the *Memorabilia* may have been composed late enough to reflect
fourth-century conditions rather than those of Sokrates' lifetime, although the conditions relevant
here probably remained the same throughout much of both centuries.

[10] For counter-claims about the level of wealth of Aiginetan merchants, see de Ste. Croix (1972: 267
n.1) and Figueira (1981: 15, 170, 282, 284–6, 321–6, 342–3). Appian (*Pun.* 12.87) compares the fortunes
of Athens' empire to merchants' profits (*emporika kerdea*) – an "increase" followed by a "massive
loss." On the profits and losses of *emporoi* and *nauklēroi* for both the classical period or later, see
also X. *Mem.* 3.4.2; Philo *De migratione Abrahami* 217; Dio Cass. 38.20.4.

[11] Cohen (1992: 123) claims that "Phormion . . . engaged in maritime trade," but the single passage he
cites ([D.] 49.31) in no way supports his claim.

[12] On whether Lampis II may be the owner or captain of a vessel, see item 2 of no. 13.

other business activities.[13] The case of Phormion II, the banker and *nauklēros*, is more complex. Two men might be regarded as trading agents of Phormion. At one point (D. 45.64) Phormion II dispatches Stephanos as his agent (πρεσβευτῆς) to plead with those from Byzantion who seized his (Phormion's) ships, but neither this mission nor what we otherwise know about Stephanos prompts us to regard him as an agent *engaged in trade* on Phormion's behalf. The other candidate, Timosthenes (no. 24), is called the friend (ἐπιτήδειος) and associate (κοινωνός) ([D.] 49.31) of Phormion II; on one occasion Timosthenes is said to engage "in commerce on his own account" (*kat' emporian idian*). Perhaps the purpose of the word *idian* ("on his own account") is to distinguish this venture from others undertaken *on Phormion's account*. Then there is the perplexing case of the slave Lampis II (no. 13). Perhaps he qualifies as the agent of his owner Dion.

Even if these tenuous inferences are correct, an entrepreneur–agent relationship between Phormion II and Timosthenes on the one hand and Dion and Lampis II on the other provide the only recorded exceptions to the rule, unless one wishes to add two less likely candidates – the above-mentioned Stephanos and Philondas (no. 26), an employee of Timotheos who accompanies a timber shipment from Macedonia to Athens.[14] Other *emporoi* and/or *nauklēroi* in the Catalogue apparently worked alone or as co-equals in pairs. Roughly a third of the fourth-century total (nineteen out of sixty-one) operated in partnerships.[15] These Erxleben (1974: 486, 490) believed to be exclusively "family undertakings," but in at least five of the ten cases they clearly are not, or the family tie is not mentioned.[16] The only exception to the two-man partnership dates from the very end of our period (the 320s): in [D.] 56 the partners Dionysodoros and Parmeniskos are accused of being part of a larger trading network organized by Kleomenes, Alexander of Macedonia's deputy in Egypt.[17]

[13] The phrase applied to Lampis I in Plut. *Mor.* 234F (ναυκλήρια πολλὰ ἔχων) means "having much property in ships" and not "having many cargoes on the sea in ships" (Loeb translation), just as the words μέγιστα ναυκλήρια in D. 23.211 mean "the greatest amount of property in ships." See further item 5 of no. 2.

[14] On Philondas' unlikely status as an *emporos*, see further item 2 of no. 26.

[15] Nos. 4 and 5 (non-family); nos. 6 and 7 (non-family); nos. 11 and 12 (family); nos. 17 and 18 (non-family); nos. 19 and 20 (family); nos. 29 and 30 (non-family); nos. 31 and 32 (family); no. 49 and sons (family); nos. 51 and 52 (family); nos. 53 and 54 (non-family). All the recorded partnerships in the classical period date from the fourth century. Was one partner legally liable for the acts of another? No: Athenian law contained no notion of partnership or corporation. See E. M. Harris' (1989) lucid and convincing explanation of how the absence of such a law clarifies certain features of several bottomry-related disputes in the corpus of speeches attributed to Demosthenes.

[16] See n.15 for a list of family and non-family partnerships.

[17] [D.] 56.7–9; see also [Arist.] *Oec.* 2.2.33. On Kleomenes' network see further Ziebarth (1896: 62–3) and Erxleben (1974: 489–90).

No large classical trading "combines," then, nor (as Appendix 2 shows) any political or economic cohesion among the one- or two-person enterprises described above. But the way the grain trade was organized might affect the place of traders at Athens in other ways. At 16–19 we saw how vital was the grain supply to Athens and at 34–5 above how grain imports were financed at Athens by bottomry loans. What if the *lenders* combined to influence official Athenian policy? That possibility becomes likelier if two further conditions are met – if lenders were themselves traders *and* citizens. Being a lender-cum-trader would deepen one's involvement in the grain trade, and being a citizen would offer a lender-trader access to the political influence denied largely foreign *emporoi*. Hence the two remaining questions of this section: Were most bottomry lenders also maritime traders? And, traders or not, were most lenders citizens?

Paul Millett recently argued for a strong overlap of regular bottomry lenders and maritime traders.[18] On the face of it the overlap makes sense: who but traders themselves, with their business contacts and firsthand experience with the complex details of such long-range commerce, were better prepared to invest their money knowledgeably? Yet the Catalogue documents only a slight overlap: out of sixty-two fourth-century active *emporoi* and *nauklēroi* only six definitely or probably made bottomry loans, as possibly did a further six.[19] We also hear of a former *emporos* (no. 8) who, having retired, devotes himself to maritime lending. Millett (1983: 37) well describes how capricious can be the differing head counts: my rosters of bottomry lenders for example differ significantly from those of Erxleben,[20] Isager–Hansen,[21] and Millett.[22]

[18] Millett (1991: 192): "The largest group of identifiable maritime creditors are professional lenders, all having some personal experience of the practicalities of maritime trade."

[19] Definite or probable lenders: nos. 11 (E), 12 (E), 13 (N), 16 (E), 22 (poss. E), and 29 (E). Possible lenders: nos. 4 (poss. E), 19 (E), 20 (E), 33 (prob. N), 34 (prob. N), and 23 (N – this particular loan was probably made before Phormion II became a *nauklēros* [see item 4 of no. 23], but with equal probability he continued to lend *after* becoming one). I exclude the unnamed Athenian (no. 8) who explains ([D.] 33.4) that he took up bottomry lending *after* retirement.

[20] See Erxleben's first set of totals for all bottomry lenders (1974: 479), together with a later, revised set (1974: 482). His short list (479) of active or retired *emporoi* who lend numbers only four as compared with my thirteen (if the retired *emporos* in [D.] 33 is added to the twelve active *emporoi* or *nauklēroi*). One might doubt if some of Erxleben's alleged instances of bottomry lending are actually such, but even if these are removed the gap between "Kapital und aktiver Handelstätigkeit" (482) remains. See further Millett's comments on Erxleben's use of the sources (1983: 37–8), which prompts Cohen (1992: 170–1) to cite Erxleben as a practitioner of "misplaced cliometrics." For other examples of the same malady, see further Cohen (1990b).

[21] Isager–Hansen (1975: 73 n.81). Almost half those named by Isager–Hansen are missing from my list in n.19 above, and vice versa. See further Marianne Hansen's detailed comparisons (1984: 79–89) of Erxleben's and Isager–Hansen's lists.

[22] Cf. those on my list (n.19 above). Millett (1991: 192–4) names only half as either casual or professional lenders (nos. 8, 11, 12, 13, 16, and 22).

The lack of a significant documented overlap between traders and lenders – only thirteen out of sixty-one – can have several explanations. Among them is the lack of sufficient information in the fourth-century Attic orators about various facets of a trader's or a lender's activity, if it does not serve a given speaker's interest to mention these in the civil suits from which most of our evidence comes.[23]

Entirely compatible with the above explanation is yet another one at odds with Millett's – that a respectable number of people other than maritime traders lent on bottomry. This is the alternative chosen by Edward Cohen in Chapter 5 of his 1992 book, where he challenged the near-orthodox view[24] that bankers did not make maritime loans, arguing that they did so on a significant scale.[25] His opening salvo (121–9) is to my mind his least effective: he cites D. 27.8–11 wherein Demosthenes describes the various items in his deceased father's estate. In D. 27.11 Demosthenes says "In addition to all these [other] items, he left 7000 dr. [as] a sea loan with Xouthos [παρὰ Ξούθῳ], 2400 dr. in Pasion's bank, 600 dr. in that of Pylades, and 1600 dr. with Demomeles the son of Demon…"[26] Cohen infers from this passage, first, that all four of these men were bankers, and, second, that the above amounts were all bottomry loans (121–9). I am not persuaded by his arguments (123–9) that Xouthos or Demomeles are bankers, and I confess to greater uncertainty about interpreting the three unnamed loans as maritime loans, solely on the strength of the condensed description in D. 27.11. Yet in the subsequent pages of his Chapter 5 (136–87) Cohen makes a stronger case for bankers' involvement in maritime lending,[27] although the proportions escape us. *Probably*, then, traders had no monopoly on bottomry lending; bankers and perhaps others engaged in it as well.

The final question of this section: Were lenders, whether traders *or* bankers,[28] mainly Athenian or foreign? Of the six traders in the Catalogue[29]

---

[23] As Millett also points out (1983: 38).

[24] See above all Bogaert (1968: 259–61), (1965: 140–56, esp. 141–4), (1986: 27–9, 47–9); de Ste. Croix (1974: 51 n.39); Isager–Hansen (1975: 84); Vélissaropoulos (1980: 303); Millett (1983: 47); and Austin (1988: 741). Thompson admits the possibility of bankers' involvement in bottomry lending (1979: 233–41) but downplays their actual significance (1979: 241). Stanley too (1990: esp. 70–1) sees a role for bankers in making maritime loans.

[25] This is the thesis of Cohen's (1992) Chapter 5, which revives older arguments to the same effect. For these see the first two references in n.7 to the Catalogue, to which should be added the other references in Cohen's n.115 on p. 137.

[26] Cohen's translation (1992: 121) of D. 27.11: "But [he also left] maritime loans: 7,000 dr., a sea loan (*ekdosis*) with Xouthos, 2,400 dr. at the bank of Pasiōn, 600 at that of Pyladēs, 1,600 with Dēmomelēs the son of Dēmon…"

[27] The cogency of Cohen's case for bankers as bottomry lenders has been acknowledged by Figueira (1994: 111–13), Morris (1994: 355), and Shipton (1994: 82 and 1997: 419 n.139).

[28] I can find no documented overlap at all of maritime trading with banking. See further n.11 above.

[29] See n.19 above.

who definitely or probably lend on bottomry, only two (nos. 16 and 22) are Athenians (to whom should be added the Athenian [no. 8] who took to lending after he retired from trading);[30] among possible lenders, only one (no. 23) out of six. Probably something like the same proportions hold for bankers – a sizable number foreign[31] – even if the most successful of them, the metics Pasion and Phormion, did receive Athenian citizenship. One conclusion and a further inference follow: much of the "professional business sector" in Athens was in the hands of non-Athenians, and, whether traders or bankers, their "nationality" denied them political access to and hence leverage on the Athenian "government."[32]

THE FIFTH-CENTURY EVIDENCE

Were *emporoi* as a rule poor in the fifth century as well? The evidence is sparse. Apart from commonsense doubts about radical change in this respect from the fifth to the fourth centuries, our best clue comes from the evidence for bottomry lending. Were the loans that furnished poor *emporoi* with the necessary capital for trade in the fourth century also available in the fifth? Until the 1970s the earliest reference to a Greek bottomry loan was thought to appear in [Lys.] 32.6. There the speaker refers to the maritime loans made (ναυτικά . . . ἐκδεδομένα) by the Athenian, Diodotos, who died in a battle at Ephesos in 409 B.C. ([Lys.] 32.4–15, esp. 6–7).[33]

Then in 1976 David Harvey described an earlier reference to a maritime loan in a fragment of Eupolis' *Marikas*, dated 421:[34] Harvey (1976: 233)

---

[30] Having earned "a moderate amount" ([D.] 33.4) from trading, he ceased making this way (in Cicero's words [*Off.* 1.151]) "from the deep sea to the harbor," where he earned his living by bottomry lending. Few former maritime traders in classical Athens probably took Cicero's next step – "from the harbor to the fields" (*Off.* 1.151), probably settling instead in Piraeus to engage in other business activity.

[31] See for example Cohen (1992: 145).

[32] On the "foreign leverage" issue, see further the third paragraph of Appendix 2. On the proportion of foreigners vis-à-vis Athenians among those who made maritime trading or banking their principal activity: Thompson devotes two articles (1978 and 1982) to arguing that "the citizen of Athens did not abandon economic activity to the metic" (1978: 423). Both pieces largely ignore the distinctions between different categories of people (e.g., citizen *emporoi* or *nauklēroi* as distinct from citizen bankers) that more specific, detailed studies such as this are devoted to investigating. (On Thompson's assumptions and tone, see further Millett [1991: 162–3].) Osborne (1991: 119–42) suffers from a similar lack of precision. He speaks repeatedly of wealthy Athenians being "forced into the market" or of their "involvement in the market" but fails to specify how. As *rentier* owners of manufacturing concerns or as active owner-managers? Or as bottomry lenders of either the "casual" or "professional" variety (to use Millett's distinction)?

[33] For a breakdown of the loans left in Diodotos' estate, see Millett (1991: 168).

[34] *P Oxy.* 2741 = Eupolis *PCG* F 192.96–8. The possibility that *P Oxy.* 2741 fr. 1B col. 2 might refer to a bottomry loan had already been suggested by Lobel in the *editio princeps* (*Oxyrhynchus Papyrus* 35 [1968] no. 2741, pp. 55–73). Harvey's arguments for this reference as the first genuine evidence for

added that "Eupolis, like Lysias [in 32.6] expected his audience to understand what seems to be no more than a passing reference to a maritime
loan – in other words, the maritime loan was already a familiar institution
in 421." How far back does this "familiar institution" date? Probably to the
second quarter of the fifth century, argued de Ste. Croix (1974: 44 and n.13),
who connected it with the growing trade in grain with Athens.

Four other pieces of evidence have been cited to show that bottomry
lending existed earlier than the fourth century. None is convincing: from
Thgn. 1197–1202 Bravo (1977: 5–7) somehow inferred that Theognis secured
a loan in order to engage in maritime commerce. Hasebroek (1928: 24 and
n.3) thinks *to nautikon* in X. [*Ath. pol.*] 1.12 refers to bottomry loans, but
Meiggs (1972: 264 n.1) is surely right: "The meaning here of *to nautikon*
is service in the triremes." P. Calligas[35] assumes that the debts recorded
on lead plaques found on Corcyra and dating from *c.* 500 B.C. are debts
incurred through bottomry loans; but, as Austin and Vidal-Naquet say
(1977: 155 n.21), "there is nothing in the inscriptions to prove this." Erxleben
(1974: 469) thinks Isok. 7.32–5 refers to bottomry lending. There the rich
are said to help the poor enter both *emporia* and the "trades" (ἐργασίας)
almost certainly by means of loans. One can only guess about this passage:
my hunch is that it represents nothing more than Isokrates' attempt to
contrast the sordid money-grubbing of his own day (7.25) with the good
old days, when the rich lent to the poor out of generosity, without worrying
overmuch about repayment.[36]

Probably no later than the mid-fifth century, then, bottomry loans made
maritime trade a possibility for even poor men. The proportions were very
likely the same as in the fourth – the majority poorer, with wealthy exceptions. The only corroborating bits of evidence are unfortunately either
late or unhelpful: Plutarch says that Perikles encouraged citizens to enter
emporia, rope-making, weaving, leatherworking, and other humble occupations (*Per.* 12.6).[37] And there may be an ounce of historical truth in the
passage (7.32–5) by Isokrates just mentioned – that at some point in the
past certain poorer people carried on *emporia*.

One final point: the sixteen fourth-century *emporoi* and *emporoi-
or-nauklēroi* in the Catalogue who were *not* poor come from all over the

---

a bottomry loan have been accepted by de Ste. Croix (1974: 44 and n.13), McKechnie (1989: 193–4
n.23), Davies (1992: 24), Austin (1994: 561 n.117), and Millett (1991: 190).

[35] (1971): 79–94, esp. 86. See also Chadwick (1973) and (1990).

[36] Millett's comments on this passage (1989: 25–8) are far more perceptive than Erxleben's (1974: 471–3)
or Bravo's (1977: 4–5).

[37] Cf. Eupolis (*CAF* F 122 = *PCG* F 135) and X. *Mem.* 3.7.6.

eastern Mediterranean and Black Sea areas. That as many as five[38] of the sixteen are Athenians follows from the nature of the evidence. Yet neither for Athens nor for anywhere else in the Greek world is there evidence that *emporoi* and *nauklēroi* formed part of anything like a "merchant aristocracy" in the classical period.[39]

---

[38] Nos. 8, 16, 22, 39, and 40.

[39] Aristotle says the "merchant sort" (*emporikon* [*eidos*]) at Aigina and Chios belonged to the "popular element" (*demos*) as distinct from the "notables" (*gnorimoi*) (*Pol.* 1291b 17–24). Knorringa (1926: 58, 67) takes Thuc. 3.72.3 and 74.2 to mean that *emporoi* "formed the aristocratic element" in Corcyra, but the *emporoi* he refers to may have lived in the "boarding houses" (ξυνοικίας) and not the "homes" (οἰκίας) (Thuc. 3.74.2) on Corcyra. On Knorringa's claim (1926: 59) that Corcyra was "preeminently fitted for trade by its situation," cf. de Ste. Croix (1972: 75).

CHAPTER 5

Official attitudes towards maritime traders

INTRODUCTION

What was the official attitude – legislative, administrative, and political – of classical Greek poleis to those trading with them? Athens' response of necessity occupies center stage because most of our evidence comes from there. The surviving bits of evidence from elsewhere show that other poleis also depended upon imports of vital goods, and like Athens these other poleis did what they could to attract and control maritime traders. I first examine Athens' efforts and in the penultimate section turn to the efforts of other poleis, by concentrating on the fourth century and adding references to the fifth where appropriate. I also deal almost exclusively with Athens' grain trade because we know something about those engaging in it, whereas we glimpse only a single *emporos* or *nauklēros* (no. 27) engaging in the vital timber trade with Athens, and even there the circumstances are not typical.[1]

In each prytany the Athenian assembly held a plenary session devoted (among other things) to the grain supply;[2] any aspiring politician furthermore was expected to know enough about it to render expert advice.[3] Such an intense concern follows from Athens' unparalleled dependence on grain[4] (described at 16–19 above), which in turn meant an unparalleled dependence on those bringing it – the *emporoi* and *nauklēroi* previously described as "professional" (Chapter 1), foreign (Chapter 3), and (in the case of *emporoi* as least) relatively poor (Chapter 4). Athens' concern for grain influenced these *emporoi* and *nauklēroi* at four stages of their work: when

---

[1] See further item 2 of no. 27.   [2] [Arist.] *Ath. Pol.* 43.4.

[3] X. *Mem.* 3.6.13; cf. Arist. *Rh.*1360a 12–13.

[4] See esp. nn.3 and 7 of Ch. 2. Athens' dependence on imported grain did not render it *utterly* dependent on maritime traders. It resorted to at least two other means of securing grain. In 374/3 B.C. the Athenian assembly levied a tax, to be paid in grain, on its north Aegean islands of Lemnos, Imbros, and Skyros; it further specified how and by whom the collected grain was to be auctioned off at Athens (Stroud 1998). Second, in the 360s it negotiated an agreement (*IG* ii² 207) to purchase grain direct from a Mysian satrap see further Osborne (1981: 52–4, 1982: 61–80) and Engen (1996: 53–4, 93–8, 429–30 nn. 102–13), for yet other references.

they came to Athens to take out loans; when, having sailed from Athens, they arrived at the source of the grain; when they sailed back to Athens; and when they actually arrived there.

STAGE ONE: ATTRACTING MARITIME TRADERS TO ATHENS

Most of the *emporoi* and *nauklēroi* trading with Athens were not only foreign but (as I argue in Chapter 6) non-resident as well. Most also relied on bottomry loans to finance their trading.[5] In fourth-century Athens they normally borrowed from citizens or metics,[6] who were required by Athenian law to lend only on ventures returning to Athens.[7] So by taking out loans at Athens *emporoi* and *nauklēroi* obliged themselves to return there.[8] The question thus becomes, why would non-resident *emporoi* and *nauklēroi* come to Athens in the first place to take out loans?

In the fifth century they surely came because of the profit margins guaranteed by Athens' prosperity and power,[9] whereas in the fourth Athens was forced to take the following special steps to attract them:

1 By the mid-fourth century[10] Athens could promise non-resident *emporoi* embroiled in legal disputes at Athens a speedier procedure,[11] even if we cannot be certain about the details:[12] see further Appendix 3 for discussion

---

[5] For reasons discussed above in at 34–5.

[6] Even without consulting the somewhat unreliable figures of Erxleben (1974: 479, 487) and of others, we could guess the conclusion – that most lenders at Athens were if not citizens then at any rate metics. A foreigner's investment would probably keep him in Athens throughout the venture on which he lent, and that very likely came close to outrunning the specified time when a *xenos* became a *metoikos*. See Whitehead (1977: 8–9) on the length of that "specified time."

[7] See D. 35.51 for the text of the law; cf. D. 35.50; [D.] 56.5–6, 13.

[8] Non-Athenian, non-resident *emporoi* and *nauklēroi* escaped the Athenian law requiring citizens and metics to transport grain only to Athens. (Various versions, normally tailored to suit the case at hand, appear in [D.] 34.37; D. 35.50; Lykourg. *Leoc.* 27; cf. [D.] 58.12.) Whereas Athens could thus control and discipline citizens and metics, it could not do the same to other foreigners, lest they be put off coming to Athens. As I stress in the text, these *xenoi* had to be lured to Athens by one means or another. But, once they arrived and took out loans, they too were "caught" (as Erxleben [1974: 496] points out) by the law punishing citizens and metics for lending money on any vessel carrying grain (and perhaps other specified goods) to a port other than Athens (see the references in n.7 above); cf. the Athenian law requiring shipowners and supercargoes to sail to the port to which they had agreed to sail ([D.] 56.10). The Athenian polis thus faced the double obligations of attracting traders *and* of protecting borrowers. On the latter see [D.] 34.52; 56.48–50; 34.50 (an opaque source, on which see further item 2 of no. 15).

[9] As Austin and Vidal-Naquet (1977: 116) and Hopper (1979: 78) suggest. For fifth-century evidence of Athens' preoccupation with its grain supply, see de Ste. Croix (1972: 49 n.97), coupled with Davies' brief review of the controversy concerning when Athens' dependence began (1992: 301 and nn.53–4). See further the discussion and references in at 16–19 above.

[10] On the date and substance of the Athenian *dikai emporikai* see Appendix 3.

[11] I do not mean to imply that rapid procedure was the sole advantage offered. See further Appendix 3.

[12] The precise way in which procedure was accelerated by the *dikai emporikai* depends on how one interprets the category (*dikai emmenoi*) into which they fell. See Appendix 3 for the two principal interpretations.

of the *dikai emporikai*. In the fifth the category of legal actions called δίκαι ἀπὸ συμβόλων were surely meant in part at least to facilitate the settlement of lawsuits arising out of trade with Athens by *emporoi* or *nauklēroi* from allied states.[13] A privilege granted *en bloc* to Phaselites may have been intended mainly to further expedite the settlement of disputes arising out of bottomry loans.[14] That privilege consisted of the right to appear before the Athenian Polemarch; other fifth- and early fourth-century Athenian magistrates called *xenodikai* and *nautodikai* may have also indicated a special official concern for *emporoi*, but the tiny amount of evidence about both offers no basis for any plausible guess as to their actual roles.[15] In the fourth century Athens also offered *emporoi* and *nauklēroi* legal protection from frivolous prosecutions.[16]

2 In the first half of the fourth century Athens offered non-resident *emporoi* from Sidon exemption from the obligations of a metic, if for some reason their work kept them in Athens beyond the time when *xenoi* became *metoikoi*.[17] Another exemption on a smaller scale: in the latter stage of the Peloponnesian War those who imported ships' oars to Athens were exempted from the 1 percent harbor tax.[18]

3 In the second half of the fourth century Athens granted Phoenician *emporoi* from Kition in Cyprus permission to acquire a plot of land on which to found a sanctuary of Aphrodite "just as the Egyptians built a sanctuary of Isis."[19] As in the case of the Sidonians mentioned above, this privilege represented an effort to accommodate Phoenician *emporoi* and (perhaps) Egyptian *emporoi* who may have resided elsewhere and only used the sanctuaries on visits.[20]

4 *Emporoi* and *nauklēroi* knew that Athens was disposed to reward special services in aid of her grain supply.[21] In times of shortage, particularly at

---

[13] See above all de Ste. Croix's discussion (1961: 95–108).   [14] See n.29 of Ch. 3.

[15] See Cohen (1973: 163–84) for a discussion of the Athenian *xenodikai* and *nautodikai* in the fifth century.

[16] [D.] 59.10–11. Baseless charges were punished with larger fines, arrest, and "other penalties."

[17] See further n.22 of Ch. 3.

[18] See the second decree published in Walbank (1978: 316, lines 14–15) with his commentary (esp. 321–4) and MacDonald (1981). Perdikkas II earlier had granted Athens the exclusive right to purchase Macedonian oars (*IG* i³ 89, line 31).

[19] See n.23 of Ch. 3.   [20] As Whitehead (1986: 161) suggests.

[21] See X. *Hier.* 9.9; Aen. Tact. 10.12; cf. X. *Vect.* 3.3–14. On the use of grants of *proxenia* in connection with grain-related services, see Marek (1984: 359–75). Burke (1992: 207 n.34) summarizes Marek's (1984) and Walbank's (1978) tabulations of *proxenia* grants for such services. (Walbank deals only with the fifth-century Athenian grants; Marek [1984: 361–4] tabulates classical and hellenistic grants by numerous poleis.) Burke (1992: 208, 210) believes the people so honored by Athens with either *proxenia* or *enktesis* to be exclusively "men engaged in trade," but fewer than half of Engen's entries (1996: nos. 1–29) for the years 415–323 B.C. even possibly fall into that category. On the political implications of fourth-century grants of *proxenia*, see further Perlman (1958). Marek (1985) correctly

the end of the classical era, Athens honored men who donated grain, or sold it at low prices, or donated or advanced the money with which to buy it. One of these was a *nauklēros*,[22] and the others were probably or possibly *emporoi* or *naukleroi*.[23]

5 Particular mention should be made of Athens' efforts on behalf of Hera-kleides of Salamis in Cyprus (no. 60). Not only did it honor him for the services described in item 2 of no. 60; it also dispatched an Athenian envoy to demand the return of his sails from the Herakleots who had seized them (see item 2 of no. 60). Yet never, as far as we know, did Athens grant citizenship to either Herakleides or any other active *emporos* or *naukleros* for services rendered in the classical period.[24]

STAGE TWO: ASSISTING AND CONTROLLING
OUTWARD-BOUND TRADERS

The forementioned state measures might have helped to attract *emporoi* or *naukleroi* to Athens, where they took out bottomry loans. Then they set sail, arriving eventually (after an intermediate stop or stops)[25] at the source of the grain, most commonly Pontos.[26] Note next how the long arm of Athens reached the *emporos* or *naukleros* even in ports far from Athens.

1 A trader arriving in Pontos in the fourth century, for example, received exemption from duty and priority of lading solely on the strength of his returning to Athens with grain.[27] In times of shortage the Bosporan

---

denies the *proxenos*' economic role as a modern-day consular trade representative. Instead he sees trade-related *proxenia* grants as rewarding and hence promoting foreigners' generosity in supplying grain.

[22] No. 60.

[23] Nos. 51–9. See also the earlier fourth-century honors for nos. 49 and 50. In the fifth century Athens also honored two *naukleroi* (nos. 47 and 48) for their services.

[24] For the actual honors awarded Herakleides see item 2 of no. 60. For those (if known) awarded other *emporoi* and *naukleroi*, see item 2 of nos. 47–8 and item 1 of nos. 51–9. Phormion II (no. 23), successor to the banker and businessman Pasion, received citizenship (as had Pasion). But the services for which Phormion was honored probably resembled Pasion's and therefore did not include efforts to supply Athens with grain in Phormion's role as *naukleros*. The only other man to receive Athenian citizenship, Chairephilos (no. 39), had probably retired from saltfish trading by the time he was thus rewarded. In any case I regard him as one of the weakest of all the "possible" candidates in the Catalogue. The grant of Athenian citizenship was, in Whitehead's words (1977: 159), "primarily a tool of international diplomacy." See further Osborne (1983: 186–221) for the sorts of people who received citizenship as well as for the relevant documentation. Cf. D. 23.211, where Demosthenes calls it "shameful that these Aiginetans . . . have never to this day given citizenship to Lampis [no. 2], who of all Greeks owns the greatest amount of property in ships, and who fitted out their *polis* and port; they grudgingly thought him worthy only of exemption from the metic tax . . ."

[25] See for example the scheduled itinerary in the only surviving text (probably genuine) of a bottomry contract (D. 35.10–13). Casson (1991: 105–7) and Davies (1993: 222–5) provide translations.

[26] As J. K. Davies mentioned in lectures, the purpose of going to Pontos (to return with grain) is so obvious as to remain unstated in the bottomry contract preserved in D. 35.10–13.

[27] D. 20.31; [D.] 34.36.

ruler sent away traders returning elsewhere, granting export rights only to those bound for Athens.[28] Athens secured such privileges (as well as outright gifts) from rulers of grain or timber-producing states by assiduously bestowing honors and negotiating treaties.[29]

2 An *emporos* or *nauklēros* arriving from Athens in a foreign port found resident *proxenoi* anxious to help, partly because Athens rewarded their help with official honors.[30]

3 At certain destinations the *emporos* or *nauklēros* found that Athens used power rather than diplomacy to guarantee the supply of necessities. Such was probably[31] the case in Athens' monopoly of *miltos*[32] ("ruddle" or "red ochre") from Keos, described in an Athenian copy (dated 350 B.C.) of decrees by three poleis on Keos.[33] For our purposes the crucial feature is how intrusively the decrees controlled the activities of the traders themselves. Shippers were ordered to transport the *miltos* in vessels designated by the Athenians, and a trader's ship or goods would be confiscated if he transported *miltos* to anywhere other than Athens. Even the freight charge paid to shipowners by the producers was set (at one obol per talent of *miltos*).[34]

STAGE THREE: ASSISTING AND CONTROLLING TRADERS
RETURNING TO ATHENS

Between his departure from, say, Pontos and his arrival back at Athens an *emporos* or *nauklēros* continued to feel the impact of Athens' determination

---

[28] Isok. 17.57.

[29] On Athens' relations with Bosporan rulers see esp. Burstein (1978 and 1993); Isok. 17.57; D. 20.29–41; [D.] 34.36; Strabo 7.46; *IG* ii² 212 = *Syll.*³ no. 206 = Tod no. 167 = Rhodes no. 9 = Harding no. 82. On its relations with Macedonian rulers, see Meiggs (1982: 119, 123, 127–32) and Borza (1987). Primary sources: *IG* i³ 61 = ML no. 65 = Fornara no. 128 (Perdikkas II); *IG* i³ 89 esp. lines 55 ff. (Perdikkas II); *IG* i³ 117 = ML no. 91 = Fornara no. 161 (?Archelaos); *IG* ii² 102 = Tod no. 129 = Harding no. 43 (Amyntas III); cf. Philoch. *FGrH* 328 F 119 together with Plut *Per.* 37.4 (445/4 B.C.); Hdt. 7.158.4 (481 B.C.). Athens also honored the King of Sidon in Phoenicia (*IG* ii² 141 = *Syll.*³ no. 185 = Tod no. 139 = Harding no. 40 (370s or 360s B.C.).

[30] Of those grouped under the rubric, "Very unlikely candidates" in the "Introduction" to the Catalogue, nos. 1–8 probably constitute such a collection of *proxenoi*.

[31] Whether Keos drafted the decrees voluntarily or under compulsion from Athens is unknown. The surviving Kean decrees so carefully follow the formula of Athenian inscriptions that Austin and Vidal-Naquet (1977: 296) believe they were originally drawn up at Athens.

[32] *Miltos* was used (among other things) for painting the hulls of ships; see further the references to *miltos* in Tod no. 162, p.185.

[33] *IG* ii² 1128 = Tod no. 162 = Wickersham–Verbrugghe (1973: no. 61). Cf. the following two Athenian treaties with poleis of Keos: *IG* ii² 111 = *Syll.*³ no. 173 = Tod. no. 142 = Bengtson (1975: no. 289) = Wickersham–Verbrugghe (1973: no. 44, (362 B.C.) and *IG* ii² 404 = (1973: Wickersham–Verbrugghe (1973: no. 56) (*c.* 356 B.C.). Cf. also *IG* xii 5.594 = *Syll.*³ no. 172 = Tod. no. 141 (a treaty between Keos and Histiaia *c.* 363 B.C.).

[34] Tod no. 162, lines 30–1, 28, and 13–14.

to provide herself with necessities and (in certain cases) deny them to others.

1 In the early years of the Peloponnesian War, for example, Athens stationed special officials at the Hellespont; the only surviving testimony to these "guardians of the Hellespont" (*Hellespontophylakes*) shows that they were at least charged with deciding where grain shipments from the Black Sea were and were not to go.[35] Later in 410 merchantmen sailing out of the Black Sea were forced to pay a very high duty of 10 percent to Athenians stationed opposite Byzantion.[36] Athens also sought to control traders' activities in other theaters of the Peloponnesian War. To the *naukleros* Lykon of Achaia (no. 47), for example, it granted permission to trade in all waters under its control except the Gulf of Korinth.[37] And, finally, in the fourth century[38] an Athenian decree made the conveying of arms or ships' tackle to Philip of Macedonia a capital offense.[39]

2 In the fourth century *emporoi* and *naukleroi* en route to Athens sometimes found themselves accompanied by Athenian triremes, whose job was to prevent the seizure of grain ships by hostile or hungry states.[40]

3 *Emporoi* and *naukleroi* aboard the grain ships bound for Athens also had to cope throughout the fourth century with the threat of pirates.[41] Athens' most dramatic recorded response was to send a colony to the

---

[35] *IG* i³ 61 = ML no. 65 = Fornara no. 128 (430 or the early 420s B.C.). Here the Methoneans are granted the right to export a certain amount of grain annually from Byzantion, if they apply in writing to the "guardians of the Hellespont" (*Hellespontophylakes*), who are instructed neither to prevent these shipments nor to allow others to do so. See further *IG* ii² 55+ = *ATL* II D 21 = Hill (1951: B 83 [428/7 B.C.]) and *IG* ii² 58 = Hill (1951: B 84, esp. lines 15–19 [c. 426 B.C.]). Cf. *IG* ii² 28, lines 17 ff. (387/6 B.C.).

[36] X. *Hell.* 1.1.22, which says that Alkibiades established this 10 percent duty in 410 B.C. On this passage see further Krentz (1989: 100) and Polyb. 4.44.4. Hopper (1979: 75–6) wants to associate this duty with the *Hellespontophylakes* mentioned in lines 36–7 and 39–40 of an Athenian decree dated c. 426/5 B.C. (*IG* i³ 61), on which see n.35 above.

[37] See further items 1 and 2 of no. 47.

[38] On the date of the decree see Aeschin. 1.80.   [39] D. 19.286.

[40] Athenian convoys: Diod. Sic. 15.34.3 but cf. X. *Hell.* 5.4.60–1; [D.] 50.17–20; Philoch. *FGrH* 328 F 162 but cf. D. 18.87–8 and Theopomp. *FGrH* 115 F 292; *IG* ii² 408 lines 8–10; *IG* ii² 1628 lines 37–42; ?[D.] 56.9. See also Thuc. 2.69.1; X. *Hell.* 1.1.36; [D.] 50.4–6; D. 17.20; and more generally 18.301.

[41] On the threat of piracy to Athens as well as to other states and their response, see Ormerod (1924 rp. 1967) Ch. 4; Ziebarth (1929: 9–19, 100–17); Michell (1959: 306–10); Isager–Hansen (1975: 55–7); Hopper (1979: 81–3, 196–7); Ducrey (1968: 171–94); Garlan (1978 and 1989b); Nowag (1983: 113–97, archaic period only); Casson (1988); McKechnie (1989: 101–41, esp. 117–19); Pritchett (1991: 312–63); and de Souza (1995). For present purposes [D.] 58.53–4, 56 is the most crucial fourth-century source reference, apart perhaps from the first reference mentioned in n.40 above. For an excellent survey of piracy throughout ancient Greco-Roman history, see now de Souza (1999).

Adriatic in 325/4;[42] its explicit purpose (lines 216–30) was to secure a supply of grain for Athens and, by means of this new naval base, protect seafarers from attacks by Etruscan pirates.

STAGE FOUR: ACCOMMODATING AND CONTROLLING TRADERS RETURNING TO ATHENS

Athens remained intent on both accommodating *and* controlling[43] the *emporoi* and *nauklēroi* after they arrived back at Athens with shipments of grain:

1 Athenian law controlled *emporoi* by having public officials compel them to bring to the city of Athens two-thirds of the grain they imported.[44] These officials were called "overseers of the import market" (*epimeletai tou emporiou*) – a supervisory post that probably entailed further control of maritime traders.[45]

2 Polis laws and decrees accommodated *emporoi* and *nauklēroi* by punishing anyone who brought false accusations against them;[46] by providing a public slave as official coin tester in Piraeus "for [the] *nauklēroi, emporoi*, and [all] the others";[47] and by controlling the activities of the grain sellers (*sitopolai*). Of course Athenian laws[48] regulating the *sitopolai* and the prosecutions[49] resulting from violations thereof primarily served the interests of citizen consumers; but, as the speaker in [Lys.] 22 makes clear, they were also meant to "gratify and render more zealous" the *emporoi*,[50] against whom the *sitopolai* in this instance had combined.

---

[42] *IG* ii² 1629 lines 145–232 = Tod no. 200 = Rhodes no. 22 = Harding no. 121.

[43] For a full listing by various officials of "what Athenians [of the fourth century] . . . thought required public administration and control," see Davies (1993: 230–2). For an overview of the officials variously responsible for grain, see Gauthier (1981: 19–28) and Figueira (1986).

[44] [Arist.] *Ath. Pol.* 51.4, on which see further Rhodes (1981: 579) and Gauthier (1981).

[45] [Arist.] *Ath. Pol.* 51.4. I owe the translation of *epimeletai tou emporiou* to Figueira (1986: 150). On the Athenian *epimeletai tou emporiou* see further D. 35.51; [D.] 58.8, 9, 26; Din. 2.10; s.v. the term in Harpokration, ed. Bekker (*Anecdota Graeca*) and in the *Suda* also the Athenian inscriptions cited in Stroud (1974: 181 n.92).

[46] [D.] 58.10–13, 53–4; cf.8–9.

[47] Lines 37–8 of an inscription edited by Stroud (1974: 157–88).

[48] Athenian laws concerning the *sitopolai*: **A.** Law forbidding anyone in Athens to accumulate by purchase more than fifty phormoi of grain at a time: [Lys.] 22.5–7. (On the term συμπρίασθαι in [Lys.] 22.5–7, see Figueira [1986: 152–5] and Tuplin [1986: 495–8].) **B.** Law forbidding the *sitopolai* to add more than one obol to the retail cost: [Lys.] 22.8, cf. perhaps [Arist.] *Ath. Pol.* 51.3. **C.** Law requiring the *sitophylakes* to see that unground grain in the agora was sold at a fair price: [Arist.] *Ath. Pol.* 51.3; cf. perhaps [Lys.] 22.8.

[49] [Lys.] 22 *passim*. On the functions of the *sitopolai*, see further Rhodes (1981: 577–8), Gauthier (1981: esp. 19–28), and Figueira (1986).

[50] [Lys.] 22.21, cf.17.

OFFICIAL ATTITUDES OUTSIDE ATHENS

This section has no pretensions to being an exhaustive account. I omit interstate agreements altogether and cite only examples sufficient to illustrate the similarity of official attitudes elsewhere to those at Athens, in order to generalize further in this chapter's Conclusion.[51]

Like classical Athens, other Greek poleis normally consumed rather than exported their produce and yet sometimes still ran short, even if Greek agricultural production rose throughout the classical period.[52] When shortages occurred, the classical solution differed from the archaic: whereas archaic poleis sent hungry people to where the food was (through colonization), classical poleis brought the food to hungry people,[53] relying on the same official mechanisms and the same maritime traders that Athens relied on.

Other poleis' need for imported grain in fact may have preceded that of Athens in the classical period, if recent efforts to downdate Athens' need are correct.[54] At Abydos in 480 B.C., Xerxes saw grain ships from Pontos sailing to Aigina and the Peloponnese.[55] From Teos survives the earliest attempt by a classical polis to regulate the grain trade: a law (*c.* 475–470 B.C.) required Tean officials to put to death anyone preventing the import of grain or trying to re-export it; the perpetrators also were to be publicly cursed three times a year.[56]

Poleis other than Athens also negotiated with Bosporan rulers for grain[57] and with Macedonian rulers for timber.[58] Like Athens too other poleis

---

[51] The most helpful short survey of steps taken by Greek states to secure food is by Jameson (1983); the most helpful longer treatment, Garnsey (1988), whose first two chapters constitute an excellent general introduction to the surviving Greek evidence, which is itemized in unreflective fashion by Ziebarth (1929: 118–40) and Hopper (1979: 83, 88, 94–5, 114–15, and esp. 190–9).

[52] Morris (1994: 362–5) outlines the case for the increase in agricultural production: his notes provide the bibliography.

[53] I owe the contrast to Davies (1992: 26).

[54] On the controversy, including references, see further 16–19 above.

[55] Hdt. 7.147.2. Cf. Demosthenes' remarks (23.211) on Aigina's refusal to reward with citizenship the metic Lampis' enormous services. For references to subsequent shipments of grain to poleis other than Athens, see n.6 of Ch. 2.

[56] ML no. 30 = Fornara no. 63 = Arnaoutoglou no. 70. Other poleis forbade the export of grain, e.g., Selymbria ([Arist.] *Oec.* 2.2.17; cf. [X.] *Ath. pol.* 2.11–12). On an ingenious solution at Klazomenai to the shortage of food, see [Arist.] *Oec.* 2.2.16.

[57] *Syll.*³ no. 212 = Tod no. 163 = Wickersham and Verbrugghe (1973: no. 62) (Mytilene and Leukon, Bosporan ruler, *c.* 350 B.C.).

[58] *Syll.*³ no. 135 = Tod no. 111 = Pouilloux no. 25 = Harding no. 21 (two treaties between Amyntas III and the Chalcidians, early fourth century).

regularly imposed duties on both imports and exports[59] and appointed special officials to oversee transactions in their ports.[60]

Most Greek trade laws focus on securing imports, but scholars have found cases of what they regard as economic imperialism. A Thasian law from the late fifth century for example stipulates measures to ensure the quality of Thasian wine, forbids the import of foreign wine into that portion of the mainland opposite Thasos, and specifies the polis' share of revenues as well as the magistrates involved.[61] De Ste. Croix doubted that the decree qualified as *bona fide* economic imperialism,[62] and both Finley and de Ste. Croix attacked Pouilloux's incorporation of this text into a larger argument for *Athenian* commercial imperialism.[63] As for the claim, contested at far greater length by de Ste. Croix, that the so-called Megarian decree also qualified as an act of Athenian economic imperialism,[64] it is a waste of effort on all sides to devote so much print to an issue for which there is so little evidence.

CONCLUSION

How far were Greek poleis prepared to go to secure necessities? Jameson[65] is right to stress the limited nature of state intervention in trade. No Greek polis, either of the archaic or classical periods, went to war over grain or timber as did the United States in "Operation Desert Storm" over oil.[66] Harding[67] correctly cautions Hornblower about claiming that "in

[59] *SEG* xi 1026 = Pleket no. 8 = Arnaoutoglou no. 39 (Kyparissian law on import and export duties, fourth or third century). See also the texts cited by Arnaoutoglou at the top of page 42 and Vélissaropoulos (1980: 223–8).

[60] *IG* xii suppl. 348 = Pleket no. 9 = Arnaoutoglou no. 42 (Thasian harbor regulations, third century). For non-Athenian *sitophylakes* of the hellenistic period, see the references in Figueira (1986: 151 n.5).

[61] *IG* xii suppl. 347 = Pleket no. 2 = Arnaoutoglou no. 36. For bibliography, see Stanley (1980: 88–93). Vélissaropoulos (1980: 138–9, 191–4), and Salviat (1986: 145–96).

[62] De Ste. Croix (1972: 43 n.80): "Among other provisions, this law forbids the import of foreign wines into the Thasian Peraea in Thasian ships (II 8–10). The purpose of this clause could hardly have been anything but the simple desire of Thasian landowners to ensure the sale of their own produce in the area on the mainland which they controlled, free from all except local competition, while reserving to themselves the right to import into their island such foreign wine as they wanted."

[63] Pouilloux (1954); de Ste. Croix (1972: 43 n.80); Finley (1965: 28–32). For an extended argument against the claim that the so-called "Athenian coinage decree" (ML no. 45) qualified as a prime example of Athenian economic imperialism, see now Figueira (1998: esp. 15–16, 227–39, 552–8). For a description of the view he combats, see also 2–11.

[64] De Ste. Croix (1972: 225–89). MacDonald provides the subsequent bibliography in (1983: 385), to which should be added Sealey (1991: 152–8) and Pritchard (1991: 77–85).

[65] Jameson (1983: 11).

[66] See further Vélissaropoulos (1980: 6) on what classical Greek states never attempted to control.

[67] Harding (1995: 108).

Athens' case, imperialism and the search for grain imports had always gone together."[68] From Tean imprecations upon Athenian market regulations and convoys, the various modes of official Greek interference fell short of commercial imperialism.[69] In fact, as Harding points out, Athens' honorary decrees in return for trade-related services amount to "the [diplomatic] reverse of imperialism."[70]

Four other points are worth noting about official responses, with the emphasis as usual on Athens. First, neither Athens nor any other polis in the classical period possessed its own merchant fleet or offered preferential treatment to its own citizen traders.[71] Second, it is misleading to say, as does Hasebroek,[72] that Athens intervened in trade *only* to secure vital necessities for its citizens and not in the interests of the *emporoi* and *nauklēroi* who carried the goods. The foregoing demonstrates that Athens obviously *did* act on behalf of maritime traders, due simply to the huge overlap[73] of their interests with those of the Athenian citizen body. On the other hand the foregoing confirms Hasebroek's more general and basic contention that Athens' official interest in trade was limited to an "import" interest.

Yet, one wonders, third, if Hasebroek sufficiently stressed the intensity of this import interest, at least with regard to its impact on traders rather than on trade. At virtually every stage of their work, both in and out of Athens, *emporoi* and *nauklēroi* trading with Athens felt the impact of "government interference," of Athens' official determination to both attract *and* control them. This persistent intersection of political and of economic activity (the former on the part of the state, the latter of the part of the trader) can only be explained, as Hasebroek insisted,[74] by that distinctively Greek institution, the polis, in this instance an Athenian polis committed to dependence on external sources of food.

The fourth feature worth noting about Athens' attitude to traders is its narrow focus, which further confirms Hasebroek's emphasis on the importance of the polis framework with regard to the maritime trader's place and role in classical Greece. One thing alone interested Athens about the

[68] Hornblower (1991b: 170).
[69] I suspect that as a practitioner of commercial imperialism Karthage serves as a revealing foil to Greek poleis of the classical period. Unfortunately almost no relevant evidence survives for Karthaginian activity prior to the third century B.C. For a judicious analysis of Karthaginian imperialism in the classical period, see Whittaker (1978). The lack of archaic or classical evidence prevents Niemeyer (1989) and Günther (1993) from explaining in what specific respects Karthaginian expansion in the sixth and fifth centuries, doubtless led by Karthaginian aristocrats, was commercial in nature.
[70] Harding (1995: 108).
[71] Thus de Ste. Croix (1972: 393–6), Austin (1994: 161), and Cartledge (1998: 15).
[72] Hasebroek (1928: 102, 116, 151).   [73] Cf. Austin and Vidal-Naquet (1977: 295 n.5).
[74] Hasebroek (1928: Ch. 3 *passim*).

emporoi and *nauklēroi* trading there – the service they provided the polis. If the *emporoi* were (as I claim) largely poor and non-resident, Athens in no sense "held it against them"; instead it did whatever was necessary to guarantee that poor, transient *emporoi* brought their grain to Athens. Three cases demonstrate how disposed was Athens to ignore everything about a trader except the vital service he performed. Fifth-century Athens *may* have even ignored one of the essential duties of a citizen in excusing citizen *emporoi* from military service.[75] And the fourth-century *dikai emporikai* guaranteed that legal emphasis was placed on Lampis' *nauklēria* and *emporia*, not on his possible status as a chattel slave.[76] Finally, an Athenian decree[77] honoring Herakleides of Salamis called him an *emporos*, in spite of his almost certainly being a *nauklēros*, a term probably connoting[78] his activity in *emporia* as well. That an official decree used the less inclusive word (*emporos*) might testify best of all to how carefully focused was Athens' official interest: it strictly limited its notice of Herakleides to the service he provided by bringing grain; everything else about him, including even his shipowning, it ignored.

[75] All the evidence is late and possibly unreliable. In Ar. *Plut.* 904 and *Eccl.* 1027 an Athenian citizen can avoid some public duty by claiming to be an *emporos*. The scholiasts on both passages and the *Suda* (s.v. *Emporos eimi skeptomenos*) claim that the public duty is military service. Böckh and Fränkel 1 (1886: 109–10 and note "e") accept this but discount the further claim (schol. *Plut.* 904) that *emporoi* were exempt from payment of *eisphora* as well.

[76] On Lampis II see further item 2 of no. 13. The case of Lampis might make it more accurate to say that the *dikai emporikai* were not so much "supranational" (Cohen [1973: 59, 61, 70, 74]) as simply transcending the normal barriers of legal status.

[77] On the decree honoring Herakleides of Salamis in Cyprus, see item 2 of no. 60.

[78] On the frequency with which shipowners engaged in *emporia*, see 12–13 and item 2 of no. 41.

CHAPTER 6

Unofficial attitudes toward maritime traders

THE "SOCIAL STATUS" OF MARITIME TRADERS

Having dealt with Athenian legal and administrative mechanisms, I now turn to the Athenians themselves. What were the attitudes adopted by Athenian society at large towards the *emporoi* and *nauklēroi* trading with Athens? In Chapter 5 we saw the vital service they performed for both citizens and others within the polis. Can we, in addition to identifying the economic role *emporoi* and *nauklēroi* played, say anything about their "social status"? How seriously, in other words, did their largely foreign[1] origins influence Athenian estimations? Or, again, how respectable was the work they did?

That they did real work for a living may have earned maritime traders the blanket disapproval of the Athenian leisure class. Davies[2] shows how during the classical period the composition of this leisure class changed, with newcomers whose sources of wealth were more diverse, but there is no evidence that it changed its view of those without leisure. In particular we should not misread an aristocrat's eagerness[3] for imports as social approval of those who brought them.

How far down the social scale did this leisure ideal go? Relative estimations are another matter, and have to do with the various ways in which different Athenian strata viewed the sort of work a maritime trader did. Nowadays the corporal reserves his envy for the sergeant. He acknowledges the higher status of the major, but the gap fails to engage his aspiration. The major reserves *his* disdain for the lieutenant; the corporal and the private

---

[1] A number of *emporoi* and *nauklēros* such as Konops (no. 63), were clearly non-Greek and freed-men. For doubts about how contentious an issue was one's barbarian or slave birth in Athens, see above all Whitehead (1977: 111–14). As Whitehead says (121), "If the Athenians cared whether their metics were Hellenic or non-Hellenic, free-born or slave-born, they did not care enough to legislate about it."

[2] Davies (1984: 38–72).

[3] See for example X. *Vect.* 3.3–5 and *Eq. mag.* 4.7; Isok. 8.21; cf. Plut. *Lys.* 3.4.

are in a world apart. Can we, at Athens, compare the major to the working farmer, the lieutenant to the skilled craftsman, the sergeant to the maritime trader, the corporal to the retail seller, and the private to the hired laborer? That is roughly the pecking order described by Plato and Aristotle.[4] Did most Athenians share it?

Most scholars appear to think so. Historical sociologists tell us that those who engaged professionally in any sort of commerce were well down the social ladder in agrarian societies, except in the so-called ports of trade.[5] And to the current Finley-inspired consensus on the low status[6] of Greek maritime traders have been added darker speculations about their undoubted habitat in Athens, Piraeus. It was "a world apart,"[7] a "sacrilege" to the traditional Athenian elite,[8] full of foreign cults, brothels, and unconventional views about money-making and working for a living.[9]

MARITIME TRADERS: PRIMARILY *XENOI* OR *METOIKOI*?

But perhaps such a "rhetoric of otherness" is premature, at least as it relates to the social status of maritime traders: when we say that someone has a certain social status at Athens, we mean that he evokes certain sorts of estimations

---

[4] I (very tentatively) draw Plato's hierarchy of respectability from his most comprehensive discussions of the various occupations in *Resp*. 369d–371e and *Plt*. 287b–290a. Plato often lumps together *emporoi* and *kapeloi* (*Prt*. 313c, 314a; *Leg*. 918d, 919d; *Grg*. 517d; *Resp*. 371d, 525c). He also occasionally couples *naukleros* or *naukleros* with both (*Leg*. 842d; *Plt*. 289e–290a) or with one or the other (with *emporoi*, *Leg*. 831e; with *kapeleia*, *Leg*. 643e). At one point or another characterizes all three as menial or illiberal (*Leg*. 644a, 919d; *Grg*. 517d–518a), but takes a special slap at *kapeloi* (*Resp*. 371c–d; *Leg*. 705a; 919a,c,e; 920a–c). For evidence of Plato's relative regard for craftsmen, see *Leg*. 902d–e; *Criti*. 109c; Morrow (1960: 145); cf. *Grg*. 517e–518a. For Aristotle's hierarchy see esp. *Pol*. 1290b 40 ff.; cf. 1291b 18 ff. and 1328b 3 ff. Aristotle both subsumes *emporia* under (1291b 4–5) and distinguishes it from (1291b 19–20) the category termed *agoraios*. On differences between the views of Plato and Aristotle and for astute comments on Aristotle's perspective, see further Meikle (1995: 73–4, 125–6).

The sole passage suggesting that the *emporos* is happy in his work: Antiphanes *CAF* F 151 = *PCG* F 149. Other non-philosophical sources rank professional *emporia* as a humble occupation but assign it no definite rank in a hierarchy of such occupations (Plut. *Per*. 12.6; X. *Mem*. 3.7.6; *Vect*. 4.6; Isok. 7.32–3; on [Lys.] 22 see next section and Seager [1966: 179]). Xenophon hints that *naukleros* may be more respectable than *emporia* (*Mem*. 1.6, 8; *Eq. mag*. 9.2; cf. [Arist.] *Rh. Al*. 1424a 29–30, where there are textual problems).

On the respectability of various occupations see further Austin and Vidal-Naquet (1977: 11–18); Brunt (1973: 9–34); Newman (1887a: 96–126); Hopper (1979: 18–21); Aymard (1967: esp. 324–33); Balme (1984). They all pay little or no attention to the "relative deprivation" emphasized in the portion of my text to which this note refers.

[5] E.g., Crone (1989: 18–20, 173); Nolan and Lenski (1999: 177–9).

[6] E.g., McKechnie (1989: 178), Millett (1991: 191), and Davies (1998: 235).

[7] The title of von Reden's article (1995b: 24–37).   [8] Von Reden (1995b: 28).

[9] On these various unsavory features, see further Vélissaropoulos (1977), Mossé (1983), and von Reden (1995b). For more sober, less evocative discussions of Piraeus as a commercial center, see further Garland (1987: 58–100) and Roy (1998). On foreign cults located there see Garland (1987: 101–11).

in the minds of Athenians. But if he by-and-large goes unnoticed apart from the crucial food he brings, can he be said to *have* a social status?

It partly depends on how many maritime traders, instead of residing at Athens, only paid brief visits there. Some scholars[10] assume that throughout the classical period the *emporoi* and *nauklēroi* trading at Athens were metics. I suggest on the contrary that right through the classical period the majority of them were probably not metics but *xenoi*.[11] The metic or *xenos* status of many in the Catalogue is vague enough for it to be of little or no help,[12] and the other evidence is meager, but there still remain sufficient reasons.

In the first place, David Whitehead showed persuasively[13] that metics at Athens were far from privileged; in fact, as Philippe Gauthier argued, it was a privilege to be *excused* from metic status.[14] Would foreign *emporoi* and *nauklēroi* therefore want to become metics? Whereas foreign craftsmen (*technitai*) and retail sellers (*kapeloi*) were virtually obliged by the nature of their work to do so, the same was not true of *emporoi* and *nauklēroi*; there was no bar to their trading with Athens while residing elsewhere. Why, then, would maritime traders choose to forsake the prerogatives of citizenship in their native poleis[15] for the obligations of metics at Athens?

Second, the various kinds of sources in which maritime traders appear may also suggest that they only visited Athens as *xenoi* and therefore were seldom "underfoot." Apart from references in the comedies, fourth-century philosophical works, and the court cases, we would know practically nothing about them. The portrayal of maritime traders in Greek comedy does not illumine the issue at stake here, and only the obligation to be systematically comprehensive prompts Plato and Aristotle to notice maritime traders, while the speeches in the pseudo-Demosthenic corpus dealing with the admissibility of bottomry suits obviously reflect no general interest. The sole non-legal and non-philosophical attention paid to traders is found in

---

[10] Clerc (1893: 397); Knorringa (1926: 68); Cohen (1973: 52); Gomme (1937: 42–66, esp. 58–62).

[11] In his 1935 article Finley (1935: 332) rightly criticizes the scholiasts and late lexicographers as unreliable sources for terminology, but he singles out an error that was never made: Hesychios never defines *emporos* as *metoikos*; his definition of *emporos* is in fact commonsensical but incomplete. It is *emporios*, a word appearing nowhere else, that Hesychios equates with *metoikos*.

[12] Probably nos. 11 and 12 and possibly nos. 9 and 33 are metics; nos. 30 and 66–70 definitely are. Possibly nos. 1, 10, 19, 20, and 34 are *xenoi*; no. 29 probably is. Note how few and how indefinite are the candidates.

[13] Whitehead (1977: 57–58); see also n.17 of the Catalogue.

[14] Gauthier (1972: 119) was the first to point this out.

[15] On whether a metic retained his citizenship in his home polis, see Whitehead (1977: 71–2) and Isager–Hansen (1975: 69). McKechnie (1989: 181) makes the excellent point that his absence from his home polis during the summer probably weakened a maritime trader's ties to it, particularly (I would add) if it precluded the military service expected from citizens. See further McKechnie (1989: 181–3).

Xenophon's *De vectigalibus*; and that work, I will next show, provides some of the best evidence for my claim.

Third, whenever anyone mentions why metics are needed at Athens, it is never for *emporia* but for the crafts and retail trades (*kapeleia*). This is true from Themistokles[16] in the early fifth century right down to Plato and Xenophon in the fourth. Both of the latter in fact *systematically* distinguish *emporoi* from metics. Xenophon in *Vect.* believes that Athens needs more *emporoi* and metics, but he makes the clearest possible distinction between them. He devotes *Vect.* 2 exclusively to discussing how to attract more metics and a better class of metic. Then with *Vect.* 3 he shifts abruptly from (as he puts it in a summary [3.5] of both sections) those who εἰσοικίζοιντο ("make themselves at home here") to those who ἀφικνοῖντο ("visit"). These visitors are solely *emporoi* and *nauklēroi*, and what is needed to attract *them* is altogether different from what Xenophon hopes will attract metics. In *Vect.* 2 Xenophon grumps about the barbarian element among the metic population; in *Vect.* 3 he seems prepared to treat royally *all* visiting *emporoi* and *nauklēroi*, Greek or barbarian.[17] *These* barbarians, in other words, are different.

My purpose in citing *De vectigalibus* is more fundamental than to show that at the time of its writing most of those trading at Athens were *xenoi* and not metics. That metics and *emporoi* occupy such completely separate compartments of an unphilosophical mind like Xenophon's perhaps testifies to more than the contemporary reality; it may testify to a long-term reality as well.

Plato in the *Laws* also distinguishes *emporia* from metic tasks,[18] but the rigor of the separation in a philosophical account is less revealing than in the parts of *Vect.* just cited. It is still worth quoting one passage, if only because it so nicely describes a pattern of activity that I believe fits *emporoi* and *nauklēroi* throughout the classical period.

Next we must consider how to receive the visitor from abroad. There are four types of foreigners which call for mention. The first is like a migratory bird who comes back regularly, usually during summer. Like birds many of them fly over the seas, traders [*emporeuomenoi*] avid for profit, and come in the summer season to visit foreign cities. Magistrates appointed to deal with these must receive them in market places, harbours and public buildings, near the city but outside it.[19]

---

[16] Diod. Sic. 11.43.3 (probably anachronistic, it must be acknowledged); cf. [X.] *Ath. pol.* 1.12; on the meaning of *to nautikon* in this passage, see Meiggs (1972: 264 n.1). For further source references and his comments, see Whitehead (1977: 116–21). On *technon* instead of the *teknon* of the MSS in X. *Vect.* 2.2, see Gauthier (1976: 62–3).

[17] Cf. Aen. Tact. 10.12.   [18] See above all Saunders (1962: 65–79).

[19] *Leg.* 952d–953e; Austin and Vidal-Naquet's translation (1977: 376).

The above three considerations offer a basis for criticizing the following argument by Philippe Gauthier.[20] He claims that from shifts in Athenian judicial procedures for metics and foreigners in the classical period we can deduce changes in their relative proportion. In the fifth century there were legal facilities[21] at Athens for three groups of foreigners – metics, *xenoi* from states bound by treaty agreements with Athens, and certain other privileged strangers (such as *proxenoi*). The absence of clear evidence that still other *xenoi* – Gauthier calls them "simples *xenoi*" – were so accommodated suggests that very few of these traded with Athens in the fifth century. We ought to think, then, of fifth-century Athens as a place where prosperity prompted foreigners (including *emporoi*) to stay long enough to become metics, and in many cases even to install themselves and their families.

Gauthier thinks that there appeared (probably in the 350s) a new judicial arrangement[22] whereby matters relating to bottomry contracts were handled by a new kind of court. The distinctive features of this new arrangement were that now cases were decided *ratione rei*, not *ratione personae* as earlier, and the procedure had been speeded up. Gauthier believes this new system was designed to cope with a new situation in the wake of the Social War. With Athens less prosperous, fewer *emporoi* now became metics. When treaty arrangements lapsed, those *xenoi* once covered by such arrangements now became "simples *xenoi*." For its grain supply Athens needed foreign *emporoi*, and these new courts reflected the need, by offering a rapid procedure for settling disputes arising from bottomry loans – loans on which the grain trade depended.

This then is Gauthier's argument. He makes two claims about the place of traders at Athens in the fifth century. The first is that most *xenoi* then trading there were not "simples *xenoi*" but were from states bound to Athens by treaty agreements. This is quite plausible. If we exempt Kyrene and Syracuse, other Greek poleis of any consequence were for at least the last half of the fifth century allies of either Athens or Sparta. When Sparta's allies were at war with Athens, they certainly did not trade there; and, if traders from states allied with Athens visited there, chances are that these states would have wanted and obtained interstate agreements.

[20] Gauthier (1972: 111–26, 132–6, 149–56).
[21] Cf. Lewis' criticisms of Gauthier's scheme (1975: 262–3). For a more plausible view, see de Ste. Croix (1961: 100–1).
[22] This new arrangement (the *dikai emporikai*) is the subject of Appendix 3.

Gauthier's second claim is more questionable. He believes that a substantial number of foreigners trading with Athens in the fifth century were metics, perhaps even metics "installés pour longtemps" (1972: 110). If my previous arguments carry weight, it becomes more likely that most maritime traders at Athens fell instead into the category of *xenoi* bound by interstate agreements. Much depends on when metic status at Athens acquired the burdensome obligations that Whitehead well describes; it would appear the natural consequence of Perikles' citizenship law of 451/0 B.C., but the term *metoikos* is already in official use before 460 B.C., with what requirements we know not.[23]

Gauthier also claims that in the fourth century metics at Athens became less durably installed. Given the lack of evidence, this seems to me unknowable. That the *total* number of metics (durably installed or otherwise) declined is likely. Since most foreigners were attracted to Athens because of her commercial prosperity, the loss of empire undoubtedly led to a drop in the number of metics. We should probably be careful not to exaggerate the decline: fourth-century Athens remained the commercial hub of the Aegean and thus continued to attract many craftsmen and retail traders who became metics.

The loss of empire had another result as well. If, as I claim, most of the *emporoi* and *nauklēroi* had been *xenoi* long before the *dikai emporikai*, then these new arrangements do not reflect a changing proportion of metics to *xenoi* among maritime traders; they represent instead Athens' response to the need, emphasized by Xenophon in *Vect.*,[24] for more *emporoi* – more of the *xenoi* who, with a decline in Athens' prosperity, were now taking their goods elsewhere. At any rate these *xenoi* were the very *emporoi* the speaker in [Lys.] 22 wished to attract in 386 B.C., well before what Gauthier considers the immediate cause of the *dikai emporikai* – the outcome of the Social War. As I point out in Chapter 3 above, the speaker in [Lys.] 22.21 urged the jury to "court" the *emporoi* by voting the grain dealers guilty, thus implying that if the *emporoi* were not courted they might take their grain elsewhere. If the Athenian law barring citizen and metic *emporoi* from taking grain elsewhere was in effect in 386 B.C.,[25] then the speaker must have had in mind *emporoi* who were *xenoi*.[26]

---

[23] *IG* i[3] 244 C, line 8. See Whitehead (1986: 148) and Davies (1992: 299–300 and nn.51–2). Whitehead (1986: 148) sees the requirements of the *metoikia* as developing throughout the fifth century.

[24] *Vect.* 3.3–5.   [25] See n.6 of Ch. 3.

[26] Aeschin. 1.40 mentions "the maritime traders and the other non-resident foreigners" (*ton emporon kai ton allon xenon*).

CONCLUSION

> Neither stone blocks
> Nor ships' timbers
> Nor even the carpenters' art
> Can make a polis.
> But where there are men
> Who know how to preserve themselves
> There one finds walls and a city as well.
>
> Alkaios LP F 426[27]

If, then, most of those trading with Athens in the classical period were *xenoi* and not metics, they may have remained largely "out of sight" at Athens. Did they also remain "out of mind"? Not if the attitudes of several citizen juries are any indication. "I am an *emporos*" (*Ego d' eimi emporos*) says one trader to an Athenian jury, confident that the jurors will attend to that as well as to his citizen status.[28] And it is another jury's anxiety about attracting foreign *emporoi* on which the speaker in [Lys.] 22 ultimately plays:

The *sitopolai* [graindealers] have confessed that they combined against the *emporoi*, and for offering this admission they are now characterised as τοὺς ὁμολογοῦντας παρανομεῖν [men who admit to breaking a law]. How can the jury not condemn those who admit their guilt? Whether in fact the *sitopōlai* had ever confessed to the offence for which they were supposed to be on trial, as Lysias makes them do in the interrogation, is a point which must remain in doubt. The emphasis in the peroration, despite the blatant arrogation of the law to the cause of the *emporoi*, is all upon the expediency of humouring them, and so the orator's strategy reaches its fulfilment and the *sitopōlai*, arraigned for buying more corn than the law allowed, may see themselves, the charge forgotten, condemned for the mythical delict of conspiring against the *emporoi*.[29]

Furthermore, as I stressed at 55–9 above, that upper-class, self-consciously Athenian writer Xenophon devotes not a word in the *De vectigalibus* to any facet of maritime traders' social status, concentrating instead on their indispensability to Athens as bringers of food.

---

[27] I quote Rahe's translation (1992: 30); the portion on the ancient world in his 1992 book has been reprinted as Rahe (1994a). See also Page (1955: 434).

[28] D. 35.49. On Androkles' citizenship see the references in item 4 of no. 16. Androkles appealed not only to the jurors' concern for *emporoi* but also (D. 35.26) to their sense of citizen solidarity and to a certain amount of anti-foreign sentiment against Phaselites (see as well D. 35.1–2). Seager's comment (1966: 179) on another plea also applies here: "The card was a dangerous one to play, for the jury might have remembered that many of the *emporoi* were also foreigners." Androkles' bold claim to be an *emporos* contrasts markedly with the Athenian metics' refusal to identify themselves *as metics* on their tombstones at Athens, on which see Whitehead (1986: 33–4, 57).

[29] Seager (1966: 177) commenting on [Lys.] 22.17, 21.

Hasebroek thus stands vindicated in spite of himself, at least with regard to Athens. He showed that official interest in traders was an import interest, limited to attracting and controlling the men who played such a vital economic role. He perceived, in other words, the extent to which the polis framework shaped official attitudes. What he failed to perceive was its impact on the attitudes of Athenian society at large. He and others after him thought that Athenians might attend primarily to aspects of a trader's low social status – to his relative poverty, foreign birth, or particular occupation, for example.[30] Hasebroek failed to carry his own "substantivist" thesis far enough because he never realized that at Athens the civic dependence on imported food replaced considerations of social status in the minds of individual Athenians as well. This crucial feature of the trader's "place" distances Athens from other pre-modern, agrarian societies. For at Athens "the economy was not [merely] embedded in society; the economy and the society were embedded in the polity."[31]

---

[30] Hasebroek (1928: esp. 8–12); for mention of some very recent adherents of this view, see n.6 above.

[31] Rahe (1992: 29), echoed by Cartledge (1998: 9) as follows: "It is simply not possible to overstate the degree to which ancient Greek life – communal and private, individual and collective – was politicized." There is almost no evidence as to how maritime traders were regarded at poleis other than Athens. It probably depended on how vital their services were. The more a polis relied on imports of necessities, the more it and its citizens probably focused on a trader's indispensable economic role. In poleis whose dependence on imports was less crucial, certain aspects of his social status may have become more important. See further X. *Eq. mag.* 4.7.

CHAPTER 7

Archaic modes of exchange and the personnel involved c. 800–475 B.C.

INTRODUCTION[1]

In 1983 Paul Cartledge wrote a brief article reaffirming Johannes Hasebroek's basic insights into the place of trade and traders in the world of archaic Greece. Like Hasebroek, Cartledge assumed that, in order to talk sensibly about archaic trade or traders, one had to locate them in a sound socio-economic context. He defended Hasebroek's framework – an overwhelmingly agrarian economy and society, with a ruling class drawing its wealth and prestige from landowning, not commerce, so that the dominance of market relationships or commercial aristocracies were fantasies of those who improperly modernized a world with quite low levels of commercial and manufacturing activity.[2] Cartledge's piece capped a three decade-long effort by substantivist-minded ancient historians, led in Britain by M. I. Finley and G. E. M. de Ste. Croix, to convince their colleagues that this alternate way of looking at Greco-Roman economic activity captured more of the ancient reality.

Were other ancient historians persuaded? Consider recent estimates of archaic market activity. James Redfield speaks of the period 750–700 B.C. as "a time when traders were beginning to transform society . . ." and concludes that "by the middle of the sixth century this reconstruction was more or less complete. . ."[3] And Robin Osborne recently wrote, "In this paper I argue that the archaic world *was* a world of interdependent markets."[4] As for the role of the Greek aristocrats in commerce: In 1994 J. N. Coldstream observed that "unlike later Greek aristocrats, those of the eighth and seventh

---

[1] The references cited in this chapter are far from comprehensive, much less exhaustive. I cite mainly recent works that have been of particular use.

[2] Cartledge (1983). One of Cartledge's principal aims was to show how Bravo in his 1977 article and Mele in his 1979 book revert to a more modernizing and hence implausible stance. Cartledge usefully summarizes the main points of both works; Mele himself also provides useful summaries on 40, 74, 99, 102, 106–9, esp. 108–9.

[3] Redfield (1986: 31, 51).   [4] Osborne (1996: 31).

centuries did not disdain the role of trader."[5] Speaking as well of the early archaic period, David Tandy began a 1997 book by claiming that "the traders were mostly *aristoi*";[6] and in the same year Walter Donlan argued for "the much heavier engagement of aristocrats in organized international trade in the years prior to *c.* 675 B.C."[7]

That two such contrasting perspectives continue to appeal to ancient historians raises a troubling question: Is it possible to resolve these differences empirically? Or is the surviving archaic evidence so meager, unrepresentative, and (in certain cases) corrupt that *both* the above alternatives are equally compatible with it, so that *all* interpretations of the place of traders in archaic Greek life boil down to a clash of viewpoints? If the answer is yes, then archaic economic history is a fool's game, an exercise in rumor-mongering and special pleading, and Benedetto Bravo's (curiously postmodern) hermeneutic ventures into etymology[8] are the best one can expect in a field short on "facts."

I once was convinced that an empirical inquiry into the place of archaic traders was impossible and was initially reluctant to include an archaic chapter. I was wrong: we *can* go from knowing less to knowing *slightly more* about the place of those who engaged in archaic exchanges, as long as we observe three rules of thumb.

First, we must begin by trying "to form an overall picture of how and to what extent material goods changed ownership" instead of first "accumulating evidence for the existence of trade."[9] Second, we must resist the temptation to infer prematurely from archaeological findings about *trade* any conclusions about the place of archaic *traders*; a given set of material remains is compatible with various sorts of social structures.[10] Third, we must admit to cautious *guesswork* in any attempt to identify the personnel involved in archaic exchanges. If what follows strikes the reader as unduly cautious and tentative, he or she should note that from Hasebroek right down to the present the better studies of archaic trade and traders suffer from a tendency to claim too much for their valuable insights.[11]

The main questions raised in the chapter are: Who engaged in the interregional transfer of goods by sea in the archaic period? If different sorts of people did, can we gauge their relative wealth, prestige, and above all their proportions? And did these proportions change throughout the archaic

[5] Coldstream (1994: 53), joined by Starr (1977: 192).   [6] Tandy (1997: 4).
[7] Donlan (1997: 666).   [8] Esp. Bravo in his 1977 article as well as Bravo (1980 and 1984).
[9] Grierson (1959: 125).   [10] These are points Finley stressed in (among other works) (1975: 87–101).
[11] Hasebroek for example virtually excluded Greeks from archaic trade as an occupation (1933: 17–19, 21, 48, 66–9) and (1931: 31, 33–9, 147–8, 270).

period? For present purposes it helps to divide the period under considera-
tion into two parts: *c.* 800 to *c.* 625 B.C., and *c.* 625 to *c.* 475 B.C. The lower
terminus is the highly conjectural date from which maritime traders could
first rely on bottomry loans.[12] At the other end is the rough date posited by
Boardman for regular Greek (Euboean) traffic with and probably settlement
at Al Mina in Syria.[13]

THE PERIOD FROM C. 800 TO C. 625 B.C.

I begin with the evidence from the Homeric epics and hymns, assuming with Raaflaub[14] that Homer does indeed picture a single society. In
an analysis showing a sophistication missing from earlier accounts, Sally
Humphreys comments on

[the] complicated interaction...between the travels and guest-friendships of
nobles, war, raiding and piracy, and the development of trade...The *hetairoi*
[companions] who rowed...[the] ship [of a nobleman] might take goods for exchange, or hope to acquire them abroad by raiding, piracy or military service...
[so that] a rigid distinction between 'trade' and the transfer of goods through war,
raiding, hospitality and gift-exchange cannot be imposed [on the activities of such
hetairoi].[15]

Greek aristocrats, sailing in their own oared longships with other nobles[16]
and perhaps with their dependents,[17] probably account for a fair portion
of the goods exchanged by sea in the period 800–625 B.C.[18] The Samian
Kolaios, often called the earliest "merchant" mentioned in the sources,[19]
may have been such an aristocrat, sailing with a crew of Samian companions

---

[12] On the earliest date for bottomry loans, see further 40–2 above.

[13] Boardman (1990: 186 and 1999: 270–5); cf. Snodgrass (1994: 4–5) and the references cited therein
for a later date.

[14] Raaflaub (1997a) above all, as well as (1998).

[15] Humphreys (1978: 160, 167–9). Her point is best exemplified by Snodgrass (1980: 123–59), which
joins Cartledge (1983) as still the two most convincing overviews of archaic trade and traders. On
the role of Homeric gift-exchanges in particular see Coldstream (1983), Stanley (1986), esp. Morris
(1986), Hooker (1989), Crielaard (1993), and above all von Reden (1995a: 13–57).

[16] E.g., the ἄνδρες...ἐσθλοί ("noble men") in the *Homeric Hymn to Pythian Apollo* 392; cf. Mele (1979:
80–1).

[17] E.g., *Op.* 643–4.

[18] For descriptions of the mix of activities described in the text, see Austin and Vidal-Naquet (1977:
40–4), Nowag (1983: 56–61, 113–16, 128–39), Stanley (1986), Kopcke (1990: 123–8), and Jackson
(1993). For an important documented example of a warrior-raider-trader, see Popham and Lemos
(1995). For Mele's view of these voyages undertaken by Homer's nobles and their *hetairoi* (which he
terms "*prēxis* commerce"), see (1979) Chs. VIII and IX, esp. the useful summaries on 74 and 108 as
well as (1986: 71–80).

[19] By, e.g., Jeffery (1976: 212–13).

(*hetairoi*) and perhaps dependents to Spain, from which they brought back to Samos unprecedented profits.[20] Humphreys[21] and Snodgrass[22] note that upon their return home a dedication was made by the entire crew, not just by Kolaios.

Nor should we doubt that from the eighth through the early seventh centuries a landowner might load his produce on a small, coast-hugging boat and sell it elsewhere. Hesiod offers testimony to that effect,[23] and we know this practice extends into the classical period and well beyond. More commonly in the archaic period, perhaps, a peasant or larger landowner would carry surplus produce to the local market for sale (once markets developed),[24] taking to sea only when such a market was not conveniently available.

So far, then, no mention of people we can properly call "maritime traders," a phrase that requires definition. At 7–12 I showed how dangerous and possibly misleading it is to speak even in the classical period of maritime trade as a "profession," much less as one characterized by "specialization." For the archaic period, especially the earlier part thereof, caution must be magnified a thousandfold. I advisedly apply the term "maritime trader" to the following two elastic categories: (a) free men who derive much if not most of their livelihood from going to sea, whether for a season or longer, in search of goods they ultimately resell for their own profit; and (b) free or unfree men who take to sea, whether for a season or longer, principally on behalf of a wealthy landowner for whom they obtain goods by trade abroad.[25] Both sorts, "independent maritime traders" and

---

[20] Hdt. 4.152. There Herodotus calls Kolaios a *nauklēros*. I would guess (as does Vélissaropoulos 1980: 27) that Kolaios is no "shipowner" in the commercial sense the word *nauklēros* bore in the classical period, when it normally referred to one whose livelihood depended on the ownership of a single merchant vessel on which he sailed and engaged in trade himself (Vélissaropoulos [1980: 48–9] and 12–14 in this volume). The same reservations apply to Plutarch's reference to Solon's *nauklēros* (*Sol.* 25.6). Hasebroek unnecessarily discounts the story of Kolaios as fifth-century propaganda (1928: 69 n.1 and 1931: 270). For views other than those presented in the text, see Jeffery (n.19 above), Boardman (1999: 114, 213), and Mele (1979: 96–7 and 41).

[21] Humphreys (1978: 168).

[22] Snodgrass (1980: 138–9 and 1983: 17). That Kolaios was a proper maritime trader or at least a "shipmaster" engaged solely in maritime trade remains strongly implicit in Snodgrass' two accounts.

[23] *Op.* 618–32; cf. Mele (1979: 53). These are the only lines from *Works and Days* that, post-Mele, one can cite with a degree of confidence as an example of a farmer's short-range, coastal sailing to dispose of surplus produce.

[24] Austin and Vidal-Naquet (1977: 43): "There are no fairs in Homer and the *agora* has no economic function, but is only a meeting place."

[25] Bravo devotes his 1974 article and particularly his 1977 article to showing that such agent traders were the main but not the only archaic carriers of goods exchanged inter-regionally by sea (see further 69–74). Vélissaropoulos (1980: 28, 36, 336) wrongly believes agent traders the only sort of maritime traders in the archaic period.

"agent traders" alike, go to sea mainly if not exclusively in order to trade (albeit with different ends in mind), unlike the aristocrats and their *hetairoi* mentioned earlier, for whom trading is only one of a mix of the activities Humphreys[26] and Mele[27] well describe.

If the term "maritime trader" be thus understood, then I would argue that the "traders" (*prekteres*) mentioned in *Od*. 8.162 are early maritime traders, perhaps of the "independent" rather than the "agent" sort, although Bravo[28] disagrees. There (8.159–64) the Phaiakian noble Euryalos taunts Odysseus by saying, "You don't strike me as a man of games, but as one who travels in a many-benched ship, a master (*archos*) of *prekteres* – a man who oversees the cargo, in charge of the merchandise and of greedily-sought profits."

Hesiod also testifies to an inter-regional commerce (*emporien, Op*. 646)[29] different in scope and personnel from the coastal voyages farmers such as himself might make to vend their surplus produce. Unfortunately *Works and Days* reveals precious little *unambiguous* information about either sort of trading, *far* less than Mele claims to draw from it; Mele, for example, tries to find in *Works and Days* the same mix of aristocratic activity that he and Humphreys see in the Homeric epics, but he is not at all convincing.[30]

What drove archaic Greeks to sea for purposes of trade – trade, I mean, unmixed with the raiding, gift-giving, and so forth that characterized the activities of aristocrats and their *hetairoi*? Poverty. The skimpy sources say as much,[31] and further evidence lies in the canon of prestige preventing rich landowners from doing it. As part of the mixed activities resulting in the acquisition of goods for their own use or consumption aristocrats could "engage in trade" without jeopardizing their status. But trade undertaken in the service of another, or the persistent buying in order to sell or selling in order to buy, all in quest of profit[32] – these activities would disqualify

---

[26] Humphreys (1978: 160–9).

[27] Mele's account (1979: esp. Ch. 8 and 108) of the mixed activities aristocrats and their *hetairoi* engaged in constitutes one of the most plausible portions of his book.

[28] Bravo (1977: 33–4) and (1984: 100–14). See also Mele (1979: 81–2, 58) and (1986: 71–80).

[29] Hesiod is the earliest Greek source to use the phrase *ep' emporien* to refer to a maritime trading venture. In Homer the word *emporos* means "passenger on a ship," not "maritime trader" (*Od*. 2.319 and 24.300).

[30] Mele (1979: esp. 46 and 74 as well as 41, 43, 45, and 63); on Mele see Cartledge's comments (1983: 8–12). Both Bravo (1977: 10–13) and Mele (1979: 18–21, esp. 20–1) think Hesiod an aristocrat, albeit a poor one, and Starr (1977: 123–8) views him as a "semi-aristocrat." See as well the later exchange of views in Bravo (1984: esp. 141–9) and Mele (1986: esp. 80–5). Millett (1984) forcefully criticizes all the above views and convincingly argues that Hesiod is no aristocrat but rather a peasant. See also Nowag (1983: 170–9).

[31] Hesiod *Op*. 647 and possibly 634 and 637–8; Thgn. 179–80, ?1197–1202; Solon 13.41–6 (West). See also Austin and Vidal-Naquet (1977: 55); cf. Starr (1982: 421, 425). For a qualified dissent as regards Aegina's archaic maritime traders, see Figueira (1981: 15, 170, 282, 284–6, 306, 321–6, 342).

[32] Much of this sentence is a slightly modified translation of Aymard's formulation in (1967: 330). See as well Austin and Vidal-Naquet (1977: 13) and Bravo (1977: 24).

one socially as an aristocrat. Humphreys thinks that "little but an ideological hairline divided the noble who voyaged in order to come home loaded with valuable gifts... or to exchange iron for copper... from the 'commander of sailors out for gain... always thinking of his cargo'[*Od*. 8.159ff.]."[33] Odysseus' angry reply (*Od*. 8.165–85) to the charge that he himself was such a "commander" suggests that the ideological divide was wider than Humphreys claims.

In Chapter 6 I argued that traders' indispensability to classical Athens as suppliers of imported food displaced otherwise negative evaluations of their social status. But archaic poleis relied much less on imported foodstuffs,[34] so that from Homer on, something other than the service maritime traders provide attracts attention; we read disparaging remarks about the sort of work they do,[35] and about how nice it would be not to do it.[36] In short the ideological divide between aristocrat and maritime trader loomed wide throughout the archaic period.

Where did maritime traders get the wherewithal to trade in the period *c*. 800–625 B.C.? There is no likelier source of both ship and cargo than wealthy landowners,[37] so that for the earlier archaic period Bravo's "agent theory" has a special appeal, even if throughout the archaic period not a single explicit reference occurs in the sources to one who trades as the agent of another.[38]

In addition to these agent traders, could poor, independent maritime traders somehow finance voyages in search of goods they brought back to the Greek world and sold to whomever they wished? I strongly suspect the answer is "yes" but can cite no evidence; and in any case how different

---

[33] Humphreys (1978: 167).

[34] Bravo (1983: 211) exaggerates archaic poleis' need for grain, a need he argues is based not on the growth of an urban *demos* but on bad harvests. This highly speculative claim is partly refuted by Jameson (1983: esp. 8, 12–13) in an article in the same collection. The attack launched by Peter Garnsey on efforts to date Athens' dependence on grain to the late archaic period is documented and discussed at 16–19 above. For persuasive arguments against the flow of grain to archaic Greece from the Black Sea region in particular, see Ščeglov (1990) and Tsetskhladze (1994: esp. 124), also Arafat and Morgan (1994: 129).

[35] *Od*. 8.159–64 and Thgn. 679. Solon is exceptional in the sympathetic way he, a landed gentleman, speaks not only of the maritime trader but also the agricultural laborer and the craftsman (West, *IE²* 13.43–50). We can discount Plutarch's little sermon on the attractions of maritime trading in *Sol*. 2.3; he cites no reliable evidence.

[36] Hes. *Op*. 236; Pind. *Ol*. 2.61–7.

[37] As both Hopper (1979: 25) and Salmon (1984: 150) point out.

[38] The Berezan tablet, dated *c*. 500 B.C. and elaborately discussed by Bravo in his 1974 and 1977 articles, is the only archaic document to offer any support for his theory that wealthy landowners dispatched agents to do their trading. The tablet nowhere explicitly says this, so that I find it impossible to draw any such clear conclusion from it. In his 1980 article Bravo (879–85) offered what he termed an improved text and translation of the Berezan tablet; his interpretation there and in his 1983 piece remains essentially unchanged. See also Chadwick (1973) and (1990).

really were such men from the agents mentioned above? In the period 800–625 B.C. who but landed aristocrats were best qualified to provide independent traders with both goods and vessel? And given the nature of the goods with which they returned to Greece – probably metals and finished luxury items[39] – who but the aristocrats were the likeliest customers?

We know far too little about seaborne exchanges in the period 800–625 B.C. to assign proportions to each of the groups mentioned above. Suffice it to say that the travels of Greek aristocrats and their *hetairoi* and dependents must account for a certain amount. It is also true that Phoenicians[40] and Etruscans[41] played a role in sea trade with the Greek world. But we can reasonably doubt that all exchanges with places such as Al Mina[42] and Pithekoussai[43] were in the hands of Greek landowners or Phoenicians; some if not many such exchanges very likely were carried on by Greek *prekteres* – agent or independent – whom we may legitimately call "maritime traders."[44] Who could resist citing Matthew Arnold's lines heralding their appearance?

> As some grave Tyrian trader, from the sea,
> Descried at sunrise an emerging prow
> Lifting the cool-hair'd creepers stealthily,
> The fringes of a southward-facing brow
> Among the Aegean isles;
> And saw the merry Grecian coaster come,
> Freighted with amber grapes, and Chian wine,
> Green bursting figs, and tunnies steep'd in brine;
> And knew the intruders on his ancient home...
>
> "The Scholar Gypsy"

[39] See further Humphreys (1978: 167); Snodgrass (1980: 123–43 and 1983, both stressing as well shipments of marble); Bass (1986 and 1991); Ridgway (1992b: 93–103); Whitbread (1995: esp. 20–4); Foxhall (1998: 298–300).

[40] From the wealth of publications on Phoenician trade and traders, I have found the following particularly helpful: Gras *et al.* (1989: 79–127); Niemeyer (1990); Aubet (1993: 102–18). On Phoenicians at Pithekoussai and elsewhere in the West, see Ridgway (1992b: 111–18 and 1994). Hopper (29–33) provides the source references.

[41] For an overview see Ridgway (1988: 634–75); for inundation, see Gras (1985: 393–701).

[42] See Boardman (1990 and 1999: 270–5) and Popham (1994), who disagree in crucial respects with Graham (1986) and Snodgrass (1994: 4–5).

[43] Far and away the best overview of Pithekoussai is found in Ridgway (1992b), a model of its kind; see also Coldstream (1994). My non-archaeologist's hunch after examining the tables and remarks on 67–77 and 101–3 of Ridgway (1992b) is that I have seriously *underargued* for the presence of non-aristocratic maritime traders – independent or agent – at Pithekoussai. Pithekoussai also provides a point of departure for bold, intriguing suggestions by Wilson (1997) and Osborne (1998) for revising our conceptual maps of Greek settlement abroad in the archaic period.

[44] For an excellent survey of Euboean activity abroad in the early archaic period, see Ch. 2 of Ridgway (1992b) and Crielaard (1993) and, for an even more general overview, Boardman (1999: 267–82 and 298–9). All three authors remark on the importance of Greek mercantile activity in and with Cyprus in this period. See also Csapo (1991 and 1993) for the very early archaic presence of Greek merchants on Crete.

THE PERIOD FROM C. 625 TO C. 475 B.C.

What sorts of people engaged in the inter-regional exchange of goods by sea in the later archaic period? I suggest that the period from roughly 625 to 475 B.C. sees a steady rise in the number of independent maritime traders relative to other carriers of goods. We can even begin to discern *why* certain sorts of carriers might decline proportionally, in particular nobles who traveled with their *hetairoi* or dependents on multi-purpose voyages as well as men trading as agents of landowners.[45]

I focus first on the single best indicator of a late archaic increase in the number of independent maritime traders – the gradual growth, perhaps beginning in the late seventh or early sixth century, in commercial imports of grain from outside the Aegean to the Greek mainland and Greek poleis of Asia Minor. Without a shred of explicit evidence many scholars think that the search for grain prompted Greek traders to arrive at Naukratis in Egypt by the late seventh century B.C.[46] Would such trade appeal to voyaging aristocrats and their *hetairoi*? True, in the sixth century noble landowners like Solon[47] and Sappho's brother voyaged to Egypt. Herodotus, who provides the earliest reference (1.29) to Solon's visit to Egypt, says nothing about his trading there, whereas Aristotle ([*Ath. Pol.*] 11.1) says Solon traveled "both on business and to see the country" (*kat' emporian hama kai theorian*). If Aristotle is correct, then Solon probably went for the same reason the son of a prominent man in the Bosporan

---

[45] Both Figueira and Mele describe a crucial transition in the sorts of people engaged in inter-regional trade by sea and date it to the late seventh century. Figueira (1981: 264) speaks of a shift from a "piracy-based model" to "long-distance trade"; Mele (1979: esp.106–7), of *prexis* or *ergon* commerce yielding to the more specialized *emporie*. Both in quite different ways describe aspects of the same major transition I argue for, although our three accounts differ in other important respects. For other testimonies to the late seventh-century intensification of inter-regional commerce, see Braun (1982: 39) and Cook (1982: 215).

[46] Starr (1977: 165 and 1982: 427 n.9) forcefully dissents. On Naukratis see the historical overview in Sullivan (1996) as well as Austin (1970: 22–45), Boardman (1999: 117–33), Braun (1982: 32–56), and Graham (1982a: 134). It is generally agreed that Egyptians received silver, wine, and olive oil in return. This assumption that imports of grain from Egypt began to arrive in Greece *c.* 625–600 B.C. is the most crucial unsupported conjecture in this chapter, and I am nervously aware of Arafat and Morgan's telling comment (1994: 129) that "the same commodities, particularly slaves and grain, tend to be cited whenever it is necessary to invoke invisible imports." The earliest literary reference to Egyptian grain for Greece occurs in Bacchylides fr. 20B 14–16 (Snell–Maehler). As for when grain shipments from the West reach Greece: Gelon of Syracuse offers to supply Greece with grain for the duration of the Persian War (Hdt. 7.158.4). Salmon (1984: 130, 135, 144) guesses that some grain imports reached Corinth even earlier. On archaic shipments of grain to Greece, see esp. Foxhall (1998: 302–3).

[47] On Solon's voyage see the source references and discussion in de Ste. Croix (1981: 129–30). See also Hasebroek's sensible comments (1928: 13 and 1931: 263) and Mele (1979: 42). On Solon's alleged *nauklēros* (Plut. *Sol.* 25.6) see n.20 above.

kingdom sailed to Athens in the early fourth century with two shiploads of grain *hama kat' emporian kai kata theorian* – to finance a sightseeing trip.[48] Charaxos, brother of Sappho, sailed to Naukratis *kat'emporian* with a cargo of Lesbian wine, perhaps again as a way of financing his voyage.[49] But (to repeat) wealthy landowners were unlikely to engage regularly in long-distance sea trade unmixed with sightseeing or other activities, for such trade was a grubby business with most of the dangers and none of the prestige associated with the mixed activities of aristocrats, their *hetairoi*, and their dependents.

I do not mean to imply that the late archaic period sees the disappearance of voyaging aristocrats who combined raiding, piracy, and trading. In fact that description probably characterizes well the sixth-century Phokaian expansion in the West,[50] so that Phokaians founded Massalia not solely, as one source[51] has it, in the course of trade, but in the course of that mix of activities such seagoing aristocrats, their *hetairoi*, and dependents undertook.[52] Protis, called by Plutarch[53] the founder of Massalia and a maritime trader, was probably no trader but one of these voyagers. We know nothing about the traders responsible for the goods coming into and going out of archaic Massalia, but I would guess that its oligarchic elite consisted of aristocrats such as Protis.[54]

At the same time, we should doubt Humphreys' assumption[55] that the activities of raiding, trading, and gift-giving landowners *continued* to be one of the major ways in which goods were exchanged in the late archaic period. Beginning already in the early archaic age, the Greek aristocracy was transformed from a warrior elite to one preoccupied with international

---

[48] Isok. 17.3–4. See further de Ste. Croix (1981: 130) and a similar example in Diog. Laert. 6.9.

[49] On Charaxos' voyage see Strabo 17.1.33 as well as Ath. 13.596b–d, Hdt. 2.134–5, and Page (1955: 45–51). Compare the acute comments by de Ste. Croix (1981: 131) and Hasebroek (1928: 13–14 and 1931: 263) with those of Gomme (1957: 258–9); see also Mele (1979: 41). On the other alleged "traders" (e.g., Plato, Thales, and Hippokrates) see de Ste. Croix (1981: 130–1). I regard the claims for Demaratos as a trader equally dubious. Demaratos, generally alleged to have been a Bacchiad who fled from Greece to Etruria, is mentioned in the following sources: Dion. Hal. 3.46.3; Cic. *Rep.* 2.19; Livy 1.34; 4.3; Strabo 5.2.2; 8.6.20; Plin. *HN* 35.16, 152. Of these only the fullest account, by Dionysios of Halikarnassos, mentions Demaratos' trading. For other views, see Blakeway (1935: esp. 147–9); Ampolo (1976–7: 333–45); Ridgway (1988: 661–7), (1992b: 119, 143), and (1992a).

[50] See esp. Morel (1975 and 1984) and Cunliffe (1988: 13–32), also Hasebroek's apt comments (1931: 270), and Mele (1979: 43, 60, 68–9, 100). For Greek settlements in Spain, see esp. Rouillard (1991) and Shefton (1995).

[51] Arist. fr. 459 *apud* Ath. 13.576a–b.

[52] See esp. Just. *Epit.* 43.35–8 with Hdt. 1.163–7, also Livy 5.34.78.

[53] Plut. *Sol.* 2.7–8; cf. Arist. *apud* Ath. 13.576b and Mele (1979: 42).

[54] On Protis and Massalia, see the references in n.50 above and my n.32 of Ch. 3 as well as Bravo (1984: 126–9); Mele (1986: 89–93); Arafat and Morgan (1994: 126–8); and Shefton (1994).

[55] Humphreys (1978: 165–9).

games, the *gymnasion, palaistra*, and *symposion*,[56] although the pace of that transformation varied throughout the Greek world, as the case of the Phokaians in the West or the Samians[57] elsewhere demonstrates. But where the transformation *did* occur, aristocratic leisure was hardly compatible with regular maritime trading.

If voyaging aristocrats were not responsible for importing grain from Naukratis, who were? Surely *not* the agents of wealthy landowners. On their return voyage these agents normally brought the special items required by the landowners themselves,[58] whereas trade in grain bespeaks a more widespread, urgent, and regular need, one better met by men able and eager to make their living by taking grain wherever they could get the best price for it, as maritime traders did in the fourth century B.C.

Other evidence supports the argument for a growing element of independent maritime traders beginning in the late seventh century. Semonides, date uncertain but perhaps living in the second half of the seventh,[59] provides the earliest surviving reference to the word *emporos*[60] in the sense of "maritime trader." In the same period, too, although not in connection with grain imports, men began to leave a record of themselves as maritime traders: Alan Johnston dates the earliest marks (in the Corinthian or Ionic alphabets) on the feet of painted vases to "the years before 600 B.C."; but more recently the same Cypriot merchant mark on pottery found in both the northern Aegean (Mende) and in southern Italy (Policoro) has been dated to about 700 B.C.[61] Another piece of supporting evidence: vase paintings and ship models portray Greek sail-powered merchant ships as early

---

[56] For an excellent overview of that transformation, see Murray (1993: 201–19). For the crucial developments either responsible for or accompanying the transformation, see esp. Snodgrass (1993) and Raaflaub (1997b).

[57] Figueira (1981: 291 n.35) collects the principal primary and secondary references to the Samians, Polykrates, and Aeakes. To these should be added (on Polykrates) Mele (1979: 106) and de Souza (1998: 282–3), and (on Aeakes) ML no. 16 and Bravo (1980: 728–35).

[58] As Salmon (1984: 151) points out.

[59] On Semonides' dates see Campbell (1967: 184), Lloyd-Jones (1975: 15–16), and Gerber (1999: 7).

[60] Semonides: West *IE*² fr. 16. The word *phortegos* makes its only archaic appearance in line 679 (West, *IE*²) of the Theognidean corpus, unless one also wants to include the Simonidean passage in which *phortegos* appears together with *emporos* as a virtual synonym (most accessible as fr. LX in Campbell [1991: 572]). Hasebroek (1931: 261 and n.2) rightly equates the *phortegoi* in Theognis with *emporoi*. Bravo (1977: 44) plausibly assumes that in the archaic period the normal word for "maritime trader" is *emporos* and not *phortegos*. See Bravo (1977: 42–50) and (1974: 128–30) for the few source references to *phortegos* in the classical period. Bravo (1977: 49–50) wrongly thinks *phortegos* the standard word for "maritime trader" in Old Comedy. On the hellenistic career of the word *phortegos* see Bravo (1977: 44–8) and Vélissaropoulos (1980: 37–42).

[61] Johnston (1979: 51). On the date of the Cypriot merchant mark: Vokotopoulou and Christidis (1995: 6, 10) and Boardman (1999: 270). On the connection between literacy and archaic commercial exchanges, see further Johnston (1983 and 1990), Coldstream (1990), and Harris (1996).

as the late eighth or early seventh centuries. Throughout the rest of the archaic and classical periods this round-hulled vessel, built solely for trading, serves as the standard mode of transportation for independent maritime traders and their cargoes.[62] Where Greeks such as the earlier mentioned Phokaians continued to combine raiding and piracy with trading into the sixth century, oared war-galleys called pentekontors remained in use.[63] I therefore take Hdt. 1.163.2 as meaning "The Phokaians, by sailing west in pentekontors, serve as an exception to the general practice of using rounded hulls (στρογγύληισι νηυσί) for trade." And the circumstances warrant the exception: in the western Mediterranean the Phokaians could perhaps adapt their pentekontors for trading without sacrificing the ability to withstand attacks from Karthaginian and Etruscan warships and pirates.[64]

It must be acknowledged how *very little* evidence we have for the presence of independent maritime traders in the late archaic period. The relevant vase paintings and ship models are few, and some of these have not been dated decisively. I further suspect that the aristocratic bias of archaic Greek literature after Hesiod precludes adequate reference to those who engaged in certain sorts of real work for a living. For example the words *emporos* and *phortegos* (both in the sense of independent maritime trader)[65] occur only once apiece in Greek literature prior to 500 B.C., in spite of what I presume to be the prevalence of such traders (relative to other carriers of goods) in the sixth century. The sole *possible* archaic reference to a *naukleros*, in the sense of one whose livelihood depends on owning a sail-powered merchant vessel, comes not from literature but from what appears to be a *naukleros'* own dedication to Pallas Athena, and even this single reference is a dubious conjecture: the editor of *IG* i³ 642a reads *Nauklēſs* for *Naukla[ros* in *IG* i² 628.[66] Just as we have good reason to date the sail-powered merchant roundship before the late sixth century, so we are free to guess that *naukleroi*

---

[62] Humphreys (1978: 166–8 and n.13) and Snodgrass (1983: 16–18, 22) argued that "purpose-built, sail-driven merchantmen" (Snodgrass [1983:17]) played little or no role in the shipment of goods until the last quarter of the sixth century. For arguments and evidence against this view, see Reed (1984: 39–41 and nn.73–84). (I continue to be most grateful to Lionel Casson, Keith DeVries, and Michael Katzev for their advice, so generously tendered, on the ship-related issues in that article.) Since then Paul Johnston's thesis on ship models, referred to in n.81, has been published as *Ship and Boat Models in Ancient Greece* (Annapolis 1985). De Sousa (1998: 272–3) provides an overview of and recent references to archaic warships, a topic not much dealt with in Reed (1984).

[63] On Phokaian activity see further the references in n.50 above, to which should be added (on Phokaian sea power in particular) de Souza (1998: 283–5).

[64] On Carthaginian naval power see the overview in Lancel (1995: 125–31); on Etruscans and Phokaians, Gras (1985: 393–475) as well as on Etruscan pirates (514–22).

[65] See n.60 above.

[66] *IG* i³ 642a and *IG* i² 628, on the latter of which see Vélissaropoulos (1980: 11 n.1 and 28 n.103), also my n.20 above.

may have sailed their vessels to Naukratis and elsewhere before they are first mentioned *c.* 500 B.C.[67]

A new question: if the period 625–475 B.C. sees a growing number of independent maritime traders, how did they acquire the goods they carried? Probably not from bottomry loans, which perhaps appear first between 475 and 450 B.C., after the wide-spread monetarization of commercial exchanges and in response to Athens' increasing need for bulk imports of grain.[68] Faced with a total lack of evidence as to how late archaic maritime trade was financed prior to bottomry loans, we can only guess. Salmon[69] sensibly reviews certain possibilities, of which I mention only one discussed by Bravo, in order to take issue with him on a point he regards as major. For long-range trade by sea Bravo[70] can imagine only one archaic alternative to agent traders – impoverished nobles who retained sufficient resources to qualify as the likeliest candidates for loans made by rich landowners to men trading on their own. This is possible, but as so often in archaic Greek economic and social history other alternatives are just as credible, so that we have no good reason to accept Bravo's claim that the majority of independent maritime traders in the archaic period came from this element of impoverished nobles. Of course some wealthy men may have dropped in status to that of maritime traders, just as an immensely profitable voyage or voyages would have elevated others out of that status. In that latter connection the name of Sostratos the Aiginetan mentioned in Hdt. 4.152 possibly arises.[71] With regard to the vexed "Sostratos dossier," I can only

[67] Vélissaropoulos (1980: 35–6, 336) wrongly claims that the "métiers" of *emporos* (as independent maritime trader) and *nauklēros* did not exist in the archaic period; rather, archaic inter-regional trade by sea was in the hands of agent traders (1980: 28, 36, 336). At Athens "les activités commerciales se transforment en véritables professions au moment même où la polis voit son épanouisssement" (36) in the classical period. She confuses the existence of archaic *emporoi* and *nauklēroi* with the *evidence* for their existence. I have maintained that *emporos* and *nauklēros* did exist as "métiers" in the archaic period, but not until very late in that period does the polis begin to develop the political-cum-legal mechanisms for defining and dealing with them. How little we know about maritime traders in the classical period apart from the light these mechanisms throw on them. Again and again *emporoi* and *nauklēroi* appear as polis-defined *metoikoi* or *xenoi*, as figures in polis-staged legal proceedings, as recipients of polis-bestowed honors, or as victims or beneficiaries of its military and diplomatic policies. We never will have such evidence for most of the archaic period because for most of it the requisite mechanisms did not exist.

[68] See further 40–2. G. E. M. de Ste. Croix (1974: 44 and n.13): "I would hazard the guess (it can be no more) that these [bottomry] loans may perhaps have developed first about the second quarter of the fifth century, in connection with the Athenian corn trade..." Calligas (1971: 86) assumes that the debts recorded on lead plaques found on Corcyra and dating *c.* 500 B.C. are debts incurred through bottomry loans; but, as Austin and Vidal-Naquet say (1977: 155 n.21), "There is nothing in the inscriptions to prove this." Cf. Salmon (1984: 149).

[69] Salmon (1984: 148–53).   [70] Bravo (1977: 24–5).

[71] See Figueira (1981: 241–9 and notes) for a thorough discussion and full bibliography, to which should be added Johnston (1979: 44, 49, 189) and (1990: 440) as well as Gill (1994: 99–101).

stress how dangerous it is to regard as typical the few archaic individuals named in the literary sources as engaging in maritime trade, since we may hear of them precisely because they *are* exceptional.

As for the archaic trade in slaves and those who conducted it, the evidence is scanty, save for the Homeric epics. There practically everyone taking to sea – aristocrat or otherwise, Greek or Phoenician – is prepared to deal in slaves throughout the archaic period and beyond.[72] A debate[73] still exists about when slaves began to be transported to Greece in large numbers, but the evidence to resolve it is sorely lacking.

To sum up: from the eighth to the late seventh century B.C. some Greeks may have engaged in inter-regional sea trade to such an extent that we should regard them as maritime traders, with agent traders perhaps outnumbering independent ones. The period from the late seventh century to *c.* 475 B.C. sees a steady rise in the number of independent traders relative to all other carriers of goods, so that by 475 B.C. the pattern for the classical period already prevails: most of the long-distance transfer of goods was by inter-regional sea trade (as distinct from non-commercial transfers), and inter-regional trade by sea in the Greek world was largely in the hands of poorer men of low status – many if not most of them Greek – who made it their main occupation.

---

[72] On Homeric and later archaic slavery see Humphreys (1978: 161–4) and Cartledge, review of Starr (1977) in (1979: esp. 356–7). See also Garlan (1988: 29–40) as well as Garlan (1987) in English, reprinted (1989a) in French; Rihll (1996), the best survey, as well as her less-helpful, earlier piece (1993: 77–107). See also 20–5. Trade in slaves can be inferred from Solon's poems (West, *IE*² 4.17–25 and 36.8–12).

[73] In addition to 20–5 see the references in n.72 above.

CHAPTER 8

Conclusion: then and now

Certainly, there were those outside the ruling classes or élites of ancient Greece who adhered to alternative ideologies, but as long as politics dominated economics and traditional landed property-owners dominated politics, 'commercial' or 'market' mentalities or ideologies were not actually going to prevail. Cartledge (1998: 8)

INTRODUCTION

This conclusion differs both in scope and method from the rest of the book. In scope it goes from micro-historical to the macro-level; in method, from the closely empirical to the speculative. Such sea-changes are justified by a particular notion of the role a conclusion should play. The bulk of an empirical historical work should take the reader from knowing less to knowing more about a given subject. The conclusion should ask, "If true, what of it?" "What is the significance of one's findings?" To my mind, questions of significance call for comparisons, the most timely of which is a comparison between *then* and *now*, between the place of traders in the world of classical Greece and the place of their various counterparts in the society in which I live.[1]

I live in the southeastern American sunbelt, the fastest growing region in America in wealth and population. In my city professional businesspeople

---

[1] Given the scope of this conclusion, I cannot hope to satisfy the scholarly appetite for bibliography. Instead I provide a very limited list of works of near-canonical status for specialists of antiquity or their students interested in locating Greco-Roman ancient economic activity in a larger perspective. To that end these specialists might profit from reading less anthropological theory and more modern Western intellectual, business, and sociological history, with a caution about the last. Synoptic works in Historical Sociology from Marx to Michael Mann are insufficiently fine-grained to capture the distinctiveness of the Greek polis, not to mention its variety. Yet, if based directly on reliable empirical studies of smaller scope, such works on later periods can help the specialist of ancient Greece gain perspective on ancient Greek economic activity. Of these I have found the most helpful to be Anderson (1974) and Mann (1986) on medieval and early modern Europe, and Mann (1993), Baechler (1995), and Brenner (1998) on later developments.

are the wealthiest and most respected element. The nation's largest and fourth-largest banks have their headquarters here, as do 133 interstate trucking firms, a semi-equivalent of ancient maritime trading. Government at all levels exerts little control over such growth, especially in the spirit of restraint; Karl Marx would have relished a laboratory such as my region for the study of unfettered capitalism. On every count, then, the above-cited "place" of businesspeople and their relation to the state contrast vividly with the place of maritime traders in ancient Athens.

What were the most important steps in such a transformation from then to now? There are four: the first is ideological; the second, constitutional; the third, economic and political; and the fourth, the shift in the size of firms, with enormous social, economic, and political implications.

STAGE I: THE IDEOLOGICAL SHIFT

I ended Chapter 6 by stressing that, on the question of how traders were perceived, Athens differed from most other agrarian societies. Here we are more interested in the rule than the exception: *whereas professional businesspeople in pre-modern societies were socially censured, in early modern Europe they and their work were for the first time ideologically commended.*[2]

The early moderns' notions of the best person, best life, and best society contrasted sharply with those of the ancients and opened the door to commercial activity being viewed in a far more positive light. In place of the lofty virtues extolled by the ancients, European thinkers from the sixteenth through the eighteenth centuries offered nearly the opposite counsel. "Why," they inquired, "demand more of humans than they can achieve? Why not acknowledge that most humans, in the grip of their passions and interests, aim not for excellence (*arete*) but for more mundane ends – material comfort and security" ("commodious living" [Hobbes],[3] "ease, comfort, and security" [John Adams])?[4]

The best society in turn ceased to be that which *transcended* the passions and interests of mortals; it was redefined as that which employed constitutional means to channel their passions and self-interest into pursuits more accessible to most humans, such as "the preservation of property" [Locke].[5]

---

[2] By far the best introduction to the theme discussed as "Stage I" is by Hirschman (1977). For this stage and the next I also have found helpful the early modern portions of a remarkable work by Rahe (1992). The most relevant parts have been reissued in paperback as Rahe (1994a) and (1994b).
[3] *Leviathian* 2.13.14.   [4] Adams (1850–6: 193).
[5] J. Locke, *Second Treatise of Government* 9.124: "The great and *chief end* ... of men's uniting into common-wealths, a putting themselves under government *is the preservation of their property*" [author's italics]. See further his Ch. 5 ("Of Property").

"Property" – in that word lay the key to achieving the new goals of material comfort and security. For as commercial relations spread through Northern Europe, early modern thinkers began to commend new traits that secured wealth for increasing numbers of early modern Europeans. The effective pursuit of commercial interests required a set of virtues different from those heroic ones extolled by the ancients. The new virtues were "frugality, economy, moderation, labor, prudence, tranquility, order, and regularity," to cite Montesquieu's list for "a democracy founded on commerce."[6] Alexander Hamilton observed that commercial prosperity encourages "the assiduous merchant, the laborious husbandman, the active mechanic, and the industrious manufacturer."[7] And de Tocqueville remarked that the commercial pursuit of "self-interest properly understood does not inspire great sacrifices, but every day it prompts some small ones; by itself it cannot make a person virtuous, but its discipline shapes a lot of orderly, temperate, moderate, careful, and self-controlled citizens."[8]

Later Karl Marx would view the commerce of his age as a *problem*, but to early moderns it was the *solution*. How best to mute the passions and interests vented with such savagery in the religious conflicts of early modern Europe? Through commerce. "Commerce cures destructive prejudices; and this is almost a general rule, that wherever there are gentle manners and morals, there is commerce; and wherever there is commerce, there are gentle manners and morals... The natural effect of commerce is to lead to peace [Montesquieu]."[9]

STAGE 2: THE CONSTITUTIONAL SHIFT

Whereas (according to Chapter 5) ancient Greek poleis subsumed economic matters under "politics" and regularly legislated about the former in the interests of the latter, Americans in 1789 constitutionally separated "state" from "economy," assigning priority to the latter and severely delimiting the role of the former.[10]

Greco-Roman ancients made the closest possible connection between politics and the economy, whereas after Locke it became natural not only

---

[6] *De l'esprit des lois* 5.6. [7] *The Federalist* no. 12.

[8] *De la Démocratie en Amérique* 2.2.8. I use George Lawrence's translation in the edition by J. P. Mayer (New York 1969: 527). See further 2.3.18 on the contrast of American attitudes towards commerce on the one hand and nineteenth-century European attitudes on the other.

[9] *De l'esprit des lois* 20.1. On the *douceur* of commerce, see further Hirschman (1977: 56–66).

[10] The best introduction to the theme discussed here is Diamond (1977: 75–108), reprinted in Diamond (1992: 337–68, 389–95). This piece is especially valuable for ancient specialists because Diamond knowledgeably contrasts Aristotle's and James Madison's assumptions about the proper scope of a polity.

to see state and economy as separate but also to view most of life's valuable pursuits as occupying the *private* sphere. Early moderns deployed a new notion of freedom to protect the privacy of such pursuits – freedom *from* intrusion by state and church.

For James Madison this expanded private sphere was dominated by growing *commercial* interests – "a landed interest, a manufacturing interest, a mercantile interest, a monied interest, with many lesser interests…" And "the regulation of these various and interfering interests forms the principal tasks of modern legislation."[11] Madison fully comprehended the novelty of this "modern" solution, for once abandoning his characteristic modesty to exclaim that he and his fellow representatives at the constitutional convention in Philadelphia had "accomplished a revolution which has no parallel in the annals of human society." By reducing the polity to the role of refereeing disputes between largely commercial interests in the private sphere, "they reared the fabrics of governments which have no model on the face of the globe."[12] To use the words of Paul Cartledge with which this chapter opens, "politics" no longer "dominated economics"; henceforth in the American *politeia* economics would dominate politics.

STAGE 3: THE ECONOMIC AND POLITICAL SHIFT

Stages 3 and 4 describe the steps by which (again to cite Cartledge) "traditional landed property-owners" ceased to "dominate politics," so that "'commercial' or 'market' mentalities or ideologies were…actually going to prevail." As for Stage 3: *Whereas professional maritime traders at classical Athens were relatively poor (Chapter 4), and (as mostly transient foreigners) politically inert (Chapter 3 and Appendix 2), American citizens professionally engaging in commerce by the end of the nineteenth century had become the nation's wealthiest and politically most dominant element.*[13]

Some ancient historians remain fuzzy about the implications of a landed elite's investment in commerce, implying that the Greco-Roman elite's

---

[11] Both quotes are from *The Federalist* no. 10.   [12] Both quotes are from *The Federalist* no. 14.

[13] As a theorist rather than historian, de Tocqueville (as Nisbet [1988] stresses) freely applies "ideal types" (before they were so named) in the way I inveighed against in the "Introduction." I nonetheless recommend de Tocqueville's entire Vol. II instead of empirical works of history because he best captures the spirit of the American developments described as "Stage 3," albeit at an earlier date (1830s); on the place of businesspeople in American life of that period, see esp. II.2.18–20. For empirical confirmations at the nineteenth century's end, see Garraty (1968), Weibe (1967), and (more briefly) Heilbroner and Singer (1999: 151–72).

"involvement in trade" brings us to the very brink of late modernity.[14] There are a number of exemplary critiques by others[15] of such views; I want instead to stress that even in early modern Europe intercontinental and interstate *trade* became politically important much earlier than did *traders*. As late as the eighteenth century's end in Britain – the cradle of the industrial revolution – the court, aristocracy, and country gentry invested much of their substantial resources in Britain's commerce yet excluded from *even the vote* all businesspeople except the very top merchant oligarchs.[16]

STAGE 4: THE SHIFT IN SIZE

Whereas two-person partnerships formed the largest maritime trading units of the classical period (Chapter 4), today business units have reached mammoth size:[17] the largest corporation headquartered in my city, Bank of America, currently employs approximately 150,000 people nationwide.

Again as in Stage 3 we do not want to unduly antedate this development. The Medici bank at its height (in the 1470s A.D.) employed in its home and seven branch offices a total of fifty-seven people.[18] Only in the 1880s[19] did the application of instrumental rationality[20] to production and distribution result in an explosion in the size of firms, so that already by

---

[14] See for example (on classical Greece) Thompson (1978 and 1982) and Burke (1992).

[15] E.g., Garnsey's review (1984: 85–8) of d'Arms (1981) or R. Saller's review (1991: 351–7) of Engels (1990).

[16] See above all Ch. 4 of Mann (1993), with plentiful references (132–6) to the empirical works on which his conclusions are based. Mann mentions that the creators of the eighteenth-century British Industrial Revolution – the petite bourgeoisie of "small masters, jobbers, traders, engineers and independent artisans" (96) – were excluded from the vote until the parliamentary reforms of 1832 (96–7, 101–3, 120–5).

[17] For Stage 4 see above all Alfred Chandler's pioneering volumes listed in n.2 of my Introduction. The rationalization of firms emphasized later in this section is more briefly described in Porter (1992).

[18] De Roover (1963: 43–4, 92–5). In his recent *magnum opus* ("the most impressive book on the subject in any language" [L. Martines, *TLS* Oct. 31 1997: 16]) Philip Jones attacks "the legend of the bourgeoisie" as the ruling class in late medieval and early Renaissance cities, arguing instead for the (continuing) admixture of landed nobility and financial elite as the dominant element (1997: esp. 1–17, 288–332).

[19] America's biggest railroading firms grew larger earlier, thus constituting the main exception.

[20] Instrumental rationality or reason is thinking in order to calculate the optimum application of means to a given end. Its best known use is for economic or commercial ends, where the goal is stated in quantitative rather than qualitative terms, and "efficiency" is calibrated by the highest cost-benefit ratio. In its post-1880, big-business guise (to which I allude later in the text of this section), maximum *efficiency* is achieved through the maximum degree of *calculability*, *predictability*, and *control* by means of non-human technology. (These four italicized dimensions of instrumental rationality are identified and further explained in Ritzer [1996].)

the century's turn the pattern of corporate oligopoly prevailing in today's America was set.

Here, too, certain historians of Greco-Roman society on both sides of the substantivist-formalist divide miss the main points. Substantivists acknowledge recently documented cases of elite market-minded activity, while carefully sheathing them in a larger, non-market perspective, with references to the anthropological literature.[21]

As a fellow substantivist I do not doubt that members of the Greco-Roman elite engaged in economically rational activity without becoming traders. Jack Goody argues convincingly that instrumental rationality was more pervasively pre-modern *and* non-western than previously thought.[22] Even more to the point is the difference in the *scale* on which instrumental rationality was employed before and after *c.* A.D. 1880.

Prior to 1880 instrumental rationality was largely a feature of an *individual* landowner's or entrepreneur's outlook. Thereafter came the application of instrumental rationality to *institutions*. Expanding on Max Weber's insights into bureaucracy, Alfred Chandler demonstrated that in their quest for profits American firms after 1880 grew large *precisely to rationalize production and distribution*. By acquiring ownership of their raw material sources, firms "vertically integrated backwards"; when they moved beyond manufacturing into marketing, they "vertically integrated forward"; and by absorbing competing firms they "integrated horizontally." Owners ceased to manage and managers to own; an altogether new element – tier upon tier of corporate managers – replaced Adam Smith's "invisible hand" of the market with the "visible hand" of more rationalized control over the above processes throughout.[23] Begun in manufacturing, the economic rationalization of firms extended in the twentieth century to retailing on an equally massive scale, in order to achieve similar economies of scale. Perhaps the most telling indication that (in Cartledge's words) "'market' mentalities" now "prevail" with a vengeance is the recent corporate commodification of health care in America. And since the Thatcher–Reagan "revolution," markets on every continent save Africa have gained at the expense of governments in the distribution of goods and services, further enhancing the wealth, power, and status of corporate businesspeople. If there is a kernel

---

[21] E.g., Morris (1994).   [22] (1996: esp. 11–81, 226–49).

[23] These processes are best described in Chandler (1977). Talcott Parsons, one of Chandler's Harvard mentors, put him onto Max Weber, the chief intellectual influence on his works. See further on Chandler's career the final reference in n.2 of my Introduction.

of truth in that husk called the primitivist-modernist debate,[24] it is that the rise of big business in the late nineteenth century marks the point at which the world began to change on a scale comparable to that due to the agricultural revolution.

---

[24] For recent definitions of the "primitivist" and "modernizer" positions, see esp. Cartledge (1998: 6–7); he usefully distinguishes between this polarity and that termed the "substantivist-formalist," on the latter of which see further my Introduction and the notes thereto. Cartledge rightly ranks the substantivist-formalist debate as far more important.

Emporoi *and* nauklēroi: *their attested states of origin*

The following list covers only the classical period and includes the fleet, army, and slave traders discussed at 20–5 as well as other traders. In addition to straightforward cases it also includes examples from imaginative literature and hypothetical examples from other sources (e.g., D. 23.146; X. *Mem.* 3.7.6). With one exception (X. *Oec.* 8.11), it excludes cases where *emporoi* or *nauklēroi* from a certain state are probably involved but remain unspecified (e.g., Hdt. 7.147; *IG* i³ 10 = ML no. 31 = Fornara no. 68; Thuc. 2.69.1). I nowhere mention the degree of likelihood ("probably," "possibly") that someone is an *emporos* or a *nauklēros*.

ACHAIA	Lykon (no. 47). *IG* i³ 174.
AIGINA	Unnamed *emporoi*. Arist. *Pol*. 1291b 23–4.
AIGINA	Unnamed *emporoi* or *nauklēroi*. Strabo 8.6.16 (citing Ephoros).
AKRAGAS	Sopatros (no. 55). Camp (1974: 322–4).
ATHENS	Andokides (no. 41). See items 2 and 4 of no. 4, together with n.3 of Ch. 3.
ATHENS	Androkles (no. 16). D. 35.10, 14, 26.
ATHENS	Archeneos (no. 36). Lys. 12.16.
ATHENS	Chairephilos (no. 39). See items 2 and 4 of no. 39, together with n. 3 of Ch. 3.
ATHENS	Leokrates (no. 40). See items 2 and 4 of no. 40, together with n.3 of Ch. 3.
ATHENS	Megakleides (no. 31). [D.] 52.20.
ATHENS	Mikon (no. 35). [D.] 58.6.
ATHENS	Nikoboulos (no. 22). See item 4 of no. 22.
ATHENS	Philippos (no. 25). See item 2 of no. 25.
ATHENS	Phormion II (no. 23). See item 4 of no. 23.
ATHENS	Thrasyllos (no. 32). [D.] 52.20.
ATHENS	Timosthenes (no. 24). [D.] 49.31.

ATHENS	Unnamed *emporos* (no. 50). *P Oxy.* 2538.
ATHENS	Unnamed *emporos* (no. 15). [D.] 34.50.
ATHENS	Unnamed *emporos* (no. 8). [D.] 33.4–6, 23, 25–6.
ATHENS	Unnamed *emporoi*. X. *Mem.* 3.7.6.
ATHENS	Unnamed *emporoi*. Plut. *Per.* 12.6.
ATHENS	Unnamed *emporoi*. D. 23.146.
ATHENS	Unnamed *emporoi*. Thuc. 2.67.4.
ATHENS	Two unnamed? *emporoi* in Aristophanes. schol. *Plut.* 904 and *Eccl.* 1027; also *Suda* s.v. *Emporos eimi skeptomenos*.
BYZANTION	Apatourios (no. 10). [D.] 33.5.
BYZANTION	Parmenon (no. 9). [D.] 33.6, 11–12, 20.
CHIOS	Panionios. Hdt. 8.105–6.
CHIOS	Unnamed *emporoi*. Arist. *Pol.* 1291b 23–4.
CORINTH	Lykios (no. 71). *IG* iv² i 102.
CRETE	Tychamenes (no. 72). *IG* iv² i 102.
CYPRUS	S.V. KITION and SALAMIS
DELOS	Unnamed *nauklēros* (no. 44). Isok. 17.42.
EGYPT	Unnamed *emporoi*. *IG* ii² 337 = *Syll.*³ no. 280 = Tod no. 189 = Rhodes no. 16 = Harding no. 111.
HALIKARNASSOS	Apollonides (no. 17). D. 35.33.
HERAKLEIA	Lykon (no. 29). [D.] 52.3, 5, 8, 14, 19.
HERAKLEIA	Mnemon and another, unnamed *emporos* (nos. 53 and 54). *IG* ii² 408.
HERAKLEIA	Pandios (no. 56). Schweigert (1940: 332–3).
HERAKLEIA	Unnamed *emporoi*. X. *An.* 5.6.19–21.
KARTHAGE	Unnamed *emporoi*. Diod. Sic. 14.46.1.
KITION on CYPRUS	Unnamed *emporoi*. *IG* ii² 337 = *Syll.*³ no. 280 = Tod no. 189 = Rhodes no. 16 = Harding no. 111.
LYNKESTIS	Two unnamed *emporoi* (nos. 45 and 46). Diod. Sic. 11.56.3.
MASSALIA	Hegestratos (no. 5). D. 32.5, 8.
MASSALIA	Zenothemis (no. 4). D. 32.5, 8.
MEGARA	Philondas (no. 26). [D.] 49.26.
MEGARA	Unnamed Megarian (no. 49). *IG* ii² 81.

MILETOS Two unnamed *emporoi* (nos. 57 and 58). *IG* ii² 409.

MILETOS Unnamed *emporos* (no. 59). *IG* ii² 407 and *SEG* xxxii 94.

PHASELIS Apollodoros (no. 20). D. 35.1, 10, 14, 26.

PHASELIS Artemon (no. 19). D. 35.1, 10, 14, 26.

PHASELIS Unnamed *nauklēros* (no. 21). D. 35.36, 52–3, 55.

PHASELIS A body of mostly unnamed *emporoi* (D. 35.1–2) from whom examples (nos. 19–21) are drawn.

PHERAI Pyron (no. 42). Isok. 17.20.

PHOENICIA s.v. SIDON.

PHOENICIA s.v. TYRE.

PHOENICIA Unnamed *emporoi*. Hdt. 3.107.

PHOENICIA Unnamed *nauklēros* of a large Phoenician merchant vessel. X. *Oec.* 8.11.

PHOENICIA Unnamed *emporoi*. Arr. *Anab.* 6.22.4.

SALAMIS on Herakleides (no. 60). *IG* ii² 360 = *Syll.*³ no. 304 =
CYPRUS Michel no. 110.

SALAMIS on Unnamed *emporos* or *nauklēros* (no. 50). *IG* ii² 283.
CYPRUS

SAMOS Hyblesios (no. 18). See item 4 of no. 18 and n.35 in the Catalogue.

SIDON Unnamed *emporoi*. *IG* ii² 141 = *Syll.*³ no. 185 = Tod no. 139 = Harding no. 40.

SINOPE Unnamed *emporoi*. X. *An.* 5.6.19–21.

THESPIAI Euandros (no. 1). D. 21.175.

THESSALY Unnamed *emporoi*. Plut. *Cim.* 8.3–4.

TYRE Hieron and his son Apses (nos. 51 and 52). *IG* ii² 342+.

Cohesion among maritime traders

To what extent if at all did maritime traders share a common policy or a sense of unity? And, if any cohesion did exist, of what sort was it – political, economic, religious, national, or a combination of some of these?

Any sort of political cohesion is very unlikely. Chapter 3 is devoted to showing that those trading at Athens were largely non-citizens and therefore without access to the political machinery.

Not a single man known to have been politically prominent in fifth/fourth century Athens ever appears as a merchant (except Andocides, *when in exile*), and . . . not a single known merchant is found playing any part in politics.[1]

Paul McKechnie therefore (1989: 197 n.62) misses the point when he emphasizes "the influence of traders and ship captains on getting decrees passed at Athens."[2] Not only were non-citizen traders unable to exert political influence as an outside "pressure group" – a notion implying institutional arrangements that did not exist; more significantly, they did not *need* to form a pressure group.[3] In [Lys.] 22.21 an Athenian jury is urged to "court and render more zealous" the (obviously) foreign *emporoi*. This is not because the *emporoi* confront Athens as a unified group with a common political or economic policy; Athens' interest in traders[4] can be explained instead by the single, all-sufficient reason Seager (1966: 184) offers: "if nobody brought corn to the Piraeus, Athens would starve."

---

[1] De Ste. Croix, (1972: 267).

[2] In this connection see also my criticisms of works by Clavel-Lévêque (1977) and Hodge (1998) in n.32 of Ch. 3.

[3] As Seager (1966: 183–4) rightly points out. But in correctly denying their cohesion Seager wrongly deprived those trading at Athens of anything in common (such as borrowing), by mistaking for ordinary *emporoi* the plaintiffs (mostly lenders) in the pseudo-Demosthenic speeches dealing with the admissibility of bottomry suits (183–4). See further 36–40 for my criticisms of the belief that the overlap between lending and borrowing was great.

[4] See further Ch. 5 on what the Athenian polis was prepared to do to attract and control traders. For attitudes of the Athenian citizens at large to traders, see Ch. 6.

Both more recent[5] and earlier[6] scholars have claimed that maritime traders formed "guilds" or "corporations" in the classical period. In the following review of their evidence I begin with the late classical period and work backwards.

In 333 B.C. the *emporoi* of Kition ask to be allowed to found a sanctuary of Aphrodite at Athens. An assembly decree grants them the right to acquire a plot of land on which to build the sanctuary, "just as the Egyptians built a sanctuary of Isis [lines 44–5]."[7] We should probably term the implied cohesion among the *emporoi* from Kition or among the Egyptians "religious-cum-national": each group appears to be united in the worship of a divinity celebrated by its state. At 55–9 I argue that most of those trading with Athens were *xenoi* and not metics. Austin and Vidal-Naquet note that in this instance the request to found a sanctuary "is put forward by the traders (*emporoi*) of Kition, not apparently as metics but in the name of the *dēmos* of Kition…"[8] Traders doubtless formed the largest group of visitors from Kition at Athens, but of course non-traders from Kition would also use the sanctuary on visits.

In the second quarter of the fourth century Athens honored Strato, king of Sidon, and also exempted Sidonian merchants from the obligations of Athenian metics, should they on visits overstay the time when *xenoi* became metics.[9] This decree says much about Athens' willingness to accommodate Sidonian *emporoi*[10] and nothing whatever about any sense of cohesion or unity felt by the Sidonian *emporoi* themselves.

In the 390s the ruler Satyros, having assembled *tous nauklērous* in Bosporos, asked them to render help to a young Bosporan, the son of Sopaios, who had traveled to Athens and was now embroiled in a legal dispute there (Isok. 17.52). Satyros' request probably testifies neither to any

---

[5] Starr (1977: 220 n.69): "guilds of *nauklēroi*." Hopper (1979: 87): "foreign corporations of merchants."
[6] See the references to secondary works in Poland (1909: 111–16) and Busolt (1920: 193 n.1).
[7] *IG* ii² 337+ = *Syll.*³ no. 280 = Tod no. 189 = Schwenk no. 27 = Rhodes no. 16 = Harding no. 111; see also Austin and Vidal-Naquet (1977: 274–5). In the classical period non-Athenians could secure such rights as the *emporoi* from Kition requested only by special permission of the Athenian polis; see further the discussion and references in Simms (1989: 216–21), Garland (1987: 101–11), and Ferguson (1944: 67). Baslez (1988) touches on classical Athens but deals mainly with hellenistic evidence.
[8] Austin and Vidal-Naquet (1977: 275 n.2). See also Whitehead (1977: 161). Vélissaropoulos (1980: 83 n.123) assumes Aphrodite in Tod no. 189 to be Aphrodite Ourania and claims (72) that she is for "les commerçants de Chypre." But Aphrodite Ourania is not exclusively for *emporoi* and *nauklēroi*: "In Semitic cities … she was prominently a city-goddess" Farnell ([1896: 621; see also 629–31]). Thus in the Athenian corpus of inscriptions we find a *woman* from Kition offering a dedication to Aphrodite Ourania (*IG* ii² 4636).
[9] *IG* ii² 141 = *Syll.*³ no. 185 = Tod no. 139 = Harding no. 40. See also Austin and Vidal-Naquet (1977: 273–4) and Whitehead (1977: 8–9, 14–15).
[10] See further Ch. 5 on Athens' efforts to attract both these Sidonians and other traders.

professional cohesion among *nauklēroi* in Bosporos nor to any special influence they could exert back at Athens. The most natural explanation is
that these *nauklēroi* were specially qualified to help the young Bosporan
because by virtue of their work they (and *emporoi*) were the likeliest
people in Bosporos to return soon to Athens,[11] where the young man
then was.

The above cases date from the fourth century. Fortunately, fifth-century
evidence also survives for other cases of what earlier was termed "religious-
cum-national" cohesion among various groups of maritime traders. Three
fragmentary Athenian decrees[12] levy what are probably landing taxes on
nauklēroi and *emporoi*[13] for support of three shrines – at Sounion for unnamed gods,[14] at Phaleron for possibly Apollo Delios,[15] and at Athens for
the Dioscuri.[16] These convey nothing about the organization of maritime
traders along business lines into guilds or corporations.

What they illustrate above all is surely the characteristic eagerness of Greek states
to place as much of the tax burden as possible on non-citizen shoulders. The gods
could thus profit from the great boon in commercial activity that Athens in the
fifth century must certainly have experienced.[17]

The likelihood of any sort of business or corporate cohesion is further
reduced by the inability of Athenian law to recognize such. As E. M. Harris
(1989: 338) notes, "Athenian law concerned itself solely with individual
persons and did not recognize the separate legal existence of collective
entities."

Ziebarth (1896: 27, 30–3) and Poland (1909: 111–12) therefore were correct
in denying any professional cohesion implicit in the formula most commonly used to describe maritime traders – *hoi emporoi kai hoi nauklēroi*.
They might have added that the formula's ubiquity says more about the
users than about the *emporoi* and *nauklēroi* themselves; it suggests that the

---

[11] On Athens' legal efforts to ensure that traders would return to Athens from Bosporos and elsewhere,
see 47–9.

[12] *IG* i³ 8, 130, and 133.

[13] *Emporoi* or *nauklēroi* or both are explicitly mentioned in *IG* i³ 130 (lines 4–5) and *IG* i³ 133
(lines 3–4); only their vessels are mentioned in *IG* i³ 8 (line 15).

[14] *IG* i³ 8 (lines 14, 16–17).

[15] *IG* i³ 130. Apollo Delios was suggested by Lewis (1960: 190–4), whose commentary on the inscription
is most helpful, even if Parker (1996: 124–5) disputes his claim (193) that this decree legislates state
supervision of what previously had been private and voluntary. See further Vélissaropoulos (1980:
229 and nn.133–4) and the older references cited in Schlaifer (1940: 234 n.1).

[16] *IG* i³ 133. See further Vélissaropoulos (1980: 88 and n.226, esp. 229 and n.132), also (1977: 72), and
Schlaifer (1940: 233–5 nn.5–6). On the Dioscuri as (among other duties) guardians of all seafarers,
see Farnell (1921: Ch. 7).

[17] Parker (1996: 125).

users confined their notice of these men to one feature only – the economic service they provided the polis by engaging in *emporia* and *nauklēria*.[18]

Hasebroek[19] claimed that there was no evidence for any sort of political or economic cohesion among maritime traders in the classical period. He believed traders to be united only by religious ties, some of which were "national" in character. That is precisely what this review of the evidence has confirmed.[20]

[18] On the preoccupation of Athens and its citizens with the trader's economic role, see further Chs. 5 and 6.

[19] Hasebroek (1928: 30, 65, 84, 101, 168); see also his (1923: 419).

[20] What is one to make of the excerpt from the code of Solon appearing in the Digest (47.22.4)? In Ferguson's translation (1944: 64), which I have altered slightly, it reads as follows:

If a demos, or phratries, or orgeones of heroes, or those going into piracy or *emporia* make arrangements among themselves, these shall be binding unless forbidden by public writings.

Ferguson (66) argues that the law dates from the Solonic code of 594 B.C., partly because "revisions of the classical period could not conceivably be responsible for phrases like ἐπὶ λείαν or εἰς ἐμπορίαν οἰχόμενοι [going into piracy or maritime trade]." For references and further discussion see Ferguson (1944: 64–6).

The dikai emporikai

The *dikai emporikai* ("private cases involving maritime traders")[1] constitute an important category under the rubric of Chapter 5 – "Official Attitudes to Maritime Traders" – for they unmistakably reflect Athens' willingness to afford special procedures to the *emporoi* and *nauklēroi* trading with Athens in the mid-fourth century. I deal here with this topic only because the problems surrounding it require more discussion than footnotes permit.

Before broaching these problems, I must mention a number of issues on which most scholars agree. Prior to the mid-fourth century special legal procedures for maritime trade already existed,[2] but by *c.* 352 B.C. Xenophon can doubt if these are sufficiently rapid to accommodate traders: in *Vect.* 2.3 he argues for "fastest possible" legal actions, "so as not to detain anyone who wished to sail out" of Athens. By the 340s B.C. Athens seems to have responded to just such a need: the term *dikai emporikai* first appears in D. 21.176 (? 347/6); and from D. 7.12 we learn that at some point prior to the date of that speech (343/2 B.C.) "the *emporikai dikai* were not as now… monthly" (*kata mena*, elsewhere *emmenoi*).[3] So at some point between 355 and 343/2 B.C. Athens instituted more convenient "monthly" arrangements for the settlement of legal disputes involving maritime traders, doubtless to continue attracting more of them in a period when the prosperity once guaranteed by power had waned.

For present purposes we can ignore many disputed issues surrounding these new procedures, such as the nature of their antecedents and the magistrates then or later responsible. Three issues in ascending order of historical significance strike me as most relevant to an inquiry into the place of maritime traders. First, there appear to be two possible criteria for inclusion in the category of *dikai emporikai* actions: the suit had to deal

---

[1] I use Todd's translation (1993: 334).   [2] Lys. 17.5.

[3] *Emmenoi*: [Arist]. *Ath. Pol.* 52.2, on which see further Rhodes (1981: 584) and the comprehensive discusson of the *dikai emmenoi* in Cohen (1973: 12–42).

with commerce in or out of Athens, and there had to be a written contract.[4] The question: to be admissible, did a case have to meet both requirements or only one? Gernet, the most historically acute scholar to deal with this entire topic,[5] argued for only one of the two;[6] Cohen, for both.[7] Evidence sufficient to resolve their disagreement does not exist.

The second problem: What does "monthly" mean when applied to maritime suits? "Decided within a month" or "initiated every month"? Older opinion[8] assumed that the suits had to be settled within a month; Cohen argued that "monthly" referred instead to the interval at which one could bring proceedings.[9] These views are best discussed in the context of my solution to the third problem: when were these *dikai emporikai* heard, in the summer sailing season or only outside it?

This third debate hinges on a textual reading of [D.] 33.23. Unamended, the manuscript reads: "The *lexeis* [controversial in meaning] involving *emporoi* are monthly [*emmenoi*] from Boedromion [most of our September] to Munychion [most of our April] in order that they may immediately [παραχρῆμα] obtain justice and set sail [ἀνάγωνται]." Alternate translation of the final clause: "in order that they may obtain justice and sail immediately."

By emending the text so that the order of months was reversed, Paoli[10] altered the timetable for suits from *outside* the sailing season to altogether *within* it (April through September). Paoli's emendation was accepted by Gernet and Harrison;[11] Cohen advanced reasons for rejecting it and returning to the original manuscript reading, a preference also favored subsequently by McDowell and Rhodes.[12]

Against Cohen Hansen argued that there is not sufficient evidence for the view that foreign *emporoi* stayed in Athens during the winter.[13] Pages 55–9 of my Chapter 6 puts the same point more positively: we have sufficient reason to believe that most of the non-Athenians trading with Athens were

---

[4] D. 32.1 contains the clearest statement of both criteria; see also D. 32.22–3; [D.] 33.1; 34.42.
[5] Gernet (1938) remains the best commentator on the *dikai emporikai* because he attends more carefully to historical realities and thus avoids being swamped by the (often insoluble) problems involving legal terminology.
[6] Gernet (1938: 186–7).   [7] Cohen (1973: 100–14).
[8] Harrison (1971: 16, 21, 154); Gauthier (1974: 424); Isager–Hansen (1975: 85).
[9] Cohen (1973: esp. 23–36), followed by MacDowell (1976: 85) and (1978: 231–2) and Rhodes (1981: 583) and (1995: 315). Hansen (1983: 167–70) favors a combination of both alternatives.
[10] Paoli (1933: 175–86).
[11] Gernet (1954–60: I 141); Harrison (1971: 86); Gauthier (1974: 424); Isager–Hansen (1975: 85); Hansen (1983: 170–5).
[12] Cohen (1973: 42–59); MacDowell (1978: 231–2); Rhodes (1981: 583 and 1995: 316).
[13] Hansen (1983: 171).

non-resident *xenoi* rather than resident *metoikoi*,[14] in which case Paoli's emendation gains credibility, for it would be enormously inconvenient to detain in Athens beyond the limits of the sailing season traders who were resident elsewhere.

Cohen argued for the manuscript reading partly because he doubted that busy traders could spare summer sailing time for litigation.[15] But traders very likely made only a single trip per season to Bosporos[16] and afterwards, if they sailed early enough, might still have as much as a month or two before the sailing season ended. In that instance late summer actions not only filled the need expressed by Xenophon for the "fastest possible" procedures;[17] they also are far more consonant with the sequence of events described in two speeches from the Demosthenic corpus than is Cohen's alternative, as Hansen argues.[18]

The first of these is [D.] 34, in which a *dike emporike* has been brought by Chrysippos (no. 11) against Phormion 1 (no. 14) for refusing to repay the loan that financed Phormion's trip to the Bosporos. See further Hansen's persuasive case that the *dike emporike* and the ensuing proceedings make much better sense if both immediately follow Phormion's return to Athens *during the same sailing season.* (Phormion is probably a non-Athenian who may reside elsewhere.)[19] Hansen's second case is [D.] 56, in which the lenders postpone for a year their legal action to recover their money. Why? "A much more reasonable reconstruction can be obtained by assuming that *dikai emporikai* were heard during the sailing season ... The loan is taken out in Metageitnion [roughly August] and when the lenders learn about the shipwreck, it is already too late to bring a *dikē emporikē*."[20] So proceedings must be postponed until the following sailing season.

Like Hansen I prefer Paoli's emendation because it better accords with the non-resident status of most non-Athenian *emporoi and* with a plausible sequence of events in the two speeches discussed above. With that emendation in mind we can deal summarily with the second issue – about whether "monthly" actions mean actions "settled within a month" or "initiated every month." The timetable Hansen and I favor accommodates either interpretation, as long as courts sought to act before the sailing season ended, or failing that, could postpone trials until the following April or May, "so as not to detain any one who wishes to sail away" from Athens (thus

---

[14] Cf. Cohen (1973: 52): "In all probability...the great bulk of traders and merchants using the Attic market resided in Attica."

[15] Cohen (1973: 55).   [16] Thus Casson (1994a: 521).   [17] X. *Vect.* 2.3.

[18] Hansen (1983: 171–4).   [19] Hansen (1983: 171–3).

[20] Hansen (1983: 173–4); my apologies to the author for foreshortening his argument.

Xenophon in *Vect. 2.3*). Given Athens' acute need for grain, the same traders were likely anyway to return early in the next sailing season to take out loans. In either of the above scenarios the "fastest possible" principle governing these maritime laws is honored, and largely non-resident traders are spared the serious inconvenience to which Cohen's reading subjects them.[21]

---

[21] Todd's summary statement (1993: 335) nicely captures my sentiments on Cohen's twin claims: "On balance we may suspect that his argument for monthly cases is considerably stronger than that for trials in winter."

Catalogue of emporoi *and* nauklēroi

INTRODUCTION

This catalogue records the following information about an **emporos** or a **nauklēros**:

1 **What his name and state are, if known.**
2 **With what degree of certainty or uncertainty he qualifies as *emporos* or *nauklēros*.** Such designations lead to a certain clumsiness of style: I ask the reader to forgive the unmusical effect of a phrase like "a possible *emporos* who possibly lends." I resorted to these awkward formulations only in the interests of accurate tabulation.
3 **Whether he makes bottomry loans.** "Loans" in this entry always mean bottomry loans unless otherwise indicated.
4 **What his juridical status is at Athens.**
5 **If an *emporos*, whether he is poor. If a *nauklēros*, whether he is wealthier than most nauklēroi.** Different purposes dictated these different questions. On the one hand I wanted to test Hasebroek's theory that most *emporoi* were poor; on the other I already knew that *nauklēroi* were moderately wealthy by virtue of owning a ship and (probably) a slave crew. I further wanted to discover whether some were wealthier than average. It is only these wealthier *nauklēroi* who are identified as "wealthy" in the Catalogue.
6 **If he has partners in *emporia* or *nauklēria*.** Partnership here always refers to a business partnership unless otherwise indicated.

The Catalogue covers only the classical period and includes only those *emporoi* and *nauklēroi* about whom something is known individually. "Kitian *emporoi*," "Achaean *emporoi*," and the like therefore are not included.[1] In

---

[1] On Kitian *emporoi* see further Appendix 2 and *IG* ii² 337 = Tod no. 189 = *Syll.*³ no. 280 = Harding no. 111 (333/2 B.C.) and Engen (1996: 46, 114–15, 432 nn.151–4). On Achaian *emporoi* see *IG* ii² 286 (before 336/5 B.C.) and Engen (1996: 56, 101–2, 430 nn.119–21). Walbank (1990: 442) connected *IG* ii² 286 with *IG* ii² 625, which perhaps mentions the Achaian origin of these possible *emporoi*.

all but the absolutely certain cases three categories – "probably," "possibly," and "probably not" – are used to assess the degree of likelihood that some-one is an *emporos* or a *nauklēros*. The last of these three categories is excluded from tabulations in the rest of the book; I resorted to it in the first place only to show how improbable were some of the possibilities. So, if we subtract the four "probably not" entries (nos. 3, 26, 37, and 38) from the total of seventy-two, that leaves sixty-eight to be tabulated in various ways.

A clear reference to an individual *emporos* or *nauklēros* does not of itself earn him a place in the Catalogue. Some features relevant to the purposes of the Catalogue – for instance his name, his polis, the fact that he traded by land or was a lender – must also be supplied. I therefore include the two *emporoi* who helped Themistokles to escape from Greece (Diod. Sic. 11.56.3), but do not include the *nauklēros* who likewise did so (Thuc. 1.137.2–3). About the *nauklēros* we know nothing else; about the two *emporoi* (nos. 45 and 46 in the Catalogue), we know that they came from Lynkestis and traded by land.

VERY UNLIKELY CANDIDATES

The following, honored in fourth-century Athenian decrees, are *not* in-cluded in the Catalogue, on grounds that claims[2] for their status as *emporoi* or *nauklēroi* are simply too implausible:

1 **Unnamed Kyreneans** (*IG* ii² 176: 353/2 B.C.). Awarded *proxenia*.
2 **Theagenes of Naukratis** (*IG* ii² 206: 349/8 B.C.). Awarded hereditary *proxenia* and *euergesia* as well as *enktesis* for a house.
3 **Unnamed Corinthian** (*IG* ii² 229: 341/40 B.C.). Awarded an olive crown.
4 & 5 **Two unnamed Chians** (*IG* ii² 252: mid-fourth century B.C.). Awarded hereditary *proxenia* and *euergesia* as well as olive crowns.
6 **Lyko of Pydna** (*IG* ii² 339: 333/2 B.C.). Awarded hereditary *proxenia* and *euergesia*.
7 **Apollonides of Sidon** (*IG* ii² 343; Schweigert [1940: 342–3]; *SEG* xxiv 103: ?323 B.C. Second half of fourth century). Awarded hereditary *prox-enia* and *euergesia* as well as *[ges k]ai oikias enktesin* and a golden crown.
8 **Praxiades of Kos** (*IG* ii² 416: *c.* 330 B.C.). Awarded *proxenia*.

---

[2] See Erxleben (1974: 495), Hopper (1979: 115), Isager–Hansen (1975: 207 and n.55), and Casson (1954: 169 and n.6).

9 **Unnamed Bosporan** (Schweigert [1939: 27–30] and [1940: 335–9]; *SEG* xxi 298 and xxiv 102: 323/2 B.C.). Awarded commendation, golden crowns, and Athenian citizenship. See further Osborne (1981: 80–5 and 1982: 95) and Engen (1996: 71, 138–9, 434 nn.194–7).

In each of the inscriptions listed above it is either stated or implied that the recipients looked after Athenian interests or merchants from Athens in their own states. Some of the inscriptions credit those honored with regular, sustained assistance and protection. If they thus were on hand in their cities to help merchants arriving in the sailing season, how could they themselves be at sea? They are all probably local *proxenoi* of Athens who are now rewarded for their services.

Certain men honored in Olbian proxeny decrees[3] of the fourth century constitute a second group of implausible candidates. These decrees offer (in part) freedom from duty on goods imported and exported. Erxleben (1974: 488–9) wrongly inferred from the *ateleia* clause, a very common feature of proxeny decrees, that the recipients were *emporoi* or *nauklēroi*.

Nor is there any evidence that the following were *emporoi* or *nauklēroi*, apart (in certain cases) from the people they associated with:

10 **Nobas of Karthage**, to whom a Theban decree (*IG* vii 2407 = *Syll.*[3] no. 179, *c.* 364/3 B.C.) grants *proxenia*, ?*ges enktesis, ateleia*, and *asylia*. The Karthaginians were notorious maritime traders, but even the slightest evidence for Nobas as one of them is lacking.[4]

11 **Herodas of Syracuse**, who in the early fourth century appears in Phoenicia with a *nauklēros* (X. *Hell.* 3.4.1).

12 **Pythodoros of Phoenicia**: Millett (1991: 210) calls him "almost certainly a trader," but we know only that the speaker in Isok. 17.3–4 says "Pythodoros the Phoenician introduced Pasion to me, and I opened an account at his bank."

13 **Unnamed Rhodian**: *Syll.*[3] no. 1166. An unnamed person asks the oracle of Zeus at Dodona if he should engage in maritime trade. No evidence exists for his status as an *actual* trader. I mention him only because Parke thinks him a Rhodian or a member of the Rhodian colony on the basis of the dialect in this Greek inscription (1967: 269 no. 19). Were there better reason to think him a Rhodian maritime trader of the classical period, he would qualify as the only one known to us.

14 **Hagias of Corinth**: Speaking of timber merchants, Salmon (1984: 123 and n.39) remarks, "One Athenian document [*IG* ii² 1672 lines

---

[3] *I. Olb.* 5–8; *IPE* I² 20 = *Syll.*[3] 219 = Michel no. 333.

[4] On Karthaginian traders and trade, see n. 69 of Ch. 5, Whittaker (1978), and Lancel (1995: 110–33, esp. 120–5).

157–9, 170, dated 329/8] appears to mention a Corinthian in the timber business." Hagias is likelier to have been a *supplier* of timber than the *transporter* thereof: two other men in *IG* ii² 1672 (nos. 64 and 65) who deal in wooden goods are called *emporoi*; so (probably) would Hagias have been called, had he been one. On Hagias see further Meiggs (1982: 434–5, 438).

15 **An unnamed Corinthian *nauklēros?*** Salmon (1984: 147) says that the only direct evidence for the mechanisms of Corinthian trade is "the brief passage of Lycurgus which records the shipment of Epirot corn by Leocrates [on whom see further no. 40], and a shipowner mentioned in a fourth-century inscription from Troezen" [*IG* iv 823 line 27]. The editors of *IG* iv follow P. Foucart's reading of *Kori[n]thon* (*IG* iv, p. 161), but one of them, J. Prott, considers (p. 164) this reading *very* conjectural ("durchaus nicht nötig"). Eight years prior to the publication of *IG* iv in 1902, Mylonas (1894: 140) could read *Karpathon* instead of *Korinthon*.

16 **Kaphisodoros of Corinth**: Salmon (1984: 123): "At Delphi in the fourth century, a good deal of timber was imported from Sicyon – and carried by a Corinthian." His source (123 n.40) is Bourguet (1932: no. 36), dated 335 B.C. J. Bousquet considerably revised the texts concerning timber in (1977: 91–105). His more plausible emendation of no. 36 lines 14–15 virtually removes Kaphisodoros as a candidate for transporter and makes him instead only a supplier, as are all the Sicyonians mentioned in lines 1–15 of no. 36. These Sicyonians and Kaphisodoros very likely are different from the anonymous maritime traders (in Bousquet's version [pp. 94–5] of lines 20–1) who actually "transported the wood from Sicyon by sea" to Kirrha, Delphi's port in the Korinthian Gulf. See as well Meiggs' sensible comments (1982: 430–3). With less evidence I would also call the Argive Nikodamos a supplier rather than a transporter of the Macedonian beams (Bourguet [1932: no. 41 col. III. 7–14], on which see Meiggs (1982: 432–3).

Table of contents to Catalogue of Emporoi *and* Nauklēroi

Number

5	Hegestratos of Massalia (D. 32)
6	Protos (D. 32)
7	Phertatos (D. 32)
8	Unnamed Athenian ([D.] 33)
9	Parmenon of Byzantion ([D.] 33)
10	Apatourios of Byzantion ([D.] 33)
11	Chrysippos ([D.] 34)
12	Brother of Chrysippos ([D.] 34)
13	Lampis II and Dion ([D.] 34)
14	Phormion I ([D.] 34)
15	Unnamed Athenian ([D.] 34)
16	Androkles of Athens (D. 35 and elsewhere)
17	Apollonides of Halikarnassos (D. 35)
18	Hyblesios of Samos (D. 35)
19	Artemon of Phaselis (D. 35)
20	Apollodoros of Phaselis (D. 35)
21	Unnamed Phaselite (D. 35)
22	Nikoboulos of Athens (D. 37)
23	Phormion of Athens (Phormion II: D. 45 and elsewhere)
24	Timosthenes of Athens ([D.] 49)
25	Philippos of Athens ([D.] 49 and elsewhere)
26	Philondas of Megara ([D.] 49)
27	Unnamed *nauklēros* ([D.] 49)
28	Nikippos ([D.] 50)
29	Lykon of Herakleia ([D.] 52)
30	Kephisiades ([D.] 52)
31	Megakleides of Athens ([D.] 52)
32	Thrasyllos of Athens ([D.] 52)
33	Dionysodoros ([D.] 56)
34	Parmeniskos ([D.] 56)
35	Mikon of Athens ([D.] 58)
36	Archeneos of Athens (Lys. 12)
37, 38	Diodotos and Diogeiton of Athens ([Lys.] 32)
39	Chairephilos of Athens (Din. 1 and elsewhere)
40	Leokrates of Athens (Lykourgos, *Leoc.*)
41	Andokides of Athens (Andok. 1 and elsewhere)
42	Pyron of Pherai (Isok. 17)
43	Stratokles (Isok. 17)
44	Unnamed Delian (Isok. 17)

45, 46	Two unnamed Lynkestians (Diod. Sic. 11)
47	Lykon of Achaia (*IG* i³ 174)
48	Pythophanes (*IG* i³ 98)
49	Unnamed Megarian (*IG* ii² 81)
50	Ph- of Salamis in Cyprus (*IG* ii² 283)
51, 52	Hieron and son Apses of Phoenician Tyre (*IG* ii² 342+)
53, 54	Mnemon and -ias of Herakleia on the Black Sea (*IG* ii² 408)
55	Sopatros of Akragas (Camp [1974: 322–4])
56	Pandios of Herakleia on the Black Sea (Schweigert [1940: 332–3])
57, 58	Two unnamed inhabitants of Miletos (*IG* ii² 409)
59	Unnamed inhabitant of Miletos (*IG* ii² 407 and *SEG* xxxii 94)
60	Herakleides of Salamis in Cyprus (*IG* ii² 360)
61	Unnamed Athenian (*P. Oxy.* 2538)
62	Attos (*IG* ii² 1672)
63	Konops (*IG* ii² 1672)
64	Simias (*IG* ii² 1672)
65	Syros (*IG* ii² 1672)
66	Epigonos (*IG* ii² 1557)
67	Moschion (*IG* ii² 1558)
68	Unnamed *emporos* (*IG* ii² 1566)
69	Unnamed *emporos* (*IG* ii² 1577)
70	Eudemon (Lewis [1968: 371])
71	Lykios of Corinth (*IG* iv² 1 102)
72	Tychamenes of Crete (*IG* iv² 1 102)

THE CATALOGUE

Please note that in any following entries "**N. E.**" stands for "no evidence."

No. 1

1 **Euandros of Thespiai or Menippos of Karia**

2–3 **A probable *emporos* or *nauklēros*,** together with someone else who is probably a lender. Euandros won a *dike emporike* against Menippos of Karia, but a subsequent, non-emporic judgment compelled him to return the two talents awarded earlier (D. 21.175–6). Normally in the *dikai emporikai* borrowers and lenders are pitted against one another, and normally borrowers are *emporoi* or *nauklēroi*, while lenders (as

Erxleben says)[5] are not as a rule drawn from the ranks of *emporoi* or *nauklēroi*. For purposes of tabulation it is therefore both helpful and probably accurate to assume that either Euandros or Menippos is an *emporos* or *nauklēros*, while the other is probably a lender.

2 **Possibly a *xenos*.** As a rule bottomry lenders are far less mobile than borrowers; since it is said (D. 21.176) that Menippos could be found in Athens only during the Mysteries and was later recompensed for being detained there, he seems the better candidate for borrower (and hence for *emporos* or *nauklēros*). Menippos possibly qualifies as a *xenos*, too, depending of course on how long he was in Athens.

3 **Not poor.** As a result of the later, non-emporic judgment Menippos recouped (D. 21.176) the two talents awarded in the *dike emporike* to Euandros, who (as item 4 above suggests) is probably the lender.

4 **N. E.**

No. 2

1 **Lampis** I. This is not the slave Lampis (Lampis II, no. 13) who appears in [D.] 34.

2 **A *nauklēros*** (D. 23.211 and Plut. *Mor.* 787A).

3 **N. E.**

4 **A privileged metic at Aigina** (D. 23.211).[6]

5 **Wealthy.** Lampis I is "the largest shipowner in Greece" (D. 23.211) and immensely rich (Plut. *Mor.* 787A; Cic. *Tusc.* 5.40; Stob. 29.87).

6 **N. E.**

No. 3

1 **Xouthos**

2 **Probably not an *emporos*.** Included in the estate of Demosthenes the Elder are 7,000 dr. described in D. 27.11 as "a maritime loan with Xouthos" (ναυτικά...ἔκδοσιν παρὰ Ξούθῳ). The word ἔκδοσιν prompted Ziebarth, Paoli, and others[7] to call Xouthos a banker, but Bogaert (1965: 143–4) disagreed.

The only other reference to Xouthos (D. 29.36) mentions a bottomry loan, but not in such a way as to make him an *emporos*. Bogaert (1965:

---

[5] Erxleben (1974: 479, 482, 513 n.150). See also my comments at 36–40 on Erxleben's tabulation as well as Millett's valid criticisms (1983: 37–8).

[6] On Lampis I, see further de Ste. Croix (1972: 267 n.61); Vélissaropoulos (1980: 51); Figueira (1981: 282–3, 297 n.98); Millett (1983: 47); and Cohen (1992: 44 n.16).

[7] Ziebarth (1929: 86); Paoli (1930: 20 n.2); *PA* 11342; Gernet (1954–60: I 81–2, n.2).

141–6), Erxleben (1974: 493), and Millett (1991: 192) regard Xouthos as an "intermédiaire," "Makler," or "middleman," respectively.

The case of Xouthos offers a particularly good opportunity to show how improbable is the possibility that certain people are *emporoi*. There is no evidence to that effect for Xouthos, although the "middleman" thesis at least involves him in maritime commerce. But this "middleman" interpretation has been challenged by Edward Cohen. Cohen (1992: 64 n.13, 122–3) takes the phrase "with Xouthos" (παρὰ Ξούθῳ) in the previous paragraph as meaning "at the bank of Xouthos" and proceeds (121–89) to make a strong case[8] against the standard view[9] that banks did not make maritime loans.

3 **N. E.**

4 **N. E.**, in spite of Kirchner's listing Xouthos (on the strength of D. 27.11 and 29.36) as a citizen (*PA* 11343).

5 **N. E.**

6 **N. E.** The reference to what might be partnership with Xouthos in D. 29.36 is too vague.

No. 4

1 **Zenothemis of Massalia**[10]

2 **A possible *emporos*.** If the speaker in D. 32 is telling the truth, Zenothemis' role in the case at hand is not that of an *emporos*. On Demon's testimony Zenothemis borrowed money at Syracuse, money with which he never purchased grain; and, since he lied about the loan to Hegestratos, he had no claim to the cargo of grain that reached Athens on the late Hegestratos' ship. In this version Zenothemis is a criminal, but not a criminal *emporos*.

Nor does Zenothemis claim to be an *emporos*, at least not in Demon's version of the former's case. There Zenothemis claims only to be a lender. Since we never hear from Zenothemis himself, we must regard him as a possible *emporos*, a possibility strengthened by his perhaps long-term association in *emporia* with the *nauklēros* Hegestratos (on which see item 6 below).

3 **A possible lender.** Again the one-sided nature of the evidence offers the possibility that Zenothemis actually made his alleged bottomry loan (D. 32.2, 12, 14–15) to Hegestratos. Erxleben (1974: 467, 507 n.48)

---

[8] For a discussion of Cohen's challenge, see 36–40 above.

[9] For references to these denials both categorical and qualified, see 36–40 above.

[10] On Zenothemis as well as nos. 5–6 below, see Oikonomides (1978: 83–8) and Cohen (1992: 168–9).

remains more skeptical about the genuineness of the loan than do Gernet (1954–60: I 114) and Isager–Hansen (1975: 139). See also Pringsheim (1916: 13–14).

4 **A non-Athenian; N. E. as to whether a metic or *xenos* at Athens.** On the one hand Zenothemis and Hegestratos are said (D. 32.5) to have taken the money borrowed at Syracuse "home... to Massalia," their city of origin (D. 32.5,8); on the other hand the speaker (D. 32.10) vaguely tries to associate them with that (partly resident) "gang of scoundrels in the Piraeus." Gerhardt (1935: 19) thought that both Zenothemis and Hegestratos stayed long enough in Athens to be metics, but he cites no evidence.

5 **Possibly not poor.** If Zenothemis qualifies as a lender (see item 3 above), then he may not be poor.

6 **Possibly the partner of Hegestratos** (no. 5). Demon calls Zenothemis the "partner" (κοινωνός) of Hegestratos (D. 32.7), but given Demon's bias the word may mean no more than "accomplice," just as his use of ὑπηρέτης to describe Zenothemis' relation to Hegestratos (D. 32.4) may mean something like "lackey" rather than "slave." (Pearson's [1972: 256] "employee" or "first mate" seems even less likely in the present context.) Elsewhere (D. 32.4) Demon says that Zenothemis was a passenger on Hegestratos' ship. This claim may be true, but there is clearly more to their relationship: both Demon and Zenothemis (in Demon's version) allude to a business association the exact nature of which remains uncertain.

No. 5

1 **Hegestratos of Massalia**

2 **A *naukleros*** (D. 32.2, 3, 4, 8). On the possibility that Hegestratos is both shipowner and ship captain, see 12–13 and Casson (1971: 316 n.70).

3 **N. E.**

4 **A non-Athenian. N. E. as to whether a metic or *xenos* at Athens.** See further item 4 of no. 4 (Zenothemis).

5 **N. E.**

6 **Possibly the partner of Zenothemis** (no. 4). See further item 4 of no. 4.

No. 6

1 **Protos**

2 **An *emporos*** (D. 32.14–15, 18, 25).

3 **N. E.**

4 **N. E.**, in spite of Clerc's claim (1893: 398) that Protos is a metic. See also Harrison (1968: 196 and n.1) and Whitehead (1977: 48).

5 **N. E.**

6 **Partner** (D. 32.17) **of Phertatos** (no. 7).

No. 7

1 **Phertatos**

2 **A possible *emporos*.** The speaker (D. 32.17) refers to Phertatos as the partner of (or participant with) Protos (no. 6), who is an *emporos*.

3 **N. E.**

4 **N. E.**

5 **N. E.**

6 **Partner** (D. 32.17) **of Protos** (no. 6).

No. 8

1 **Unnamed Athenian** in [D.] 33

2 **An *emporos*, at least formerly;** he retired almost seven years before this speech ([D.] 33.4).

3 **A lender after his retirement as an *emporos*** ([D.] 33, esp. 4). Millett (1991: 192–3) considers him a "professional lender," making both maritime and non-maritime loans.

4 **Possibly a citizen.** That the unnamed speaker resides in Athens is never stated but is implicit in [D.] 33.4–6, 23, 25–6. That he resides there as a citizen is not at all certain, but his two references to someone from Byzantion as "the foreigner" ([D.] 33.10–11) suggest it.[11]

5 **Not poor.** The sums in which he deals in [D.] 33 confirm the speaker's claim ([D.] 33.4) to have made a "moderate amount" out of *emporia*.

6 **N. E.**

No. 9

1 **Parmenon of Byzantion**

2 **A probable *emporos*.** Parmenon arrived in Athens with Apatourios, probably on the latter's ship ([D.] 33.5). Nowhere in [D.] 33 is there a hint that Parmenon himself was a shipowner, as Erxleben (1974: 477) claims. He had been exiled ([D.] 33.6, 11–12, 20) from his home in Byzantion and

---

[11] See Vélissaropoulos (1980: 42–3). The following think the unnamed speaker at least possibly a citizen: Paoli (1930: 28); Gernet (1954–60: I 128 n.1); Whitehead (1977: 48); Erxleben (1974: 473, 476–7, 513 n.118); see in particular Erxleben's comments on 476.

resided with his family in Ophryneion, a city in the Troad conveniently near Byzantion ([D.] 33.20). The sole evidence that Parmenon might be an *emporos* is his desire to sail to Sicily from Athens ([D.] 33.20), probably for purposes of trade. Like Andokides (no. 41) Parmenon may have traded only while in exile.

3 **N. E.** The loan involving Parmenon, Apatourios, and the unnamed speaker ([D.] 33.6–8) is not a bottomry loan, according to de Ste. Croix (1974: 52); Cohen (1992: 166–7) disagrees.

4 **Possibly a metic.** At the time of his visit to Athens ([D.] 33.5) Parmenon resided elsewhere (see item 2 above) and perhaps intended to remain a *xenos* until he left Athens on his projected trip to Sicily ([D.] 33.13); but he may have been forced to remain long enough to become a metic, given his stay through the initial affair ([D.] 33.6–13), the arbitration process ([D.] 33.14–18), and the ensuing period from the collapse of the arbitration proceedings ([D.] 33.19) until he left Athens at the news of his family's death in the Troad ([D.] 33.20).[12]

5 **Not poor.** Parmenon lent ten minae to Apatourios ([D.] 33.6–12).

6 **N. E.**

No. 10

1 **Apatourios of Byzantion**

2 A *nauklēros* ([D.] 33.6, 8–9, 10–12, 25).

3 **N. E.** The loans he secured from others, including one for thirty minae from the banker Herakleides, are documented in [D.] 33.5–8, on which see further Millett (1991: 208) and Cohen (1992: 40, 145, 154–8, 166).

4 **Possibly a *xenos*.** The only clue that Apatourios, originally from Byzantion ([D.] 33.5), might be a *xenos* appears in [D.] 33.25–6, where the speaker mentions ([D.] 33.26) that Apatourios "was in town" (ἐπεδήμει) last year when "the [maritime] cases were tried" (αἱ δίκαι ἦσαν), a statement applying most naturally to a non-resident. Apatourios therefore would be a *xenos*, unless during his visit he remained beyond the point at which a *xenos* became a metic (Whitehead 1977: 7–10).

5 **N. E.** His slave crew ([D.] 33.8, 9, 11, 13) may make Apatourios no wealthier than most other *nauklēroi*, on whose probable wealth see 12–13.

6 **N. E.**

---

[12] The following by Whitehead (1977: 9) may therefore perfectly characterize Parmenon the metic: "An evidently brief *epidemia* [residence] converts foreigner into metic, whether he likes it or not (and even if he has not the slightest intention of 'changing his *oikos*' [home]); and he can stop being one at any time simply by leaving." But by mistaking Parmenon for Apatourios in [D.] 33.25–6, Whitehead (1977: 48) credits Parmenon with a visit to Athens he never made.

No. 11

1 **Chrysippos**

2 **An *emporos*.** The accepted[13] view, denied by Erxleben (1974: 476), is that Chrysippos and his brother (no. 12) are (or at least until recently have been) *emporoi*. Erxleben is proved wrong by the following passages:

  A [D.] 34.38, where the speaker[14] refers to himself and his brother as "we who have continued to import grain to your market..."

  B [D.] 34.39, where the speaker describes himself and his brother as "importing more than ten thousand medemnoi of wheat..."

  C [D.] 34.1, where the speaker describes himself and his brother as "frequenting your market for a long time..."

3 **A lender.** Several passages ([D.] 34.1, 50–2) say or imply that Chrysippos and his brother are regular bottomry lenders.[15] See also n.14.

4 **Probably a metic.** The word *metoikos* is never used to describe Chrysippos and his brother, but scholars agree[16] that they are metics. They not only remained in Athens throughout the episode in question, but also were there during previous food shortages ([D.] 34.38–9) and had a long record of business activity at Athens ([D.] 34.1–2). Whitehead[17] argues that their effort "to win a good name among you" ([D.] 34.40, with 1–2, 38) was probably common among Athenian metics. See also n.14.

5 **Not poor** ([D.] 34.38–9). See also n.14.

6 **A partner with his brother** (no. 12) ([D.] 34.38). This speech presents the possibility of different partners for different ventures, on which see n.14.

[13] Held by, for example, Paoli (1930: 25), Isager–Hansen (1975: 72 n.77 and 74 n.88), and Bogaert (1965: 142 n.3).

[14] Following Schäfer (1858: 304–5), Gernet (1954–60: I 150 and n.1) believes that more than one person speaks in [D.] 34. Chrysippos begins and ends; his associate fills the interval. It is probably (Gernet says "possibly") Chrysippos' brother who in [D.] 34.39 says that "I and my brother" donated a talent with which to buy grain. The two brothers also form the "we" who imported grain in the preceding section ([D.] 34.38). The problem is this: when at the outset ([D.] 34.1–2) Chrysippos says that "we" make bottomry loans, does he refer to the same persons who imported grain in [D.] 34.38? I assume that he does, although proof is impossible.

[15] Millett (1991: 193) classifies him as a "professional" lender. At one point Chrysippos expressly identifies himself with the lenders (as distinct from *emporoi* who borrow) in [D.] 34.51–2, but that is almost certainly because of his role in the case at hand.

[16] See for example Clerc (1893: 398); Calhoun (1926: 51); Davies, (1984: 61); Bogaert (1968: 440); Isager–Hansen (1975: 72 n.77 and 157); Erxleben (1974: 465 and 476); Whitehead (1977: 49). There are no grounds for Clerc's claim (1893: 398) that Chrysippos was originally from Bosporos.

[17] In addition to Whitehead (1977: 57–8), see also his comments (37, 51) on Eur. *Supp.* 888–900 and on Lys. 12.20. Whitehead does not cite Chrysippos and his brother as examples of "model metics," but he might have added them to his list.

No. 12

1 **The brother of Chrysippos** (no. 11)
2 **An *emporos.*** See item 2 no. 11 (Chrysippos) and especially n.14 to item 2.
3 **A lender.** See item 3 no. 11.
4 **Probably a metic.** See item 4 no. 11.
5 **Not poor** ([D.] 34.38–9).
6 **A partner with his brother** (no. 11).

No. 13

1 **Lampis 11 and Dion**
2 **Lampis 11 is repeatedly called a *nauklēros*** in [D.] 34.6, 9, 32, 33, but if (as is likely) he[18] and the crew ([D.] 34.10) are slaves, **their owner Dion probably owns the ship** as well. In that case the word *nauklēros* applied to Lampis 11 would mean "captain" and not "shipowner," although this would be the only time in the Demosthenic corpus where it is so used.[19]

The case of Lampis 11 is extremely puzzling. Given a commercial world in which there is no surviving evidence for an explicit law of agency, how can a slave be held accountable by his owner for captaining a ship, for lending (see item 3 below), and for shipping goods he himself bought ([D.] 34.36, 37)?[20] As much as anyone in this Catalogue Lampis 11 does what both *nauklēroi* and *emporoi* do, except that he may own neither a ship nor the funds with which he lends and trades. One scarcely knows how to characterize him; perhaps he falls into the "agent" category Bravo (1977) posits as the normal role for archaic traders, on which see further 64–8. Since every other *nauklēros* in the Catalogue is probably the owner or owner-captain[21] of his vessel, it would be inconsistent to include Lampis 11 by himself, when the faceless Dion may be the actual owner. I therefore resolved to group Lampis 11 and Dion together under one entry as collectively constituting a probable *nauklēros.*

---

[18] Lampis 11 is called the "servant" ([D.] 34.5, 10) of Dion. Harrison (1968: 167–8 and nn.5–6) summarizes a half-century of controversy over whether Lampis 11 was a slave, whether as a slave he could appear in court, and whether he fell into the mysterious category of χωρὶς οἰκοῦντες. The first two of the above can be answered with a probable "yes"; the last remains insoluble. See also Cohen (1973: 121 and n.48).

[19] For a possible instance in which the word *nauklēros* applies to an owner-captain, see item 1 of no. 5 (Hegestratos).

[20] Cf. Cohen's discussion (1992: 98–101) of "agency as a legal mechanism." Erxleben (1974: 477; see also 479 and 513 n.132) calls Lampis 11 "a slave in the special form of an agent working for his master." This is impossible to affirm or deny, since the surviving evidence leaves us baffled about what sort of relationship is thus implied.

[21] See the preceding n.16.

3 **The money lent by Lampis II** ([D.] 34.6, 8, 12, 22–3, 25–6, 40–1)
possibly belonged to his owner Dion ([D.] 34.5, 10). Millett (1991:
192) classifies Lampis as a "casual" lender.

4 At the end of the case in question **Lampis II resided in Athens
with his family** ((D.] 34.37).[22] Nothing is said about Dion's status in
Athens or elsewhere.[23]

5 **N. E.** In particular there is no evidence for Calhoun's claim (1926: 65)
that Dion owned many ships. Even the fact that he owned a slave crew
might make him no wealthier than other *nauklēroi*.[24]

6 **N. E.**, unless one wishes to consider the relationship between Dion and
Lampis II a "partnership." It is never referred to as such, and this singular
case leaves us completely in the dark about the form that a partnership
between Dion and Lampis II would take.[25]

No. 14

1 **Phormion** I

2 **An** *emporos* ([D.] 34.1, 6–9, 22, 23, 30, 40–2, *Hypothesis* 1).

3 **N. E.**

4 **Probably a non-citizen. N.E. as to whether he is a metic or** *xenos.*
There is no evidence that Phormion I was a citizen, and [D.] 34.50 implies
that he was not. Isager–Hansen (1975: 157)[26] think him a metic because
he spent the winter in Athens as follows:

> As Chrysippus must seek out Phormio in the perfume-dealers' quarter of
> Athens in order to present the summons, it is reasonable to assume that during
> the summer season Phormio exported perfumed olive oil, while during the
> winter (when maritime trade was at a standstill) he earned his living as a
> retailer or manufacturer of perfumes.

Isager–Hansen assume that Phormion I was at work in the perfume
shop, but [Lys.] 24.20 shows that perfume shops were among the fa-
vorite loitering places in Athens. The only other possible evidence for
Phormion's being a metic is his return to Athens, where the speaker and
Lampis II found him passing time in the perfume shop. Why would he
return unless he resided in Athens,[27] especially since he faced possible

---

[22] The speaker ([D.] 34. 37) applies to Lampis II a version of one emporic law (tailored to suit the
situation) and thus raises an insoluble problem: if this and certain other mercantile laws (*emporikoi
nomoi*) applied only to Athenian metics and citizens, why cite it against a slave?

[23] There is no evidence that Dion was either a metic at Athens (Erxleben [1974: 477]).

[24] On how wealthy *nauklēroi* were, see 16–19.   [25] See also n.20 above.

[26] Others who think Phormion I a metic: Clerc (1893: 398) and de Ste. Croix (1974: 50).

[27] I do not mean to imply that metics *necessarily* resided at Athens, only that they did so as a rule. On
this see Whitehead (1977: 7–10).

charges? On the other hand, were he a *xenos*, Phormion 1 may have been optimistic about the legal consequences and returned to Athens for any number of reasons. None of Cohen's arguments (1992: 177–8) that this Phormion is identical with the banker Phormion (no. 23 below) strike me as convincing.

5 **N. E.**

6 **N. E.** We are unable to know how seriously to take the speaker's charge ((D.] 34.28) that Lampis II was Phormion I's κοινωνός (associate [accomplice?]) in the alleged fraud.

No. 15

1 **Unnamed Athenian in** [D.] 34

2 **A probable *emporos.*** [D.] 34.50 reads in part as follows:

> For you are the same ones who punished someone with death after his conviction before the people in an *eisangelia* procedure, a man who borrowed (ἐπιδεδανεισμένον) on your exchange large sums on goods already pledged as security, a man who failed to provide his creditors with [other] securities.

Demosthenes uses the verb ἐπιδανείζω in other places ([D.] 34.22; D. 35.21, 22) to refer to bottomry lending. One would therefore expect its recipient in [D.] 34.50 to be an *emporos* or *nauklēros*, and that assumption gains strength from what immediately follows, for the speaker adds that such persons as the borrower in [D.] 34.50 cause much damage (presumably by defrauding the lenders),

> since the means for engaging in trade come not from those who borrow but from those who lend; and no ship, no shipowner, and no passenger can put to sea without the help of the lenders. ([D.] 34.51)

Gernet, however, is doubtful (1954–60: I 168 n.1):

> L'allusion est très elliptique. A ce moment-là, l'*eisangelia* –
> la procédure en question – est expressément prévue pour
> la trahison ou les délits assimilés; quelque abus qu'on en
> fit, il devait y avoir, dans le cas du condamné, autre chose
> que ce que dit l'auteur.

So the victim in [D.] 34.50 was probably an *emporos*, but we cannot be certain.

3 **N. E.**

4 **A citizen** ([D.] 34.50).

5 **N. E.**, although the father of the probable *emporos* had been a general ([D.] 34.50).

6 **N. E.**

No. 16

1 **Androkles of Athens** (*PA* 872)

2 **An *emporos*.**[28] Androkles in D. 35.49 says of himself, "I am an *emporos*" (*ego d' eimi emporos...*). Erxleben (1974: 473–4) nonetheless argues that Androkles is a lender and not an *emporos*, but wants to pose as one before the jury for two reasons, because a *dike emporike* guaranteed rapid settlement (within thirty days) and because of the good reputation of *emporoi* in the minds of Athenian jurors.

　　Erxleben is probably wrong about the way in which procedure was rapid in the *dikai emporikai*. Cohen (1973: 9–40) argues persuasively that emporic *dikai* were *emmenoi* not in the sense of judgments offered within thirty days, but in the sense of "trials recurring every month" (30, 33). In this latter sense the procedure *was* more rapid than usual,[29] and no one can doubt Erxleben's further point that Athenian juries in the second half of the fourth century attended seriously to the interests of *emporoi*.[30] But Erxleben's case really hangs on the highly improbable claim that an Athenian speaker (perhaps a fairly prominent one)[31] would thus try to deceive a jury of his fellow citizens about his occupation.

3 **Also a lender** (D. 35.3, 7–8, 10, 14, 15, 24–7, 29–30, 37–9, 43, 50, 52, 54, 55).

4 **An Athenian citizen** (D. 35.10, 14, 26).

5 **Not poor.** On his loans see item 4 above, and on other possible business activities see Erxleben (1974: 476 and 510, nn.100–4).

6 **N. E.**, at least for Androkles' activities as *emporos*.

---

[28] Bogaert (1965: 141–4, esp. 142 nn.2 and 3) denies that Androkles is a banker; see further Cohen (1992: 174–5).

[29] Cohen (1973: 27): "A preferable definition of *dikai emmēnoi* would be 'suits for which complaints (*lēxeis*) were accepted at monthly intervals and expeditiously decided by a shortened procedure'." See also Gauthier's criticisms (1974: 424–5) of Cohen's definition. The issue is discussed further in Appendix 3.

[30] Out of economic necessity, not out of regard for their social position. On this see 44–9.

[31] See Erxleben (1974: 474 and 510, nn.100–4) for further reference in the sources to an Androkles of Sphettos.

No. 17

1 **Apollonides of Halikarnassos**

2 **A *nauklēros*.** Almost all[32] of our information about Apollonides comes from a deposition in D. 35.33, where he is said to be "co-owner of the ship with Hyblesios [no. 18]." We do not know how active a joint shipowner Apollonides was. His partner Hyblesios (no. 18) was undoubtedly an active *nauklēros*, present on the ship during its voyage to Pontos and its subsequent shipwreck. The deposition in D. 35.33 suggests that Apollonides was not in Athens when the trial took place, but we are not told whether this was due to his activity – joint or otherwise – on another ship.[33]

3 **N. E.**

4 **A non-Athenian** (D. 35.33). **Otherwise N. E.**

5 **Possibly wealthy.** In addition to co-owning a vessel Apollonides also owns an unknown number of slaves who are passengers on the ship at the time of its shipwreck (D. 35.33).[34]

6 **Has a partner in shipowning** (D. 35.33).

No. 18

1 **Hyblesios of Samos**

2 **A *nauklēros*** (D. 35.11, 18, 20, 23, 33).

3 **N. E.**

4 **N. E.** Kirchner lists Hyblesios in *PA* (13893), but it appears from epigraphical evidence that the name Hyblesios is distinctively Samian.[35] Contrary to Pringsheim (1916: 99), Hyblesios is clearly not identical with the Phaselite shipowner (no. 21) mentioned in D. 35.36, 52–3, 55. Hyblesios' ship was "totally wrecked" on the return trip from Pontos (D. 35.33–5), whereas the Phaselite sailed his ship safely from Pontos to the Thieves' Harbor of Athens (D. 35.28–9, 53).

5 **N. E.**

6 **Has a partner.** The deposition in D. 35.33 states that Apollonides (no. 17) is co-owner of the ship with Hyblesios.

---

[32] Wilhelm (1889: 123) believes Apollonides the *nauklēros* in D. 35.33 to be the Apollonides of [Halikar]nassos honored in a proxeny decree (*IG* ii² 136).

[33] The ship he co-owned with Hyblesios was totally wrecked (D. 35.33).

[34] See 34–5 on how wealthy most *nauklēroi* probably were and whether they regularly owned slave crews. The slaves mentioned in D. 35.33 were passengers on the ship, i.e., slaves Apollonides owned in addition to a possible slave crew, so that Apollonides may have been wealthier than most *nauklēroi*.

[35] See further Habicht (1957: 186–8).

No. 19

1 **Artemon of Phaselis**

2 **An *emporos*** (D. 35.3, 7, 10, 14, 34, 43, 49).

3 **Both Artemon and his brother Apollodoros (no. 20) are possible lenders.** According to the speaker in D. 35, Lakritos reported (D. 35.36) that his brother lent money in Pontos to a Phaselite shipowner. "Brother" in the singular would agree with other passages suggesting that only one of Lakritos' brothers went to Pontos, although which brother is not clear.[36] It seems far likelier that both brothers of Lakritos went, since their adventures throughout the trip are cast in the plural (D. 35.24–5, 28–9, 31, 52–3).[37] Therefore either brother or both could have made the loan to the Phaselite shipowner.[38]

4 **Both brothers are possibly *xenoi* from Phaselis.**[39] Clerc (1893: 399) and Gerhardt (1935: 19) state without comment that Artemon is a metic at Athens. Isager–Hansen (1975: 170) disagree:

> It is possible that Artemon and Apollodorus are residents of Phaselis, and presumably they have the status of aliens (*xenoi*), inasmuch as the speaker does not accuse them of violating the grain laws which applied to citizens and metics.

In fact the speaker does mention (D. 35.50) the law forbidding Athenian metics or citizens to transport grain elsewhere, but in a paraphrase clearly not aimed at Artemon and Apollodoros as metics. Whereas those citing this law in other places tailor it to the case in question,[40] the speaker in D. 35.50 alludes to the law almost incidentally; it merely serves as a preface to what really interests him here – his own legal situation as a lender. On this point he not only paraphrases the law (D. 35.50), but actually has it quoted (D. 35.51). Surely he would have been as careful in referring

---

[36] The speaker says (in D. 35.16) that, according to Lakritos, Artemon was to go to Pontos, whereas the depositions (D. 35.20, 23, 34) list only Apollodoros as going. The depositions may have focused on Apollodoros because Artemon was dead and Apollodoros the sole defendant in this case (D. 35.20, 23 and Gernet [1954–60 I 169 n.2]). On the probable genuineness of the depositions, see Gernet (1954–60 I 21–3, 170–1) and Erxleben (1974: 514 n.167).

[37] Certainly Lakritos himself is not included in these plurals. He remained in Athens (D. 35.16).

[38] No other passage in D. 35 is of help. D. 35.52 may refer obscurely to this loan or (more likely) to a subsequent but related transaction. On D. 35.52 see Gernet (1954–60: I 177–8, 192 n.2) and Isager–Hansen (1975: 171).

[39] From Phaselis: D. 35.1, 10, 14, 26.

[40] The same law is applied to the slave Lampis (Lampis II, no. 13), who "resided at Athens" with his family ([D.] 34.37). The speaker in [D.] 34 therefore says the law refers to "anyone who resides at Athens" ([D.] 34.37). Leokrates (no. 40) on the other hand was an Athenian citizen engaging in *emporia*, so that when the orator Lykourgos wished to apply the above law to Leokrates, he referred to "any of the Athenians" (*Leoc.* 27).

to *their* legal situation, had Artemon and Apollodoros violated the laws governing metic lenders or metic *emporoi* who take grain elsewhere. If Artemon and Apollodoros are *xenoi*, there is only one weapon left to the speaker.[41] He can attack them for breach of a bottomry contract, and that is precisely what Androkles in D. 35 does: he not only quotes the agreement itself; he also mentions it in almost half of the fifty-six sections in the speech, and explicitly refers to the breach of contract in almost a quarter of the total.[42]

5 **N. E.**

6 **Artemon and Apollodoros were brothers of Lakritos** (D. 35.15, 41–2), **but Lakritos had no part in their business partnership.** He was (to use the speaker's words) "the brother and heir of an *emporos*" (D. 35.49) but no *emporos* himself. He studied at Athens under Isokrates (D. 35.15) and was an effective speaker and teacher (D. 35.41–2, 44; Plut. *Dem.* 28.3). He almost certainly resided at Athens as a metic (D. 35.4, 16, 41).

No. 20

1 **Apollodoros of Phaselis**

2 **An *emporos*** (D. 35.7, 10, 14, 20, 24, 34, 43).

3 **Possibly a lender.** See item 3 no. 19.

4 **Possibly a *xenos*.** See item 4 no. 19.

5 **N. E.**

6 **Partner of his brother Artemon** (no. 19).

No. 21

1 **Unnamed Phaselite** in D. 35.

2 **A *nauklēros*** (D. 35.36, 52–3, 55). On his not being identical with the *nauklēros* Hyblesios, see item 4 of no. 18 (Hyblesios).

3 **N. E.**

4 **A non-Athenian; otherwise N.E.** In D. 35 the Phaselite (D. 35.36, 52–3, 55) *nauklēros* travels to Athens but does not trade there. He sails from Pontos to the Thieves' Harbor at Athens (D. 35.53), but only to allow Artemon and Apollodoros to disembark; his cargo clearly goes on to Chios (D. 35.53–4). On this episode see Isager–Hansen (1975: 172).

---

[41] Erxleben (1974: 496) points out that even the *emporos* who was a *xenos* at Athens was bound "to the emporic law ... in the roundabout way of a contract with the lender," so that "the law had absolutely no hole."

[42] Artemon and Apollodoros may have come dangerously close to becoming metics by remaining in Athens for "more than twenty-five days" (D. 35.29) upon their return from Pontos. We do not know how long a *xenos* had to remain in Athens to become a *metoikos*. Gauthier (1972: 122) argues for a month; see also Whitehead (1977: 9).

5 **N. E.**
6 **N. E.**

No. 22

1 **Nikoboulos of Athens** (*PA* 10839)

2 **A possible *emporos*.** Nikoboulos sailed from Athens in March (D. 37.6) to Pontos (D. 37.6, 23–4). He was there for an undetermined length of time (D. 37.8, 9, 23, 25, 44) and then returned to Athens (D. 37.10, 15), probably before the end of the same sailing season. Even the strongest testimony to Nikoboulos as an *emporos* (D. 37.54) could almost as readily apply to a bottomry lender who made the voyage to Pontos in order to protect his investment.[43] In fact his reference (D. 37.54) to the dangerous voyage to Pontos is followed immediately by reference (D. 37.54) to his making loans. We might doubt if one with other business interests[44] in Athens would repeatedly absent himself if he were only a lender and not an *emporos*, but the possibility is there, especially in the case of Nikoboulos, who kept a close eye on his loans, "from not only a wish to oblige, but also to keep his money from slipping through his fingers unawares..."[45]

There is no basis for calling Nikoboulos, as Hasebroek (1933: 10) does, a "former *emporos*." Nikoboulos himself makes no distinction between his very recent voyage to Pontos (D. 37.6, 8, 9–10, 15, 23–5, 44) and his earlier ones (D. 37.54).

3 **Probably a lender.** Nikoboulos never clearly describes any of his loans as bottomry loans, but some (particularly those mentioned in D. 37.54) are good candidates, and these qualify him as a probable bottomry lender.[46] Millett (1991: 193–6) considers him the quintessential "professional" lender.

4 **Probably a citizen.** The silver mines of Laurion were state property that could be leased but not sold, despite Nikoboulos' frequent reference to his buying, selling, and owning such property (D. 37.4–5, 13–6, 29–31). Metics could lease mining property (X. *Vect.* 4.12), but there is no evidence in D. 37 that Nikoboulos was a metic. Erxleben (1974:

---

[43] That Nikoboulos lent money is obvious. At least one loan (D. 37.4) is clearly not a bottomry loan; about the others we cannot be certain. See further item 3 of no. 22.

[44] Gernet (1954–60: I 225 n.3) describes Nikoboulos as follows: "Ce citoyen d'Athènes est un homme d'affaires; non content de gagner de l'argent dans les mines et de pratiquer des prêts par ailleurs, il fait pour son compte le commerce maritime."

[45] A slightly altered version of the Paley–Sandys translation (1896:145).

[46] See no. 43 above. There is no evidence for Erxleben's suggestion (1974: 470–1) that Nikoboulos might not be a lender but instead the sort of "intermediary" described by Bogaert (1965:141–4).

475) disagrees, arguing that D. 37.24 and 55 point to Nikoboulos' metic status. In D. 37.24 Nikoboulos rejects Pantainetos' claim that the former tried to disenfranchise him by saying that even a citizen could not seek to disenfranchise another citizen, thereby implying that the state alone could do it, and not that Nikoboulos was a metic. In D. 37.55 Pantainetos reproaches Nikoboulos for certain physical disabilities and not (as Erxleben [1974: 475] claims) for his foreign accent.

5 **Not poor.** Nikoboulos accepts the description of himself as a perennial lender (D. 37.52–6). One of his non-bottomry loans is for forty minae (D. 37.4), and he jointly takes out a lease on mining property for 125 minae (D. 37.31). His stress on "small profits" (D. 37.54) and "losing nearly everything" (D. 37.10) can be dismissed as rhetorical maneuvers.

6 **N. E.**, at least not for Nikoboulos' activity as a possible *emporos*.

No. 23

1 **Phormion of Athens (Phormion II)**[47] (Davies 1971: no. 14959)

2 **A *nauklēros*.**[48] The standard view[49] relies on D. 45.64 to show that Phormion II owned an indeterminate number of merchant ships. Erxleben (1974: 491–2) on the other hand believes that Phormion II, instead of owning the ships seized in D. 45.64, merely gave bottomry loans on the security of these ships. Other passages might suggest that Phormion II is a lender (see item 3 below), but D. 45.64 clearly if briefly describes an instance of shipowning, not of bottomry lending.

3 **Possibly a lender.** The sole evidence for Phormion II as a bottomry lender appears in [D.] 49.31: "At this same time Timosthenes of Aigilia also arrived from a trip abroad, where he had engaged in commerce on his own account." Timosthenes was "a friend of" (ἐπιτήδειος) and "partner of" or "participant with" (κοινωνός) Phormion. Scholars usually[50] take Phormion II's association with Timosthenes (no. 24) to be that of lender with borrower. This relationship is possible but hardly certain: I can find no other instance in which κοινωνός refers to such a relationship; and the fact that this latest trading venture of Timosthenes is "on his own

---

[47] Phormion was a slave, then a freedman, and finally a citizen at Athens. This is not the Phormion (Phormion I – no. 14) in [D.] 34. On Phormion II see further Glover (1917: 302–35, esp. 323–35); Davies (1971: 427–42, esp. 435–6); Trevett (1992: 10–11, 13–15, 42–9). On Phormion II's connection with maritime commerce, see Cohen (1992: 44 n.16, 55, 138, 145) and my n.11 in Ch. 4.

[48] Hasebroek (1928: 14) and Heichelheim (1964: 44) wrongly think Pasion the owner of Phormion's ships.

[49] See for example Davies (1971: 436); Bogaert (1968: 57, 77); Isager–Hansen (1975: 73); Knorringa (1926: 91).

[50] See for example Erxleben (1974: 491–2); Bogaert (1968: 357); and Davies (1984: 62).

account" might imply that other ventures were *done on Phormion II's account*, by a κοινωνός in the sense of one with stronger business ties to Phormion II than that of lender to borrower.[51]

4 **Probably a metic** at the time of the (possible) bottomry loan in [D.] 49.31, **and at a later date probably an Athenian citizen** as the shipowner in D. 45.64. Davies (1971: 431–2) rightly takes the reference in [D.] 49.31 to Phormion II as the friend and partner of Timosthenes to be an indication of more autonomy than a slave would possess, so that Phormion II was by then (372/1)[52] a freedman and no longer the slave of Pasion.

The reference to Phormion II's ships appears in a speech (D. 45) dated 351 or slightly later.[53] The date of the incident described in D. 45.64 (where people of Byzantion detained Phormion II's ships) is unknown, but it almost certainly falls later than his citizenship a decade earlier (361/0 B.C.: [D.] 46.13).

5 **Wealthy.** See D. 45.54, 72; 36.55–7; also Davies (1971: esp. 435–6).

6 **Possibly has a business partner**, but it may be that the relationship of Phormion II to Timosthenes in [D.] 49.31 is only that of borrower to lender. See item 3.

No. 24

1 **Timosthenes of Athens** (*PA* 13810)

2 **A possible *emporos*.** Timosthenes appears only in an episode mentioned briefly in [D]. 49.31–2, 62. The banker Phormion II (no. 23)'s "friend" or "associate,"[54] he returns to Athens ([D.] 49.31) after a "trading venture on his own account" (*kat' emporian idian*). Perhaps the word *idian* ("on his own account") is to distinguish this trip from others taken on Phormion's account, in which case Timosthenes joins Lampis II (no. 13) as the other candidate for Bravo's (1977) category of "agent" trader. He therefore could possibly be an *emporos* or *nauklēros*; the safest guess, based on his *emporia*, is that he is an *emporos*.[55]

---

[51] On the term κοινωνός see further Cohen's useful comments (1992: 76 n.71) and Harris (1989: 339, esp. nn.1 and 2). If Phormion did lend money to Timosthenes, whose was it? At the time of the loan (372/1: see n.52 below) Pasion still managed the bank ([D.] 49.29, 59) with Phormion as his cashier (D. 45.33; [D.] 49.17). Erxleben (1974: 492) seconds Bogaert's claim (1968: 357) that the loan came not from customers' deposits but from Phormion's private capital. On possible maritime loans from banks themselves, arranged in order of likelihood, see Cohen (1992: 171–83). On bankers' lending from their own money, see Cohen (1992: 183–9).

[52] [D.] 49.30 conveniently supplies the archon for the year in which Timosthenes returns home from his *emporia*. On the date of [D.] 49 itself see further Harris (1988: 44–52), and Trevett (1991: 21–7).

[53] See Schäfer (1858: 168–9) and Paley and Sandys II (1896: xxvii–xxix and xxxviii).

[54] On what κοινωνός might mean here see item 3 of no. 23 (Phormion II, of Athens) and n.51 above.

[55] Cf. Davies (1984: 62): "Timosthenes of Aigilia…was presumably a *nauklēros*, and Phormion's association with him probably consisted in putting up the money."

3 **N. E.**

4 **A citizen** ([D.] 49.31).

5 **N. E.**

6 **A possible but unlikely partner of Phormion 11** (no. 23).

No. 25

1 **Philippos of Athens**

2 **A *nauklēros.*** Without arguing the point Schäfer (1858: 141) believed Philippos the *nauklēros* in D. 24.138 to be the same as Philippos the *nauklēros* in [D.] 49.14–18, 20–1, 48–9, 53. He is probably correct for the following reasons. Although not listed in *PA*, Philippos the *nauklēros* in D. 24 is clearly an Athenian citizen, since his son Philippos is charged with an unconstitutional proposal (D. 24.138). Philippos the *nauklēros* in [D.] 49 sails with Timotheos' fleet ([D.] 49.14), in what capacity it is not clear. His civic status is nowhere mentioned, but his treasurer is the Athenian Antiphanes of Lamptrai (Davies 1971: no. 1238), member of a prominent family (Davies 1971: no. 1916). Furthermore the references to Philippos the *nauklēros* in D. 24 and in [D.] 49 date from roughly the same quarter-century. In D. 24, dated 353 B.C., we are not told when Philippos' son was tried, but the case is mentioned (D. 24.138) in connection with another occurring in the archonship of Euandros (382/1 B.C.). Philippos the *nauklēros* in [D.] 49 sailed with Timotheos' fleet in 373/2.

3 **N. E.** There is some question whether it was Philippos who made the loan to Timotheos mentioned in ([D.] 49.14, 16–21, 48–54). The speaker (Apollodoros) discusses this in the speech, but it is not relevant here, since the loan in question was not a bottomry loan.

4 **An Athenian citizen** (see item 2 above).

5 **Probably wealthy.** No single feature of what is known about Philippos in either D. 24 or [D.] 49 guarantees his wealth. But taken together three things in [D.] 49.14–21 probably suggest that he is wealthy: while with Timotheos' fleet Philippos lent Timotheos 1,000 dr. ([D.] 49.14, 16–17); Philippos at that time had a treasurer [D.] 49.14); and that treasurer (Antiphanes) was from a prominent Athenian family (Davies 1971: no. 1916).

6 **N. E.**

No. 26

1 **Philondas of Megara**

2 **Probably not an *emporos*,** in spite of Shipton's belief (1997: 144) that he was. Philondas possibly qualifies as an *emporos* only if Timotheos' claim ([D.] 49.36) that Philondas imported timber from Macedonia

"for the sake of trade" is true, but on Apollodoros' testimony ([D.] 49.26, 28–9, 33–41, 60–1) this seems unlikely. According to Apollodoros the timber was a gift from Amyntas ([D.] 49.26, 36–7) to Timotheos; Philondas, the employee of Timotheos, merely accompanied the timber from Macedonia to Athens.

3 **N. E.**

4 **A metic at Athens** ([D.] 49.26). Philondas is a Megarian by birth ([D.] 49.26).

5 **N. E.**

6 **N. E.**

No. 27

1 **Unnamed *nauklēros*** in [D.] 49

2 **A *nauklēros*** ([D.] 49.29, 40). An unnamed *nauklēros* transported a load of timber from Macedonia to Athens and there received payment for the freight costs ([D.] 49.25–30, 33–41, 60–1). The timber was a gift from Amyntas to Timotheos of Athens for the latter's private use ([D.] 49.26, 36–7).

3 **N. E.**

4 **N. E.**

5 **N. E.**

6 **N. E.**

No. 28

1 **Nikippos**

2 **A *nauklēros*** ([D.] 50.17)

3 **N. E.** Pringsheim (1916: 18–22) and Paoli (1930: 34–41) rightly refused to accept as a bottomry loan Nikippos' loan ([D.] 50.17) to Apollodoros, although disagreement still exists.[56]

4 **N. E.**, in spite of Kirchner's inclusion of Nikippos in *PA* (10830).[57]

5 **N. E.**, apart from Nikippos' loan of 800 dr. to Apollodoros ([D.] 50.17).

6 **N. E.**

---

[56] Isager–Hansen (1975: 73 n.80) and Bogaert (1965: 142 n.3) list Nikippos as a bottomry lender without comment, whereas Gernet (1954–60: III 43 and n.5) and Erxleben (1974: 471, 477, 512 n.128) follow Pringsheim (1916: 18–22) and Paoli (1930: 34–41) in denying that Nikippos made such a loan. Erxleben is challenged on this point by Cohen (1992: 59–60 [esp. n.95], 164–5, 181). In the agreement between Nikippos and Apollodoros ([D.] 50.17), a bottomry loan appears to be Apollodoros' way of *repaying* Nikippos. See Gernet's translation of this passage, "qui n'est pas facile" (1954–60: III 43 and n.5).

[57] Thus Davies (1984: 61).

No. 29

1 **Lykon of Herakleia**
2 **An *emporos*** ([D.] 52.3, 5).
3 **A lender** ([D.] 52.20). See further Millett (1991: 207, 210) and Cohen (1992: 120, 158, 180-1).
4 **Probably a *xenos*.** As the lender of a bottomry loan ([D.] 52.20) at Athens ([D.] 52.21), Lykon might remain there long enough to await the return of the borrowers and perhaps become a metic. But when Lykon thinks he has a case against the lenders, he seeks the aid of his Athenian guest-friends ([D.] 52.3, 21, 22) and not that of Kallippos, *proxenos* of the Herakleots ([D.] 52.5, 9). Further, the speaker clearly wants ([D.] 52.3, 9) to identify Lykon's partner Kephisiades *either* by his place of residence in Athens *or* by his place of birth (on which alternative see item 4 of no. 30 and the accompanying note). He perhaps has the same motive in repeatedly referring to Lykon as "the Herakleot" ([D.] 52.3, 5, 8, 14, 19). Lykon is therefore probably a *xenos*.
5 **Not poor**, in view of his loan of forty minae ([D.] 52.20) and the sixteen minae and forty dr. deposited with Pasion[58] ([D.] 52.3).
6 **Has a partner.** On this see item 6 no. 30 (Kephisiades).

No. 30

1 **Kephisiades**
2 **A probable *emporos*,** since he is clearly the partner ([D.] 52.3) of Lykon (no. 29) in *emporia* ([D.] 52.3 – see item 6 below), and at the time of the speech ([D.] 52) is abroad "on another mercantile enterprise" ([D.] 52.3).
3 **N. E.**
4 **A metic at Athens** ([D.] 52.3, 9, 25, 29).[59]
5 **N. E.**
6 **Has a partner.** Kephisiades is an "associate" (κοινωνός) ([D.] 52.3) of Lykon of Herakleia (no. 29).

[58] On Lykon see further Millett (1991: 207, 210). On the nature of Lykon's business with Pasion, see Erxleben's sensible comments (1974: 492) on Bogaert's view (1968: 355). He thinks Bogaert interprets too narrowly Apollodoros' statement (52.3) that "Lykon ... used my father's bank just as did the other *emporoi*." See further Cohen's remarks (1992: 160–9) on "overly narrow definitions of 'maritime loan'" and his astute comments on the maritime/landed classification of Greek loans (1992: 52–60 and 1990a).

[59] Gernet (1954–60: III 72 n.2) endorsed a late-nineteenth century emendation of *en Skuro* ([D.] 52.3,9) as *en Skiro*. Subsequent authors continue to disagree about which to accept – the island of Skyros as Kephisiades' place of birth and home, or Skiron as his present place of residence in Athens; see further Diller (1937: 161 n.2), Whitehead (1977: 49–50, 67 n.102), Millett (1991: 210), and Cohen (1992: 120 [Skiros]).

No. 31

1 **Megakleides of Athens** (*PA* 9686)
2 **A probable *emporos*** ([D.] 52.20). On Akē as the destination of Megakleides and Thrasyllos' projected voyage, see n.60.
3 **N. E.**
4 **A probable *emporos* who is an Athenian citizen** ([D.] 52.20).
5 **N. E.**
6 **Partner** ([D.] 52.20) **with his brother Thrasyllos** (no. 32).

No. 32

1 **Thrasyllos of Athens** (*PA* 7342)
2 **A probable *emporos*** ([D.] 52.20).[60]
3 **N. E.**
4 **An Athenian citizen** ([D.] 52.20).
5 **N. E.**
6 **Partner** ([D.] 52.20) **with his brother Megakleides** (no. 31).

No. 33

1 **Dionysodoros**
2 **Both Dionysodoros and Parmeniskos (no. 34) are probably *nauklēroi.*** The speaker in [D.] 56 cites at Dionysodoros a law which he explicitly applies to *nauklēroi* ([D.] 56.10, 49). Dionysodoros and his partner Parmeniskos clearly have a ship at their disposal ([D.] 56.3, 7, 9, 20, 39–40, 43). Is only one of them its owner, or are they both? In the absence of evidence to the contrary we should probably assume that their partnership ([D.] 56.5, 7, 10, 42, 45) in *emporia* ([D.] 56.3, 5, 6, 11, 24, 25) extends to *nauklēria* as well.
3 **Both Dionysodoros and Parmeniskos are possible lenders** of the sort Millett (1991: 192) claims are "casual" (rather than "professional"). The speaker in [D.] 56 appears to refer to Dionysodoros as a lender in [D.] 56.17, but that loan clearly ([D.] 56.17) was not made at Athens. Erxleben (1974: 468) therefore thinks that in this instance Parmeniskos is the lender, since he is at Rhodes with the money lent by the speaker and Pamphilos, while Dionysodoros is probably back in Athens (see item 4 below). Parmeniskos is thus the likelier candidate, but the lack of evidence makes a solution impossible (as Ziebarth [1929: 15 and n.1] points out).

---

[60] The MSS give Akē as the destination of Megakleides and Thrasyllos' projected voyage ([D.] 52.20). The OCT editors of Demosthenes emended *Ake*, but Herod. 2.16–17 (Headlam–Knox ed.) confirms Akē in Phoenicia as a source of wheat (cf. Harp., s.v. *Ake*).

4 **Dionysodoros is possibly a metic, whereas Parmeniskos is possibly a *xenos*.**[61] Gernet (1954–60: III 131) cites [D.] 56.7 and 23 as indications that Dionysodoros and Parmeniskos are *xenoi* and not metics, but these passages suggest only that Dionysodoros and Parmeniskos operate from Egypt; in no way do they preclude the metic status of either at Athens. Isager–Hansen (1975: 213) present a stronger case for Dionysodoros as a *xenos*: "Darius [the speaker] dares not directly charge Dionysodorus with breach of the grain laws, and this must mean that Dionysodorus is an alien (*xenos*) and not a metic."

Dareios *is* clearly disposed to cite the appropriate law at Dionysodoros: tailoring as usual to suit the case in question, he twice cites the law obliging *nauklēroi* contracting bottomry loans at Athens on cargoes of grain to return to Athens [D.] 56.10, 49). On the other hand, Dionysodoros never appears to leave Athens. After receiving the loan in dispute, Dionysodoros stays in Athens while Parmeniskos sails away ((D.) 56.7). Two years later ([D.] 56.4, 16, 46) Dionysodoros is in Athens as the defendant in the case at hand ([D.] 56.3–4, 9–11). Nothing is said about his absence in the meantime, and at some point later than the time of the original loan he is still present to receive the lenders' complaints ([D.] 56.11). Dionysodoros therefore could possibly be a metic, but no evidence exists that Parmeniskos is. Perhaps the speaker quoted the law governing those who contract bottomry loans because it implicated both Dionysodoros and Parmeniskos as joint borrowers ([D.] 56.5–6, 45), whereas the law requiring Athenian citizens and metics to bring grain to Athens might have implicated only Dionysodoros the metic.

5 **N. E.**

6 **Dionysodoros and Parmeniskos are probably partners in both** *emporia* **and** *nauklēria* (see the references in item 1 above).[62]

No. 34

1 **Parmeniskos**

2 **A probable *nauklēros*.** See item 2 no. 33 (Dionysodoros).

3 **Possibly a lender.** See item 3 no. 33 (Dionysodoros).

4 **Possibly a *xenos*.** See item 4 no. 33 (Dionysodoros).

5 **N. E.**

6 **The partner of Dionysodoros** (no. 33).

---

[61] Bogaert (1968: 84) and Clerc (1893: 399) think Dionysodoros a metic at Athens. Gauthier (1972: 156 n.163) thinks Dionysodoros "un *xenos* [at Athens], sans doute un Rhodien." He gives no reasons.

[62] For their possible membership ([D.] 56.7–9) in Kleomenes' much larger network, see Ziebarth (1896: 62–3) and Erxleben (1974: 489–90).

No. 35

1 **Mikon of Athens**
2 **A *nauklēros*** ([D.] 58.5, 10, 12). Mikon is not the father of the speaker in [D.] 58, as Kirchner (*PA* 5003) and Isager–Hansen (1975: 72 n.78) believe. See further Davies (1971: 57–9).
3 **N. E.**
4 **An Athenian citizen** ([D.] 58.6).
5 **N. E.**
6 **N. E.**

No. 36

1 **Archeneos of Athens** (*PA* 2362)
2 **A *nauklēros*** (Lys. 12.16).
3 **N. E.**
4 **Probably a citizen.** Lysias "reached the house of Archeneos the *nauklēros*..." (Lys. 12.16). I list him as a probable citizen because nothing is said about whether Archeneos owned or rented the house.
5 **N. E.**
6 **N. E.**

No. 37 and No. 38

1 **Diodotos** (Davies 1971: no. 3885) **and his brother Diogeiton of Athens**
2 **Probably not *emporoi*.** The only evidence that Diodotos was possibly an *emporos* occurs in [Lys.] 32.4: ("Diodotos having made a great deal of money *kat' emporian*...") The final two words are enough to qualify Diodotos as possibly an *emporos*,[63] but the arguments against his being such are worth giving. I begin with his brother, Diogeiton.

The word *emporia* appears only twice in the speeches attributed to Lysias, in [Lys.] 32.4 and 32.25. In the second instance Diogeiton is involved: he dispatched to the Adriatic a vessel with a cargo worth two talents and told his daughter that her children, not he, bore the financial risk. Yet when the vessel on its return doubled the initial outlay, he claimed the profits for himself. The Greek wording of 32.25 is clumsy and misleading: Diogeiton is said to have sent out a large cargo ship, but the point of the passage is that he illegally risked his wards' money on a bottomry loan and is therefore a lender and not a shipowner.[64] More important is Diogeiton's connection with *emporia*: faced with its

---

[63] Erxleben (1974: 473) disagrees without elaborating, but the consensus is that early in his life Diodotos was probably an *emporos*. See for example Davies (1971: 152–3); Bogaert (1968: 369 n.383) and (1965: 142 and n.3, 144); Isager–Hansen (1975: 172, n.78).
[64] Thus Gernet and Bizos (1926: II 195 n.4).

exceptional success, Diogeiton said that the *emporia* had been on his own behalf. *Emporian* here means something like "affaire" (Budé), "venture" (Loeb), or (more precisely) "maritime venture." Diogeiton's connection with *emporia* in this sense carries no suggestion that he is anything but a lender.[65]

Bravo (1977: 3–4) agrees that Diogeiton is not an *emporos*, but denies that he is a bottomry lender. He thinks Diogeiton gave someone two talents (probably in cash) for a trading trip to the Adriatic. This was not a bottomry loan but instead a late instance of a practice widespread in archaic Greece, whereby a rich landowner dispatched his agent to engage in trade on the former's account (or, in [Lys.] 32.25, in the interests of the former's wards).

Diodotos as a lender makes Bravo's theory unlikelier than those of others. The casual reference to Diodotos' loans in [Lys.] 32.6 suggests that bottomry lending was at the time a well-established practice.[66] The readiest explanation, then, of [Lys.] 32.25 is that Diogeiton followed in his brother's footsteps as a bottomry lender.[67]

Diogeiton's connection with *emporia* was therefore probably confined to lending. It also seems probable that Diodotos' connection with *emporia* was the same, Diodotos "having made a great deal of money on maritime ventures" *solely as a lender of bottomry loans.*

3 **Two men who lend** ([Lys.] 32.6). Millett (1991: 193) categorizes Diodotos as a "professional" lender and offers a helpful list of *all* loans, maritime and otherwise, left in his estate.

4 **Athenian citizens** (see Davies 1971: no. 3885).

5 **Not poor** (see Davies 1971: no. 3885).

6 **N. E.**

No. 39

1 **Chairephilos of Athens** (Davies 1971: no. 15187)

2 **A possible *emporos*.** The sense in which Chairephilos was a saltfish seller (ταριχοπώλης)[68] remains unclear. We are told only that his sons were made citizens because he imported saltfish (Alexis *CAF* F 77 = *PCG* F 77).

---

[65] Thus Gernet and Bizos (1926: II 195 n.4) and Erxleben (1974: 473, 510 n.97).

[66] As de Ste. Croix (1974: 44) points out and as Bravo (1977: 4) acknowledges. On the early history of bottomry lending, see further 40–2.

[67] At the same time it must be acknowledged that a bottomry loan of two talents is much higher than the fourth-century amounts. Furthermore, both the other two unusually large amounts may represent more than one loan: the seven talents and forty minae lent (in the fifth century) by Diodotos ([Lys.] 32.6), and (in the fourth) the 7,000 dr. left by Demosthenes the Elder with Xouthos (no. 3: see D. 27.11); on the loans to Xouthos see esp. Cohen (1992: 64 n.13, 122–3); cf. Bogaert (1965: 141 n.3).

[68] Ath. 3.119f–120a; 8.339d; Din. 1.43; Hyp. fr. 184 (Jensen).

Does this mean that he remained in Athens and bought from *emporoi*, or that he himself went to sea? In either instance did he sell to retailers or to consumers? And did he in the course of his life do more than one of these, only to retire after becoming wealthy? In any case the possibility exists that at some stage Chairephilos may have been an *emporos*.

3 **N. E.** Erxleben (1974: 487) disagrees. He claims that as a metic Chairephilos specialized in lending to *emporoi* who imported saltfish. True, once Chairephilos became wealthy, lending may have been among his business activities. But how did he accumulate the money to lend? Our only evidence suggests that he acquired it by trading in saltfish.

4 **Becomes an Athenian citizen** (Din. 1.43).

5 **Not poor** (see Davies 1971: 566–8).

6 **N. E.** Alexis (*CAF* F 6 = *PCG* F 6; *CAF* F 218 = *PCG* F 221) associates Chairephilos' son, Pheidippos, with the saltfish trade, but Alexis may have in mind nothing more than the original source of Pheidippos' wealth. See also Lewis (1959: 208–38) and *SEG* xviii 36, lines 510–13.

No. 40

1 **Leokrates of Athens** (*PA* 9083)

2 **A probable *emporos*.** Lykourgos (*Leoc.* 26) says that after Chaironeia Leokrates made his way via Rhodes to Megara, where he took up residence and used the money brought from Athens to ship grain from Epiros to Leukas and thence to Corinth. Lykourgos adds (*Leoc.* 27) that Leokrates thus violated the law forbidding Athenian citizens or metics (Lykourgos here uses τις Ἀθηναίων) to carry grain to any place but Athens.

Then Lykourgos proceeds to deny what he affirmed in *Leoc.* 26–7. In response to Leokrates' claim that he left Athens on a maritime trading venture (*ep' emporian*), Lykourgos replies (*Leoc.* 58) that before leaving Leokrates was never a practicing *emporos* but rather a blacksmith. Besides, argues Lykourgos (*Leoc.* 56), "Why would the Athenian need to settle for five years in Megara as an *emporos*?" Whatever Leokrates' motives for leaving Athens, we should probably assume that *at least while based at Megara* he was a full-fledged *emporos*.

Both Hasebroek (1933: 14–15) and Erxleben (1974: 477) want to deny Leokrates this status. Their position rests on barely articulated assumptions about "professional" as distinct from "non-professional" *emporoi*. I discuss the confusions surrounding the "profession" of *emporos* at 7–12.

According to my definition Leokrates *at least at one stage in his life* was very likely an *emporos* in every crucial sense of the word.

3 **N. E.**

4 **An Athenian citizen** (*Leoc.* 8, 56). There is no evidence that he traded while resident in Athens.

5 **Not poor** (*Leoc.* 22, 58).

6 **N. E.**

No. 41

1 **Andokides of Athens** (Davies 1971: no. 828)[69]

2 **A** *nauklēros.* Other sources ([Lys.] 6.19, 49; Plut. *Mor.* 834E) testify only to his *naukleria*, but Andokides himself (Andok. 1.137) refers both to "shipownings" (*nauklērion*) and *emporia* (see also Andok. 2.11–12). By "shipownings" he might mean successive ownerships of *one* vessel; otherwise Andokides joins Lampis I (no. 2) and Phormion II (no. 23) as one of the three men in the classical period who are said to own more than one merchant ship. In spite of his engaging in *emporia* we should not hesitate to classify Andokides as a *nauklēros. Nauklēroi* may have engaged in *emporia* regularly enough for the word *nauklēros* to connote trading (see further 12–13); only once, in the case of Herakleides of Salamis (no. 60), is the less inclusive word (*emporos*) surprisingly applied to someone engaged in both shipowning and trading. See further 51–3 for a discussion of this revealing exception. Andokides testifies (1.144) that it was the poverty resulting from exile that forced him into sea trade. He appears to have taken his work seriously, traveling widely and parlaying family connections into profit (Andok. 1.144–5; [Lys.] 2.11; 6.6; Plut. *Mor.* 834E): when he returned from exile in 403/2 B.C. he was again a wealthy man ([Lys.] 6.48). His travels and success together with certain comments (Andok. 1.137, 144) suggest that Andokides pursued *nauklēria* and *emporia* for a number of years, perhaps for most of his exile. Davies (1971: 31) remarks that even afterwards

> Andokides clearly derived much profit from his trading activities in exile, and though after his return in 403/2 he was again a wealthy man . . . he continued to think and act like the businessman he had turned himself into.

Erxleben (1974: 477) and Vélissaropoulos (1980: 49–50 and 1977: 64) deny that Andokides was a *nauklēros* in any professional sense.[70] I would

---

[69] On Andokides see further the bibliography in Davies (1971: 27).

[70] See 7–12 and 12–13 on the sense in which Andokides and others were "professional" *nauklēroi* or *emporoi.*

reply that during his exile Andokides was probably as genuine a *nauklēros* carrying on *emporia* as anyone in this Catalogue who did the same. But there is never a hint that this activity extended *beyond* the period of exile.

3 **N. E.**

4 **An Athenian citizen** (see Davies 1971: 31). There is no evidence that he engaged in either *emporia* or *nauklēria* while resident in Athens.

5 **Wealthy before and after his exile** (Davies 1971: 31; [Lys.] 6.48), but during the interval engages in trade because of his (perhaps exaggerated) "utter poverty and destitution" (Andok. 1.144).

6 **N. E.**

No. 42

1 **Pyron of Pherai**

2 **A possible *emporos* or *nauklēros*.** Isokrates says (17.20) that Pyron "was accustomed to sail to Pontos."

3 **N. E.**

4 **Non-Athenian. N.E. whether he is a metic or *xenos* at Athens.** Given the ambiguity of the word *xenos*, the three references to Pyron as *xenos* in Isok. 17.23 and 25 are of little help.[71]

5 **Not poor.** That Pyron owns slaves (Isok. 17.23) does not of itself prove him wealthy, but it suggests that he is not impoverished either.

6 **N. E.**

No. 43

1 **Stratokles**

2 **A possible *emporos* or *nauklēros*.**[72] The speaker (Isok. 17.35) says Stratokles at one point was ready to "sail to Pontos."

3 **N. E.** His alleged loan (Isok. 17.35) to Sopaios' son is clearly no bottomry loan.

4 **N. E.**

5 **N. E.**

6 **N. E.**

No. 44

1 **Unnamed Delian**

2 **A *nauklēros*** (Isok. 17.42).

---

[71] On the various meanings of the word *xenos* see Finley (1935: 330 n.48); Whitehead (1977; 10–11 and nn.29–37); Vélissaropoulos (1980: esp. 48 n.205); Takabatake (1988).

[72] The only references to Stratokles occur in Isok. 17.35–7.

3 **N. E.**
4 **A non-Athenian** (Isok. 17.42). **Otherwise N. E.**
5 **N. E.**
6 **N. E.**

No. 45 and No. 46
1 **Two Unnamed Lynkestians**
2 **Probable *emporoi*.** Themistokles in flight from the land of the Molossians (471/0 B.C.) was helped as follows, according to Diodoros (11.56.3): "Finding two young Lynkestians who engaged in trade and were therefore familiar with the roads, he escaped with them." Here we are at the mercy of not only Diodorus' reliability but also that of *his* source.
3 **N. E.**
4 **Non-Athenians. Otherwise N. E.**
5 **N. E.**
6 **N. E.**

No. 47
1 **Lykon of Achaia** (*IG* i³ 174: 414–412 B.C.)
2 **A probable *nauklēros*.** Lykon is granted *proxenia* and *euergesia* and is allowed to take his ship (lines 11–12) into any of the waters under Athenian control except for the Corinthian Gulf.[73]
3 **N. E.**
4 **A non-Athenian. Otherwise N. E.**
5 **N. E.**
6 **N. E.**

No. 48
1 **Pythophanes** (*IG* i³ 98 = ML 80 = Fornara no. 149: late fifth century B.C.)[74]
2 **A probable *nauklēros*.** The inscription (lines 15–19) mentions Pythophanes' ship and goods; it also decrees that a previous award of *proxenia* and *euergesia* be reinscribed. Walbank (1978: 389–90) plausibly doubts what previously had been assumed to be his Karystian origin.
3 **N. E.**

---

[73] See further Walbank (1978: 280–4) and Engen (1996: 77–8 and 437 nn.65–6).
[74] *IG* i³ 98 is an inscription from 399/8 B.C. that records three separate decrees, the first of which dates to before 411; the second, to 411/10; and the third (a reaffirmation of the second), from 399/8. See further Walbank (1978: 390–2) and Engen (1996: 48, 78–80, 427 nn.67–8). To their bibliographies should be added *HCT* (1981: 196–7).

4 **A non-Athenian. Otherwise N. E.**
5 **N. E.**
6 **N. E.**

No. 49

1 **An unnamed Megarian** (*IG* ii² 81: *c*. 390–378 B.C.)
2 **A possible *emporos*.** He and his sons are granted *proxenia* and *asylia* for themselves and their goods in lines 6–7. See further Walbank (1990: 438) on lines 1–2 and Engen (1996: 51, 89–91 and 428 nn. 90–5).
3 **N. E.**
4 **A non-Athenian. Otherwise N. E.**
5 **N. E.**
6 **Probably a partner with his sons in a family enterprise.**

No. 50

1 **Ph- of Salamis on Cyprus** (*IG* ii² 283: before 336/5 B.C.).[75] He received a commendation and crown.
2 **Possible emporos**, since the verb ἐσιτ]ήγησεν (line 2) points to his bringing grain to Athens himself. He imported not only grain but perhaps fish too and sold the grain at a reduced rate. See further Engen (1996: 57, 102–3 and 430 nn.122–4).
3 **N. E.**
4 **N. E.**
5 **Probably not poor.** He ransomed captive Athenians from Sicily, donated a talent of silver, and sold grain at a reduced rate.
6 **N. E.**

No. 51 and No. 52

1 **Hieron and his son Apses of Tyre.** (*IG* ii² 342+: 331–324 B.C.)
2 **Possible *emporoi***: Apses conveyed (κ]εκόμικ[εν, line 3) something not here specified and also vowed to transport grain (σιτ[ηγήσει]ν, line 6) to Athens. See further Walbank (1985: 107–11), Tracy (1995: 30–3), and Engen (1996: 57, 103–6 and 430–2 nn. 125–33). These two Tyrians were awarded *proxenia*, *euergesia*, *enktesis*, a commendation, and gold crowns.
3 **N. E.**
4 **N. E.** Walbank (1985: 110) counters previous arguments that these two were metics at Athens by doubting that "the Athenians would have made a grant of the *proxenia* ... to anyone who was not in a position to carry

---

[75] I follow Engen (1996: 102) in citing the date given for this decree in *IG* ii².

out the duties of a *proxenos*...The *proxenia* was not an empty honor at Athens."

5 **N. E.**

6 **Probably operating as partners in a family enterprise.**

No. 53 and No. 54

1 **Mnemon and –ias of Herakleia** (*IG* ii² 408: 333/2 B.C.)

2 **Possible emporoi,** honored with a commendation and gold crowns for selling wheat and barley at lower than the currently inflated price. We are told that one of them "brought" the barley himself. See further Tracy (1995: 30–4) and Engen (1996: 60, 112–14 and 431–2 nn.146–50).

3 **N. E.**

4 **N. E.**

5 **Possibly not poor.** Their generosity in a time of shortage, when sale promised even greater profits, may bespeak wealth.

6 **Possible partners,** solely on the strength of their being honored jointly.

No. 55

1 **Sopatros of Akragas** (Camp [1974: 322–4] 331–324 B.C.)

2 **Possible *emporos*.** He is commended for providing grain and awarded *proxenia*, *euergesia*, and a stele in the acropolis with the decree inscribed. Further, he is offered meals at the Prytanaeum and a seat of honor at the Dionysia. Camp (1974: 324): "His invitation to dine at the prytaneion is of interest, indicating his presence at Athens and suggesting that perhaps he accompanied the grain he is being honored for supplying." Camp (1974: 323–4) also notes that he is the only Sicilian supplier of grain attested by name. See further Tracy (1995: 30–4) and Engen (1996: 63, 121–2 and 433 nn.173–4).

3 **N. E.**

4 **N. E.**

5 **N. E.**

6 **N. E.**

No. 56

1 **Pandios of Herakleia** (Schweigert [1940: 332–3] *c.* 330 B.C.)

2 **Possible *emporos*.** The surviving portion of the decree mentions only a commendation. We are told that "he himself transported" goods to Athens (lines 7–8), followed by mention of his "escort of the grain" (line 9). See further Tracy (1995: 30–4) and Engen (1996: 64, 122–4).

3 **N. E.**

4 **N. E.**
5 **N. E.**
6 **N. E.**

No. 57 and No. 58

1 **Two unnamed inhabitants, possibly from Miletos** (*IG* ii² 409: *c.* 330 B.C.). The Milesian origin largely depends on a restoration (lines 16–17).
2 **Probable emporoi, possibly honored with a commendation.** "Grain was brought by them out of ?Sinope for the Athenians" (lines 8–10). See further Tracy (1995: 30–4) and Engen (1996: 65, 126–7).
3 **N. E.**
4 **N. E.**
5 **N. E.**
6 **N. E.**

No. 59

1 **Unnamed inhabitant, possibly from Miletos** (*IG* ii² 407 and *SEG* xxxii 94: 330–326 B.C. or 321–318 B.C.). As in the previous inscription (*IG* ii² 409), his Milesian ethnic identity rests in large part on a restoration (line 12 of *IG* ii² 407).
2 **Possible *emporos*.** This brief, fragmentary decree allows us to speculate that he was rewarded with a commendation for bringing grain to Athens (lines 4–5) and for escorting other ships from Cyprus (lines 5–6) probably on the same trip. See further Walbank (1987: 165–6); Tracy (1995: 30–3); Engen (1996: 65, 127–9, 433 nn.178–9).
3 **N. E.**
4 **N. E.**
5 **N. E.**
6 **N. E.**

No. 60

1 **Herakleides of Salamis in Cyprus** (*IG* ii² 360 = *Syll.*³ no. 304 = Michel no. 110 = Schwenk no. 68)[76]
2 **A *nauklēros*.** The Athenian decrees honoring Herakleides twice (lines 30–1 and line 10) refer to him as *emporos*; but if he is not a shipowner, why would the Athenians demand the return of his sails from the Herakleots who seized them (line 39)? The inscription consists of five decrees, all inscribed in 325–4 and listed in order of time as follows:

---

[76] See further Pečirka (1966: 70–2); Casson (1991: 110–11), who includes a translation; and most recently Engen (1996: 68–70, 129–31, 136–7, 433 nn.180–3).

Group I (A, B, and C), from 330/29 B.C. or slightly later:

I.A. (lines 46–50): An assembly decree instructs the Council to frame and submit a decree honoring Herakleides.

I.B. (lines 51–65): The Council proposes a gift of a gold crown to Herakleides, "because [during a grain shortage] he sailed to Athens with grain and gave the people 3,000 medimni at [the low price of] 5 dr. each."

I.C. (lines 28–45): The assembly decrees that "whereas Herakleides was the first of the *emporoi* sailing in from overseas [in 330/29] . . . to contribute grain to the people at 5 dr.," he is to receive a gold crown; and "whereas, while sailing to Athens he was brought to land by the Herakleots and his sails were seized by them," an Athenian ambassador is to go to Pontic Herakleia and demand the return of the sails.

Group II (A and B): 325 B.C.:

II.A. (lines 66–79): The Council resolves to honor Herakleides with another gold crown as a reward for his donation (in 328/7) of 3,000 dr. for the purchase of grain.

II.B. (lines 1–27): The assembly decrees that Herakleides is to receive a second gold crown and that he and his descendants are to be *proxenoi* and *euergetai*, with rights of *enktesis ges kai oikias* and of doing military service and paying *eisphora* as if they were Athenians.

3 **N. E.**

4 **A non-Athenian. Otherwise N. E.** Scholars tend to see Herakleides as a metic; Pečirka (1966: 72) lists the earlier champions of this view, to whom should be added Hopper (1979: 112) and Engen (1996: 131). There is no evidence for Herakleides as a metic, unless (as Whitehead [1977: 30] says) his visits to Athens took him in and out of the *metoikia*. In particular the grant of *enktesis* provides no support for his residence in Athens. There is no evidence as to where the other two *emporoi*[77] who received *enktesis* actually lived, but other *enktesis* recipients probably did not reside in Athens.[78]

5 **Wealthy** (*IG* ii² 360, esp. lines 55–6 and 67–8).

6 **N. E.**

No. 61

1 **Unnamed Athenian** (*P Oxy.* 2538 in Barnes, *et al.* [1966: 38–45]).

2 **An *emporos*** (*P Oxy.* 2538, from a speech by a fourth-century B.C. Attic orator). The speaker (in lines 9–13 of fr. 1 col. 2) describes his father

---

77 *IG* ii² 342+ (no. 52 and no. 53); see also Pečirka (1966: 63).

78 See, for example, *IG* ii² 206 and 343, along with Pečirka's comments (1966: 46 and 67).

as "trading and earning his livelihood from the sea." His father traveled to Selymbria, where he became friends with a Selymbrian named Antiphanes, whose daughter he married.

3 **N. E.**

4 **Probably an Athenian citizen.** J. R. Rea, the editor of *P Oxy.* 2538, speculates that the speaker cites his father's and brother's undoubted Athenian origins with an eye to litigation pertaining to his own (38–45).

5 **N. E.**, or (to put it more accurately) not enough evidence. There is a hint that this *emporos* is hardly impoverished: the speaker mentions (lines 1–5, fr. 2, col. 4) that his father (the *emporos* or former *emporos*) sent him and his brother, accompanied by a slave, to the same school.

6 **N. E.**

No. 62 to No. 65 (*IG* ii² 1672: 329/8 B.C.)

1 **No. 62: Attos** (line 104)[79]
  No. 63: Konops (line 90)[80]
  No. 64: Simias (line 147)[81]
  No. 65: Syros (line 70)[82]

2 *Emporoi.* All four are called *emporoi* in the Eleusinian accounts.

3 **N. E.**

4 **Probably non-Athenians**, contrary to Meiggs (1982: 435–6). **Otherwise N. E.** None of the four have demotics; they are probably resident or non-resident freedmen.[83]

5 **N. E.**

6 **N. E.**

No. 66 to No. 70 (Dedications of the "freedmen's bowls" [φιάλαι ἐξελευθερικαί], *IG* ii² 1553–78, c. 323–317/16 B.C.)

1 **No. 66: Epigonos, an *emporos*** (*IG* ii² 1557, line 59, and Lewis [1959: 219 line 501]).
  No. 67: Moschion, an *emporos* (*IG* ii² 1558, line 91, *IG* ii² 1559, lines 36–7, and Lewis [1959: 219, lines 148–9]).
  No. 68: An unnamed *emporos* (*IG* ii² 1566, line 2).

---

[79] Attos sells 17 skins (as raincoats?) for the public slaves, at 4½ dr. each.

[80] Konops sells a blacksmith's forge for 30–50 dr.

[81] Simias sells three cedar poles for 210 dr. On him and Syros below see further Meiggs (1982: 363, 433–6).

[82] Syros sells doorposts for 28 ½ dr.

[83] Syros in line 70 is probably not the same as the metic Syros of Alopeke in line 140 or the metic Syros of Kollytos in *IG* ii² 1673 (lines 23, ?41, and 47).

No. 69: Another unnamed *emporos* (*IG* ii² 1577, lines 3–4).

No. 70: Eudemon, an *emporos* (Lewis [1968: 371, lines 60–1 *c.* 332–330 B.C.).

2 ***Emporoi.*** See item 1 above.

3 **N. E.**

4 **The manumissions** recorded in the above inscription **transform slaves** (some of them probably χωρὶς οἰκοῦντες ["living apart in their own establishments"]) **into *metoikion*-payers.**[84]

5 **N. E.**

6 **N. E.**

No. 71

1 **Lykios of Corinth** (*IG* iv² 1 102: *c.* 375–370 B.C.)[85]

2 **A possible *emporos* or *naukleros*.** From the temple commissioners' accounts at Epidauros, we learn that Lykios has contracts for (a) quarrying and delivering stone for the colonnade (lines 5–6), (b) delivering more stone for another purpose (lines 18–19), and (c) supplying silver fir timbers (lines 24–6) – all the above for the temple of Asklepios. Among those awarded contracts Lykios and Tychamenes (the next entry in the Catalogue) qualify as the likeliest *emporoi* or *naukleroi*, on the strength of the wider scale and range of their activity. Meiggs (1982: 361) comments on the fact that "large scale merchants [such as Lykios] did not necessarily confine themselves to a single commodity..." The inscriptions make it clear that transport by sea constituted part of the trip;[86] my guess is that a merchant operating on such a large scale also may have owned the vessels involved.[87]

3 **N. E.**

4 **N. E.**

5 **Probably not poor.** Burford (1969: 151): "Lykios was not simply a trader with ships at his command, but a businessman with far-reaching contacts, a truly professional entrepreneur."

6 **N. E.**

---

[84] On the legal aspects of these manumission lists see esp. Lewis (1959: 237–8). On the juridical status of freedman in Athens see Whitehead (1977: 16–17).

[85] Burford (1969: 54) thus dates the inscription. See in the same volume Burford's translation (212–20). My references to the line numbers are taken from *IG* iv² itself, not from the slightly different numbers in Burford's edition (1966: 254–323) and in her translation (1969: 212–20).

[86] Burford (1960: 7).

[87] On Lykios see further Burford (1969: 58, 136, 212–13); Meiggs (1982: 423–30, esp. 424); and Salmon (1984: 123).

No. 72

1 **Tychamenes of Crete** (*IG* iv² 1 102: *c.* 375–370 B.C.)[88]

2 **A possible *emporos* or *nauklēros*.** Tychamenes receives a contract to quarry and deliver cypress wood for the temple of Asklepios at Epidauros (lines 25–6). Burford (1969: 151) and Meiggs (1982: 426) assume that the cypress came from Crete, presumably transported by Tychamenes himself.

3 **N. E.**

4 **N. E.**

5 **N. E.**

6 **N. E.**

---

[88] See n.85 above and Burford (1969: 37, 151, 177–8, and 213).

Bibliography

All entries are assigned their original date of publication except in the case of later editions. If the page numbers are taken from later reprints or collections, this is noted in the entry itself.

Adams, J. (1850–6) "Thoughts on Government" (1776), in C. F. Adams, ed., *The Works of John Adams* IV. Boston.

Amit, M. (1965) *Athens and the Sea: A Study in Athenian Sea-Power*. Brussels.

Ampolo, C. (1976–7) "Demarato. Osservazioni sulla mobilità sociale arcaica," *DArch* 9–10: 333–45.

Anderson, P. (1974) *Lineages of the Absolutist State*. London.

Arafat, K., and Morgan, C. (1994) "Athens, Etruria and the Heuneberg: Mutual Misconceptions in the Study of Greek-Barbarian Relations," in I. Morris, ed., *Classical Greece: Ancient Histories and Modern Archaeologies*. Cambridge: 108–43.

D'Arms, J. H. (1981) *Commerce and Social Standing in Ancient Rome*. Cambridge MA.

Arnaoutoglou, I., ed. and trans. (1998) *Ancient Greek Laws: A Sourcebook*. London and New York.

Aubet, M. E. (1993) *The Phoenicians and the West: Politics, Colonies and Trade*, trans. M. Turton. Cambridge.

Austin, M. M. (1970) *Greece and Egypt in the Archaic Age*. Cambridge.

(1988) "Greek Trade, Industry, and Labor," in M. Grant and R. Kitzinger, eds., *Civilization of the Ancient Mediterranean: Greece and Rome* II. New York: 723–51.

(1994) "Society and Economy," in D. M. Lewis, *et al.*, eds., *CAH*² VI: 527–64.

and Vidal-Naquet, P. (1977) *Economic and Social History of Ancient Greece: An Introduction*. London.

Aymard, A. (1943) "Hiérarchie du travail et autarcie individuelle dans la Grèce archaïque," *Revue d'histoire de la philosophie et d'histoire générale de la civilisation* II: 124–46, rp. in and cited from *Études d'histoire ancienne*. Paris 1967: 316–33.

Baechler, J. (1995) *Le capitalisme* I–II. Paris.

Balme, M. (1984) "Attitudes to Work and Leisure in Ancient Greece," *G&R* 31: 140–52.

Barnes, J. W. B., *et al.*, eds. and trans. (1966) *The Oxyrhynchus Papyri* XXXI. London.

Baslez, M.-F. (1988) "Les communautés d'Orientaux dans la cité grecque: formes de sociabilité et modèles associatifs," in R. Lonis, ed., *L'étranger dans le monde grec*. Nancy: 139–58.

Bass, G. (1986) "A Bronze Age Shipwreck at Ulu Burun (Kas): 1984 Campaign," *AJA* 90: 269–96.

(1991) "Evidence of Trade from Bronze Age Shipwrecks," in N. H. Gale, ed., *Bronze Age Trade in the Mediterranean*. Jonsered: 69–82.

Bengtson, H., ed. (1975) *Die Staatsverträge des Altertums* II, 2nd ed. Munich.

Berthold, R. M. (1984) *Rhodes in the Hellenistic Age*. Ithaca NY.

Blackman, D. J. (1982) "Ancient Harbours in the Mediterranean," *IJNA* 11: 79–104, 185–211.

Blakeway, A. (1935) "'Demaratus': A Study in Some Aspects of the Earliest Hellenisation of Latium and Etruria," *JRS* 25: 129–49.

Boardman, J. (1980) *The Greeks Overseas*, new and enlarged ed. London, rp. with a new epilogue and cited from the 4th ed. London 1999.

(1990) "Al Mina and History," *OJA* 9: 169–90.

Böckh, A., and Fränkel, M. (1886) *Die Staatshaushaltung der Athener* I–II, 3rd ed. Berlin.

Bogaert, R. (1965) "Banquiers, courtiers et prêts maritimes à Athènes et à Alexandrie," *CE* 40: 140–56.

(1968) *Banques et banquiers dans les cités grecques*. Leiden.

(1986) "La banque à Athènes au IVᵉ siècle avant J. C. État de la question," *MH* 43: 19–49.

Bolkestein, H. (1958) *Economic Life in Greece's Golden Age*, new ed. Leiden.

Borza, E. N. (1987) "Timber and Politics in the Ancient World: Macedon and the Greeks," *Proceedings of the American Philosophical Society* 131: 32–52.

Bourguet, E. (1932) *Fouilles de Delphes* III: *Épigraphie*, fasc. 5: *Les comptes du IVᵉ siècle*. Paris.

Bousquet, J. (1977) *Études delphiques*. BCH suppl. 4. Paris.

Bradley, K. R. (1987) "On the Roman Slave Supply and Slavebreeding," in M. I. Finley, ed., *Classical Slavery*. London: 42–64.

Braudel, F. (1982) *The Wheels of Commerce = Civilization and Capitalism 15th Century–18th Century* II, trans. S. Reynolds. New York.

Braun, T. F. R G. (1982) "The Greeks in Egypt," in J. Boardman and N. G. L. Hammond, eds., *CAH* ² III.3: 32–56.

Braund, D. C. (1994) "The Luxuries of Athenian Democracy," *G&R* 41: 41–8.

and Tsetskhladze, G. R. (1989) "The Export of Slaves from Colchis," *CQ* 39: 114–25.

Bravo, B. (1974) "Une lettre sur plomb de Berezan: colonisation et modes de contact dans le Pont," *DHA* 1: 111–87.

(1977) "Remarques sur les assises sociales, les formes d'organisation et terminologie du commerce maritime grec à l'èpoque archaïque," *DHA* 3: 1–59.

(1980) *Sulân. Représailles et justice privée contre des étrangers dans les cités grecques* = *ANSP* 10: 675–987.

(1983) "Le commerce de céréales chez les Grecs de l'époque archaïque," in P. Garnsey and C. R. Whittaker, eds., *Trade and Famine in Classical Antiquity.* Cambridge: 17–29.

(1984) "Commerce et noblesse en Grèce archaïque. A propos d'un livre d'Alfonso Mele," *DHA* 10: 99–160.

Brenner, R. (1998) "The Economics of Global Turbulence: A Special Report on the World Economy, 1950–98," *The New Left Review* 229: 1–264.

Brun, P. (1993) "La stèle des céréales de Cyrène et le commerce du grain en Egée au IV s. av. J. C.," *ZPE* 99: 185–96.

(1973) "Aspects of the Social Thought of Dio Chrysostom and of the Stoics," *PCPhS* 19: 9–34.

Burford, A. (1960) "Heavy Transport in Antiquity," *EHR* 13: 1–18.

(1966) "Notes on the Epidaurian Inscriptions," *BSA* 61: 254–334.

(1969) *The Greek Temple Builders of Epidaurus.* Liverpool.

Burke, E. (1992) "The Economy of Athens in the Classical Era: Some Adjustments to the Primitivist Model," *TAPA* 122: 199–226.

Burstein, S. M. (1978) "*I.G.* II² 653, Demosthenes and Athenian Relations with Bosporus in the Fourth Century B.C.," *Historia* 27: 428–36.

(1993) "The Origin of the Athenian Privileges at Bosporus: A Reconsideration," *AHB* 7: 81–3.

Busolt, G. (1920) *Griechische Staatskunde* I, ed. H. Swoboda. Munich.

Calhoun, G. M . (1926) *The Business Life of Ancient Athens.* New York.

Calligas, P. (1971) "An Inscribed Lead Plaque from Korkyra," *BSA* 66: 79–94.

Camp II, J. M. (1974) "Proxenia for Sopatros of Akragas," *Hesperia* 43: 314–24.

(1982) "Drought and Famine in the 4th Century B.C.," *Hesperia* Suppl. 20: 9–17.

Campbell, D. A., ed. (1967) *Greek Lyric Poetry: A Selection of Early Greek Lyric, Elegiac and Iambic Poetry.* Basingstoke and London.

ed. and trans. (1991) *Greek Lyric* III: *Stesichorus, Ibycus, Simonides, and Others.* Cambridge MA and London (Loeb Classical Library no. 476).

Cartledge, P. (1979) Review of Starr (1977), *Phoenix* 33: 354–7.

(1983) " 'Trade and Politics' Revisited: Archaic Greece," in P. Garnsey, *et al.*, eds., *Trade in the Ancient Economy.* Berkeley: 1–15, 181–2.

(1998) "The Economy (Economies) of Ancient Greece," *Dialogos* 5: 4–24.

Cartledge, P., Millett, P., and Todd, S., eds. (1990) *Nomos: Essays in Athenian Law, Politics and Society.* Cambridge.

Casson, L. (1950) "The Isis and her Voyage," *TAPA* 81: 43–56.

(1954) "The Grain Trade of the Hellenistic World," *TAPA* 85: 168–87, rp. in *Ancient Trade and Society.* Detroit MI 1984: 70–95.

(1971) *Ships and Seamanship in the Ancient World.* Princeton, rp. Baltimore 1995.

(1988) "Piracy," in M. Grant and R. Kitzinger, eds., *Civilization of the Ancient Mediterranean: Greece and Rome* II. New York: 837–44.

(1991) *The Ancient Mariners: Seafarers and Sea Fighters of the Mediterranean in Ancient Times*, 2nd ed. Princeton.

(1994a) "Mediterranean Communications," in D. M. Lewis, *et al.*, eds., *CAH* ² vi. Cambridge: 512–26.

(1994b) *Ships and Seafaring in Ancient Times*. Austin TX.

Cawkwell, G. L. (1984) "Athenian Naval Power in the Fourth Century," *CQ* 34: 334–45.

Chadwick, J. (1973) "The Berezan Lead Letter," *PCPhS* 19: 35–7.

(1990) "The Pech-Maho Lead," *ZPE* 82: 161–6.

Chandler, A. D., Jr. (1962) *Strategy and Structure: Chapters in the History of the Industrial Enterprise*. Cambridge MA.

(1977) *The Visible Hand: The Managerial Revolution in American Business*. Cambridge MA.

(1990) *Scale and Scope: The Dynamics of Industrial Capitalism*. Cambridge MA.

Clavel-Lévêque, M. (1977) *Marseille grecque. La dynamique d'un impérialisme marchand*. Marseilles.

Clerc, M. (1893) *Les métèques athéniens*. Paris, rp. and cited from New York 1979.

Cohen, E. E. (1973) *Ancient Athenian Maritime Courts*. Princeton.

(1990a) "A Study in Contrast: 'Maritime Loans' and 'Landed Loans' at Athens," in G. Nenci and G. Thür, eds., *Symposion 1988*. Cologne and Vienna: 57–79.

(1990b) "Commercial Lending by Athenian Banks: Cliometric Fallacies and Forensic Methodology," *CPh* 85: 177–90.

(1992) *Athenian Economy and Society: A Banking Perspective*. Princeton.

(1993) "The Athenian Economy," in R. M. Rosen and J. Farrell, eds., *Nomodeiktes: Greek Studies in Honor of Martin Ostwald*. Ann Arbor: 197–206.

Coldstream, J. N. (1977) *Geometric Greece*. London.

(1983) "Gift Exchange in the Eighth Century B.C.," in R. Hägg, ed., *The Greek Renaissance of the Eighth Century B.C.: Tradition and Innovation*. Stockholm: 201–6.

(1990) "The Beginnings of Greek Literacy: An Archaeologist's View," *Ancient History: Resources for Teachers* 20: 144–59.

(1994) "Prospectors and Pioneers: Pithekoussai, Kyme and Central Italy," in G. R. Tsetskhladze and F. De Angelis, eds., *The Archaeology of Greek Colonisation: Essays Dedicated to Sir John Boardman*. Oxford: 47–59.

Collingwood, R. G. (1939) *An Autobiography*. Oxford.

Connor, W. R. (1971) *The New Politicians of Fifth-Century Athens*. Princeton, rp. with a new Preface. Indianapolis 1992.

Cook, J. M. (1982) "The Eastern Greeks," in J. Boardman and N. G. L. Hammond, eds., *CAH* ² iii.3: 196–221.

Crielaard, J. P. (1993) "The Social Organization of Euboean Trade with the Eastern Mediterranean during the 10th to 8th Centuries B.C.," *Pharos* 1: 139–46.

Crone, P. (1989) *Pre-Industrial Societies*. Oxford.

Csapo, E. (1991) "An International Community of Traders in Late 8th–7th c. B.C.: Kommos in Southern Crete," *ZPE* 88: 211–16.

(1993) "A Postscript to 'An International Community of Traders in Late 8th–7th c. B.C. Kommos'," *ZPE* 96: 235–6.

Cunliffe, B. (1988) *Greeks, Romans and Barbarians: Spheres of Interaction.* London.

Davidson, J. (1997) *Courtesans and Fishcakes: The Consuming Passions of Classical Athens.* London.

Davies, J. K. (1971) *Athenian Propertied Families 600–300 B.C.* Oxford.

(1984) *Wealth and the Power of Wealth in Classical Athens.* Salem NH.

(1992) "Society and Economy," in D. M. Lewis, *et al.*, eds., *CAH* ² v: 287–305.

(1993) *Democracy and Classical Greece*, 2nd ed. Cambridge MA.

(1998) "Ancient Economies: Models and Muddles," in H. Parkins and C. Smith, eds., *Trade, Traders and the Ancient City.* London and New York: 225–56.

Diamond, M. (1977) "Ethics and Politics: The American Way," in R. H. Horwitz, ed., *The Moral Foundations of the American Republic.* Charlottesville, rp. in Diamond, M. *As Far as Republican Principles Will Admit*, ed. W. A. Schambra. Washington DC 1992: 337–68, 389–95.

Diller, A. (1937) *Race Mixture among the Greeks.* Urbana IL, rp. and cited from Westport CN 1971.

Donlan, W. (1997) "The Homeric Economy," in I. Morris and B. Powell, eds., *A New Companion to Homer.* Leiden: 649–67.

Ducrey, P. (1968) *Le traitement des prisonniers de guerre dans la Grèce antique.* Paris.

Ehrenberg, V. (1951) *The People of Aristophanes: A Sociology of Attic Comedy*, 2nd ed. Cambridge, rp. and cited from London 1974.

Eiseman, C. J. and Ridgway, B. S. (1987) *The Porticello Shipwreck: A Mediterranean Merchant Vessel of 415–385 B.C.* College Station TX.

Elayi, J. (1987) "Al Mina sur l'Oronte à l'époque perse," in E. Lipinski, ed., *Phoenicia and the East Mediterranean in the First Millennium B.C.* Leuven: 249–66.

(1988) *Pénétration grecque en Phénicie sous l'empire perse.* Nancy.

Engels, D. W. (1990) *Roman Corinth: An Alternative Model for the Classical City.* Chicago.

Engen, D. T. (1996) "Athenian Trade Policy, 415–307 B.C.: Honors and Privileges for Trade-Related Services." Diss. UCLA.

Erxleben, E. (1974) "Die Rolle der Bevölkerungklassen im Aussenhandel Athens im 4. Jahrhundert v.u.Z.," in E. C. Welskopf, ed., *Hellenische Poleis* I. Berlin: 460–520.

Fantasia, U. (1993) "Grano siciliano in Grecia nel v e iv secolo," *ASNP* III 23: 9–31.

Farnell, L. R. (1896) *The Cults of the Greek States* II. Oxford.

(1921) *Greek Hero-Cults and Ideas of Immortality.* Oxford.

Ferguson, W. S. (1944) "The Attic Orgeones," *HThR* 37: 61–140.

Figueira, T. J. (1981) *Aegina: Society and Politics.* Salem NH.

(1986) "*Sitopolai and Sitophylakes* in Lysias' 'Against the Graindealers': Governmental Intervention in the Athenian Economy," *Phoenix* 40: 149–71.

(1994) Review of Cohen (1992), *BMCR* 5: 109–13.

(1998) *The Power of Money: Coinage and Politics in the Athenian Empire.* Philadelphia.

Finley, M. I. [Finkelstein] (1935) "*Emporos, Nauklēros*, and *Kapēlos*: A Prolegomena to the Study of Athenian Trade," *CP* 30: 320–36.

(1962) "The Black Sea and Danubian Regions and the Slave Trade in Antiquity," *Klio* 40: 51–9, rp. with a Bibliographical Addendum in and cited from Finley 1981: 167–75, 271–3.

(1965) "Classical Greece," in *Deuxième conférence internationale d'histoire économique, Aix-en-Provence, 1962* 1: *Trade and Politics in the Ancient World*. Paris: 11–35.

(1975) "Archaeology and History," in *The Use and Abuse of History*. London.

(1977) "Aulos Kapreilios Timotheos, Slave Trader," in *Aspects of Antiquity: Discoveries and Controversies*, 2nd ed. Harmondsworth: 154–66.

(1981) *Economy and Society in Ancient Greece*, ed. B. D. Shaw and R. P. Saller. London.

(1985) *The Ancient Economy*, 2nd ed. Berkeley, rp. with a new forward by I. Morris and cited from this "updated edition." Berkeley 1999.

Foxhall, L. (1998) "Cargoes of the Heart's Desire: The Character of Trade in the Archaic Mediterranean World," in N. Fisher and H. van Wees, eds., *Archaic Greece: New Approaches and New Evidence*. London and Swansea: 295–309.

Gabrielsen, V. (1994) *Financing the Athenian Fleet: Public Taxation and Social Relations*. Baltimore and London.

(1997) *The Naval Aristocracy of Hellenistic Rhodes*. Aarhus.

Garlan, Y. (1978) "Signification historique de la piraterie grecque," *DHA* 4: 1–16.

(1987) "War, Piracy and Slavery in the Greek World," in M. I. Finley, ed., *Classical Slavery*. London: 7–21.

(1988) *Slavery in Classical Greece*, trans. J. Lloyd. Ithaca.

(1989a) "Guerre et esclavage," in *Guerre et économie en Grèce ancienne*. Paris: 74–92.

(1989b) "Les pirates," in *Guerre et économie en Grèce ancienne*. Paris: 173–201.

Garland, R. (1987) *The Piraeus from the Fifth to the First Century B.C.* London.

Garnsey, P. (1984) Review of d'Arms (1981), *CPh* 79:85–8.

(1985) "Grain for Athens," in P. A. Cartledge and F. D. Harvey, eds., *Crux: Essays Presented to G. E. M. de Ste. Croix on his 75th Birthday*. London: 62–75, rp. in and cited from Garnsey (1998) 183–200.

(1988) *Famine and Food Supply in the Greco-Roman World: Responses to Risk and Crisis*. Cambridge.

(1992) "The Yield of the Land in Ancient Greece," in B. Wells, ed., *Agriculture in Greece*. Stockholm: 147–53, rp. in and cited from Garnsey 201–13.

(1998) *Cities, Peasants and Food in Classical Antiquity: Essays in Social and Economic History*, ed. W. Scheidel. Cambridge.

Garnsey, P., Hopkins, K., and Whittaker, C. R., eds. (1983) *Trade in the Ancient Economy*. Berkeley.

Garnsey, P., and Morris, I. (1989) "Risk and the Polis: The Evolution of Institutionalised Responses to Food Supply Problems in the Ancient Greek State," in P. Halstead and J. O'Shea, eds., *Bad Year Economics: Cultural Responses to Risk and Uncertainty*. Cambridge: 98–105.

Garnsey, P., and Whittaker, C. R., eds. (1983) *Trade and Famine in Classical Antiquity*. Cambridge.

Garraty, J. A. (1968) *The New Commonwealth 1887–1890*. New York.

Gauthier, P. (1972) *Symbola: Les étrangers et la justice dans les cités grecques*. Nancy.

(1974) Review of Cohen (1973), *REG* 87: 424–5.

(1976) *Un commentaire historique des* Poroi *de Xénophon*. Geneva and Paris.

(1981) "De Lysias à Aristote (*Ath. pol.*, 51, 4): le commerce du grain à Athènes et les fonctions des sitophylaques," *RD* 59: 5–28.

(1982) Review of Bravo (1980), *RHDFE* 60: 553–76.

Gerber, D. E., ed. and trans. (1999) *Greek Iambic Poetry*. Cambridge MA and London (Loeb Classical Library no. 259).

Gerhardt, P. (1935) *Die attische Metoikie im vierten Jahrhundert*. Diss. Königsberg 1933.

Gernet, L. (1909) *L'approvisionnement d'Athènes en blé au Ve et au IVe siècle*. Paris, rp. and cited from New York 1979.

(1938) "Sur les actions commerciales en droit athénien," *REG* 51: 1–44, rp. in *Droit et société dans la Grèce ancienne*. Paris 1955, rp. and cited from New York 1979: 173–200.

ed. (1954–60) *Démosthène, Plaidoyer civil* I–IV. Paris.

Gernet, L., and Bizos, M. eds. (1924, 1926) *Lysias: Discours* I–II. Paris.

Gill, D. W. J. (1994) "Positivism, Pots and Long-Distance Trade," in I. Morris, ed., *Classical Greece: Ancient Histories and Modern Archaeologies*. Cambridge: 99–107.

Glover, T. R. (1917) *From Pericles to Philip*. London.

Goitein, S. D. (1968–93) *A Mediterranean Society: The Jewish Communities of the Arab World as Portrayed in the Documents of the Cairo Geniza* I–VI (V and VI co-authored with P. Sanders). Berkeley.

ed. and trans. (1973) *Letters of Medieval Jewish Traders*. Princeton.

Gomme, A. W. (1937) "Traders and Manufacturers," in *Essays in Greek History and Literature*. Oxford.

(1957) "Interpretations of Some Poems of Alkaios and Sappho," *JHS* 77: 255–66.

Goody, J. (1996) *The East in the West*. Cambridge.

Goudineau, C. (1983) "Marseilles, Rome and Gaul from the Third to First Century BC," in P. Garnsey, *et al.*, eds., *Trade in the Ancient Economy*. Berkeley: 76–86, 192–6.

Graham, A. J. (1982a) "The Colonial Expansion of Greece," in J. Boardman and N. G. L. Hammond, eds., *CAH*² III.3: 83–162.

(1982b) "The Western Greeks," in J. Boardman and N. G. L. Hammond, eds., *CAH*² III.3: 163–95.

(1986) "The Historical Interpretation of Al Mina," *DHA* 12: 51–65.

Gras, M. (1985) *Trafics tyrrhéniens archaïques*. Rome.

Gras, M., *et al.* (1989) *L'univers phénicien*. Paris.

Grierson, P. (1959) "Commerce in the Dark Ages: a Critique of the Evidence," *Transactions of the Royal Historical Society* 9:125.

Grote, G. (1888) *A History of Greece* I. London: v–vi.

Günther, L.-M. (1993) "Die karthagische Aristokratie und ihre Uberseepolitik im 6. und 5. Jh. v. Chr.," *Klio* 75: 76–84.

Haas, C. J. (1985) "Athenian Naval Power before Themistocles," *Historia* 34: 29–46.

Habicht, C. (1957) "Samische Volksbeschlüsse der hellenistischen Zeit," *AM* 72: 180–95.

Hadjidaki, E. (1996) "Underwater Excavations of a Late Fifth Century Merchant Ship at Alonnesos, Greece: The 1991–1993 Seasons," *BCH* 120: 561–93.

Hansen, M. (Marianne) (1984) "Athenian Maritime Trade in the 4th Century B.C.: Operation and Finance," *C&M* 35: 71–92.

Hansen, M. H. (1983) "Two Notes on the Athenian Dikai Emporikai," in P. Dimakis, ed., *Symposion 1979*. Cologne: 167–75.

Harding, P. (1995) "Athenian Foreign Policy in the Fourth Century," *Klio* 77: 105–25.

Harris, E. M. (1988) "The Date of Apollodorus' Speech against Timotheus and Its Implications for Athenian History and Legal Procedure," *AJP* 109: 44–52.

(1989) "The Liability of Business Partners in Athenian Law: The Dispute between Lycon and Megacleides ([Dem.] 52.20–1)," *CQ* 39: 339–43.

Harris, W. V. (1980) "Towards a Study of the Roman Slave Trade," in J. H. D'Arms and E. C. Kopff, eds., *The Seaborne Commerce of Ancient Rome: Studies in Archaeology and History*. Rome: 117–40.

(1989) *Ancient Literacy*. Cambridge MA.

(1996) "Writing and Literacy in the Archaic Greek City," in J. H. M. Strubbe, et al., eds., *ENERGEIA: Studies On Ancient History and Epigraphy Presented to H. W. Pleket*. Amsterdam: 57–77.

Harrison, A. R. W. (1968 and 1971) *The Law of Athens*. Oxford I (1968) and II (1971).

Harvey, F. D. (1964) "The Use of Written Documents in the Business Life of Classical Athens," *Pegasus* 2: 4–14.

(1966) "Literacy in the Athenian Democracy," *REG* 79: 585–635.

(1976) "The Maritime Loan in Eupolis' 'Marikas' (P. Oxy. 2741)," *ZPE* 23: 231–3.

Hasebroek, J. (1923) "Die Betriebsformen des griechischen Handels im IV. Jahrh.," *Hermes* 58: 393–425.

(1928) *Staat und Handel im alten Griechenland*. Tübingen. Page references are to the translation by L. M. Fraser and D. C. Macgregor (1933) *Trade and Politics in Ancient Greece*. London.

(1931) *Griechische Wirtschafts- und Gesellschaftsgeschichte bis zur Perserzeit*. Tübingen.

Heichelheim, F. M. (1964) *An Ancient Economic History* II, trans. J. Stevens. Leiden.

Heilbroner, R., and Singer. A. (1999) *The Economic Transformation of America: 1600 to the Present*, 4th ed. Fort Worth.

Hill, G. F. (1951) *Sources for Greek History between the Persian and Peloponnesian Wars*, new ed. by R. Meiggs and A. Andrewes. Oxford.

Hirschman, A. D. (1977) *The Passions and the Interests: Political Arguments for Capitalism before Its Triumph*. Princeton.

Hodge, A. T. (1998) *Ancient Greek Finance*. London.

Hooker, J. T. (1989) "Gifts in Homer," *BICS* 36: 79–90.

Hopkins, K. (1983) "Introduction," in P. Garnsey *et al.*, eds., *Trade in the Ancient Economy*. Berkeley: ix–xxv.

Hopper, R. J. (1979) *Trade and Industry in Classical Greece*. London.

Hornblower, S. (1991a) *A Commentary on Thucydides* i. Oxford.

   (1991b) *The Greek World 479–323 B.C.*, rev. ed. London and New York.

   and Greenstock, M. C., eds. and trans. (1983) *The Athenian Empire*, 3rd ed. London.

Humphreys, S. C. (1978) "Homo Politicus and Homo Economicus," in *Anthropology and the Greeks*. London: 159–74.

Isager, S., and Hansen, M. H. (1975) *Aspects of Athenian Society in the Fourth Century B.C.* Odense.

Jackson, A. (1993) "War and Raids for Booty in the World of Odysseus," in J. Rich and G. Shipley, eds., *War and Society in the Greek World*. London and New York: 64–76.

J.A.C.T (The Joint Association of Classical Teachers) (1984) *The World of Athens: An Introduction to Classical Athenian Culture*. Cambridge.

Jameson, M. (1983) "Famine in the Greek World," in P. Garnsey and C. R. Whittaker, eds., *Trade and Famine in Classical Antiquity*. Cambridge: 6–16.

Jeffrey, L. H. (1976) *Archaic Greece*. London.

Johnston, A. W. (1979) *Trademarks on Greek Vases*. Warminster UK.

   (1983) "The Extent and Use of Literacy: The Archaeological Evidence," in R. Hägg, ed., *The Greek Renaissance of the Eighth Century B.C.: Tradition and Innovation*. Stockholm: 63–8.

   (1990) "Supplement," in L. H. Jeffery, *The Local Scripts of Archaic Greece*, 2nd ed. Oxford.

Johnston, P. (1985) *Ship and Boat Models in Ancient Greece*. Annapolis.

Jones, A. H. M. (1940) *Athenian Democracy*. Oxford.

Jones, P. (1997) *The Italian City-State: From Commune to Signoria*. Oxford.

Jordan, B. (1975) *The Athenian Navy in the Classical Period*. Berkeley.

Katzev, M. L. (1972) "The Kyrenia Ship," in G. F. Bass, ed., *A History of Seafaring Based on Underwater Archaeology*. New York: 50–2.

Keen, A. (1993) "Grain for Athens," *Electronic Antiquity* 1.6.

Kingsley, B. M. (1986) "Harpalos in the Megarid (333–331 B.C.) and the Grain Shipments from Cyrene," *ZPE* 66: 165–77.

Knorringa, H. (1926) *Emporos: Data on Trade and Traders in Greek Literature from Homer to Aristotle*. Amsterdam.

Kopcke, G. (1990) *Handel*. Göttingen.

Krentz, P., ed. and trans. (1989) *Xenophon, Hellenika I–II.3.10*. Warminster UK.

Lancel, S. (1995) *Carthage: A History*, trans. A. Nevill. Oxford.

Lewis, D. M. (1959) "Attic Manumissions," *Hesperia* 28: 208–38.

   (1960) "Apollo Delios," *BSA* 55: 190–4.

   (1968) "Dedications of Phialai at Athens," *Hesperia* 37: 368–80.

   (1975) Review of Gauthier (1972), *CR* 25: 262–3.

Lloyd-Jones, H. (1975) *Females of the Species*. London.

Lombardo, M. (1988) "Marchands, transactions économiques, écriture," in M. Detienne, ed., *Les savoirs de l'écriture. En Grèce ancienne.* Lille: 159–87.

MacDonald, B. R. (1981) "The Phanosthenes Decree: Taxes and Timber in Late Fifth-Century Athens," *Hesperia* 50: 141–6.

   (1983) "The Megarian Decree," *Historia* 32: 385.

MacDowell, D. M. (1976) Review of Cohen (1973), *CR* 26: 84–5.

   (1978) *The Law in Classical Athens.* London.

McGraw, T. K., ed. (1988) *The Essential Alfred Chandler: Essays Toward a Historical Theory of Big Business.* Cambridge MA.

McKechnie, P. (1989) *Outsiders in the Greek Cities in the Fourth Century BC.* London and New York.

Mann, M. (1986) *The Sources of Social Power* I: *A History of Power from the Beginning to A.D. 1760.* Cambridge.

   (1993) *The Sources of Social Power* II: *The Rise of Classes and Nation-States, 1760–1914.* Cambridge.

Marek, C. (1984) *Die Proxenie.* Frankfurt am Main.

   (1985) "Handel und Proxenie," *MBAH* 4: 67–78.

Meiggs, R. (1972) *The Athenian Empire.* Oxford.

   (1982) *Trees and Timber in the Ancient Mediterranean World.* Oxford.

Meikle, S. (1995) *Aristotle's Economic Thought.* Oxford.

Mele, A. (1979) *Il commercio greco arcaico. Prexis ed emporie.* Naples.

   (1986) "Pirateria, commercio e aristocrazia: Replica a Benedetto Bravo," *DHA* 12: 67–109.

Meritt, B. D. (1945) "Attic Inscriptions of the Fifth Century," *Hesperia* 14: 129–32.

Michell, H. (1957) *The Economics of Ancient Greece,* 2nd ed. Cambridge.

Miller, M. C. (1997) *Athens and Persia in the Fifth Century BC: A Study in Cultural Receptivity.* Cambridge.

Millett, P. (1983) "Maritime Loans and the Structure of Credit in Fourth-Century Athens," in P. Garnsey, *et. al.,* eds., *Trade in the Ancient Economy.* Berkeley: 36–52.

   (1984) "Hesiod and His World," *PCPhS* 30: 84–115.

   (1989) "Patronage and its Avoidance in Classical Athens," in A. Wallace-Hadrill, ed., *Patronage in Ancient Society.* London and New York: 15–47.

   (1990) "Sale, Credit and Exchange in Athenian Law and Society," in P. Cartledge *et al.,* eds., *Nomos: Essays in Athenian Law, Politics and Society.* Cambridge: 167–94.

   (1991) *Lending and Borrowing in Ancient Athens.* Cambridge.

Morel, J.-P. (1975) "L'expansion phocéenne en occident: dix années de recherches (1966–1975)," *BCH* 99: 853–96.

   (1984) "Greek Colonization in Italy and the West (Problems of Evidence and Interpretation)," in T. Hackens, *et al.,* eds., *Crossroads of the Mediterranean: Archaeologia Transatlantica* II. Providence RI and Louvain-La-Neuve: 123–61.

Morris, I. (1986) "Gift and Commodity in Archaic Greece," *Man* 21: 1–17.

   (1994) "The Athenian Economy Twenty Years after *The Ancient Economy,*" *CPh* 89: 351–66.

(1999) "Foreword" to M. I. Finley, *The Ancient Economy*, updated ed. Berkeley: ix–xxxvi.

Morrow, G. R. (1960) *Plato's Cretan City*. Princeton.

Mossé, C. (1962) *La fin de la démocratie athénienne*. Paris.

(1983) "The World of the *Emporium* in the Private Speeches of Demosthenes," in P. Garnsey, *et al.*, eds., *Trade in the Ancient Economy*. Berkeley: 53–63.

Moysey, R. A. (1976) "The Date of the Strato of Sidon Decree (*IG* ii² 141)," *AJAH* 1: 182–9.

Murray, O. (1993) *Early Greece*, 2nd ed. Cambridge MA.

Mylonas, K. D. (1894) "ΕΠΙΓΡΑΦΗ ΕΚ ΤΡΟΙΖΗΝΟΣ," *BCH* 18: 137–44.

Newman, W. L., ed. (1887a) *The Politics of Aristotle* i. Oxford.

Newman, W. L., ed. (1887b) *The Politics of Aristotle* iv. Oxford.

Niemeyer, H. G. (1989) *Das frühe Karthago und die phönizische Expansion in Mittelmeerraum*. Göttingen.

(1990) "The Phoenicians in the Mediterranean: A Non-Greek Model for Expansion and Settlement in Antiquity," in J.-P. Descoeudres, ed., *Greek Colonists and Native Populations*. Canberra and Oxford: 469–89.

Nisbet, R. (1988) "Tocqueville's Ideal Types," in A. S. Eisenstadt, ed., *Reconsidering Tocqueville's Democracy in America*. New Brunswick NJ: 171–91.

Nolan, P., and Lenski, G. (1999) *Human Societies: An Introduction to Macrosociology*, 8th ed. New York.

Nowag, W. (1983) *Raub und Beute in der archaischen Zeit der Griechen*. Frankfurt am Main.

Oikonomides, A. N. (1978) "The Alleged 'Carthaginian Blockade' of the Western Mediterranean and the Adventures of a Massaliot 'Tramp Ship' (Demosthenes xxxii)," *AncW* 1: 83–8.

Ormerod, H. A. (1924, rp. 1967) *Piracy in the Ancient World*. Chicago.

Osborne, M. J. (1981–3) *Naturalization in Athens* i (1981), ii (1982), iii–iv (1983). Brussels.

Osborne, R. (1987) *Classical Landscape with Figures: The Ancient Greek City and its Countryside*. London.

(1991) "Pride and Prejudice, Sense and Subsistence: Exchange and Society in the Greek City," in J. Rich and A. Wallace-Hadrill, eds., *City and Country in the Ancient World*. London and New York: 119–45.

(1996) "Pots, Trade and the Archaic Greek Economy," *Antiquity* 70: 31–44.

(1998) "Early Greek Colonization? The Nature of Greek Settlement in the West," in N. Fisher and H. van Wees, eds., *Archaic Greece: New Approaches and New Evidence*. London and Swansea: 251–69.

Page, D. (1955) *Sappho and Alcaeus*. Oxford.

Paley, F. A., and Sandys, J. E., eds. (1896 and 1898) *Select Private Orations of Demosthenes*, 3rd ed. rev. Cambridge: i (1898), ii (1896), rp. as a single volume New York 1979.

Paoli, U. (1930) *Studi di diritto attico*. Florence.

(1933) *Studi sul processo attico*. Padua.

Parke, H. W. (1967) *The Oracles of Zeus*. Cambridge MA.

Parker, R. (1996) *Athenian Religion: A History*. Oxford.

Parkins, H., ed. (1997) *Roman Urbanism: Beyond the Consumer City*. London.

Pearson, L., ed., (1972) *Demosthenes: Six Private Speeches*. Norman OK.

Pečirka, J. (1966) *The Formula for the Grant of Enktēsis in Attic Inscriptions*. Prague.

Perlman, S. (1958) "A Note on the Political Implications of Proxenia in the Fourth Century B.C.," *CQ* 8: 185–91.

Pleket, H. W., ed. (1969) *Epigraphica II: Texts on the Social History of the Greek World*. Leiden.

Poland, F. (1909) *Geschichte des Griechischen Vereinswesens*. Leipzig.

Popham, M. R. (1994) "Precolonisation: Early Greek Contact with the East," in G. R. Tsetskhladze and F. De Angelis, eds., *The Archaeology of Greek Colonisation: Essays Dedicated to Sir John Boardman*. Oxford: 11–34.

Popham, M. R., and Lemos, I. S. (1995) "A Euboean Warrior Trader," *OJA* 14: 151–7.

Porter, G. (1992) *The Rise of Big Business: 1860–1920*. Arlington Heights IL.

Pouilloux, J. (1954) *Recherches sur l'histoire et les cultes de Thasos* I. Paris.

ed. and trans. (1960) *Choix d'inscriptions grecques: Textes, traductions, et notes*. Paris.

Pringsheim, F. (1916) *Der Kauf mit fremdem Geld*. Leipzig, rp. and cited from New York 1979.

Pritchard, D. (1991) "Thucydides, Class-Struggle and Empire," *Ancient History: Resources for Teachers* 21: 77–85.

Pritchett, W. K. (1971) *Ancient Greek Military Practices* I, rp. as *The Greek State at War* I. Berkeley 1974.

(1991) *The Greek State at War V*. Berkeley.

Raaflaub, K. (1997a) "Homeric Society," in I. Morris and B. Powell, eds., *A New Companion to Homer*. Leiden: 624–48.

(1997b) "Soldiers, Citizens, and the Evolution of the Greek *Polis*," in L. G. Mitchell and P. J. Rhodes, eds., *The Development of the Polis in Archaic Greece*. London and New York: 49–59.

(1998) "A Historian's Headache: How to Read 'Homeric Society'?," in N. Fisher and H. van Wees, eds., *Archaic Greece: New Approaches and New Evidence*. London and Swansea: 169–93.

Rahe, P. (1992) *Republics Ancient and Modern: Classical Republicanism and the American Revolution*. Chapel Hill.

(1994a) *Republics Ancient and Modern* I: *The Ancien Régime in Classical Greece*. Chapel Hill.

(1994b) *Republics Ancient and Modern* II: *New Modes and Orders in Early Modern Political Thought*. Chapel Hill.

(1994c) *Republics Ancient and Modern* III: *Inventions of Prudence: Constituting the American Regime*. Chapel Hill.

Reden, S. von (1995a) *Exchange in Ancient Greece*. London.

(1995b) "The Piraeus – A World Apart," *G & R* 42: 24–37.

Redfield, J. (1986) "The Development of the Market in Archaic Greece," in B. L. Anderson and A. J. H. Latham, eds., *The Market in History*. London: 29–57.

Reed, C. (1984) "Maritime Traders in the Archaic Greek World: A Typology of Those Engaged in the Long Distance Transfer of Goods by Sea," *AncW* 10: 31–44.

Rhodes, P. J. (1981) *A Commentary on the Aristotelian Athenaion Politeia*. Oxford, rp. with addenda and cited from Oxford 1993.

ed. and trans. (1986) *Greek Historical Inscriptions 359–323 B.C.*, 2nd ed. London.

(1995) "Judicial Procedures in Fourth-Century Athens: Improvement or Simply Change?," in W. Eder, ed., *Die athenische Demokratie im 4 Jahrhundert v. Chr.* Stuttgart: 303–19.

Ridgway, D. (1988) "The Etruscans," in J. Boardman, *et al.*, eds., *CAH* ² IV: 634–75.

(1992a) "Demaratus and His Predecessors," in G. Kopcke and I. Tokumaru, eds., *Greece and Egypt between East and West: 10th–8th Centuries BC*. Mainz: 85–92.

(1992b) *The First Western Greeks*. Cambridge.

(1994) "Phoenicians and Greeks in the West: a View from Pithekoussai," in G. R. Tsetskhladze and F. De Angelis, eds., *The Archaeology of Greek Colonisation: Essays Dedicated to Sir John Boardman*. Oxford: 35–46.

Rihll, T. (1993) "War, Slavery, and Settlement in Early Greece," in J. Rich and G. Shipley, eds., *War and Society in the Greek World*. London and New York: 77–107.

(1996) "The Origin and Establishment of Ancient Greek Slavery," in M. L. Bush, ed., *Serfdom and Slavery: Studies in Legal Bondage*. London and New York: 89–111.

Ritzer, G. (1996) *The McDonaldization of Society*, rev. ed. Thousand Oaks CA.

Roebuck, C. (1950) "The Grain Trade between Greece and Egypt," *CPh* 45: 236–47.

Roover, R. de (1963) *The Rise and Decline of the Medici Bank 1397–1494*. Cambridge MA.

Rouillard, P. (1991) *Les Grecs et la péninsule ibérique du VIIIe au IVe siécle avant Jésus-Christ*. Paris.

Roy, J. (1998) "The Threat from the Piraeus," in P. Cartledge, *et.al.*, eds., *Kosmos: Essays in Order, Conflict and Community in Classical Athens*. Cambridge: 191–202.

Ste. Croix, G. E. M. de (1961) "Notes on Jurisdiction in the Athenian Empire," *CQ* 11: 94–112.

(1972) *The Origins of the Peloponnesian War*. London.

(1974) "Ancient Greek and Roman Maritime Loans," in H. Edey and B. S. Yamey, eds., *Debts, Credits, Finance and Profits*. London: 41–59.

(1981) *The Class Struggle in the Ancient Greek World from the Archaic Age to the Arab Conquests*. Ithaca NY.

Sallares, R. (1991) *The Ecology of the Ancient Greek World*. London.

Saller, R. (1991) Review of Engels (1990), *CPh* 86: 351–7.

Salmon, J. B. (1984) *Wealthy Corinth: A History of the City to 338 BC*. Oxford.

Salviat, F. (1986) "Le vin de Thasos: amphores, vin et sources écrites," in J.-Y. Empereur and Y. Garlan, eds., *Recherches sur les amphores grecques = BCH Suppl.* 13. Paris: 145–96.

Sarikakis, T. C. (1986) "Commercial Relations between Chios and Other Greek Cities in Antiquity," in J. Boardman and C. E. Vaphopoulou-Richardson, eds., *A Conference at the Homereion in Chios 1984*: 121–31.

Saunders, T. J. (1962) "The Metic in Plato's Laws." Diss. Cambridge.

Sčěglov (=Chtcheglov), A. (1990) "Le commerce du blé dans le Pontseptentrional (seconde moitié du viième–vème siècle)," in O. Lordkipanidzé and P. Lévêque, eds., *Le Pont-Euxin vu par les Grecs: Sources écrites et archéologie*. Paris: 141–59.

Schäfer, A. (1858) *Demosthenes und Sein Zeit* iii 2: *Beilagen*. Leipzig, rp. and cited from New York 1979.

Schlaifer, R. (1940) "Notes on Athenian Public Cults," *HSPh* 51: 233–5.

Schweigert, E. (1938) "Inscriptions from the North Slope of the Acropolis," *Hesperia* 7: 269–70.

(1939) "Greek Inscriptions," *Hesperia* 8: 1–90.

(1940) "Greek Inscriptions," *Hesperia* 9: 309–57.

Schwenk, C. J. (1985) *Athens in the Age of Alexander: The Dated Laws & Decrees of the 'Lykourgan Era' 338–322 B.C.* Chicago.

Seager, R. (1966) "Lysias against the Corndealers," *Historia* 15: 172–84.

Sealey, R. (1991) "An Athenian Decree about the Megarians," in M. A. Flower and M. Toher, eds., *Georgica: Greek Studies in Honour of George Cawkwell* = *BICS Suppl.* 58. London: 152–8.

Shefton, B. B. (1994) "Massalia and Colonization in the North-Western Mediterranean," in G. R. Tsetskhladze and F. De Angelis, eds., *The Archaeology of Greek Colonisation: Essays Dedicated to Sir John Boardman*. Oxford: 61–86.

(1995) "Greek Imports at the Extremities of the Mediterranean, West and East: Reflections on the Case of Iberia in the Fifth Century BC," in B. Cunliffe and S. Keay, eds., *Social Complexity and the Development of Towns in Iberia* = *PBA* 86: 127–55.

Shipley, G. (1987) *A History of Samos 800–188 BC*. Oxford.

Shipton, K. M. W. (1994) Review of Cohen (1992), *The Financial History Review* 1: 81–2.

(1997) "The Private Banks in Fourth-Century B.C. Athens: A Reappraisal," *CQ* 47: 396–422.

Simms, R. R. (1989) "Isis in Classical Athens," *CJ* 84: 216–21.

Snodgrass, A. M. (1980) *Archaic Greece: The Age of Experiment*. London.

(1983) "Heavy Freight in Archaic Greece," in P. Garnsey, *et al.*, eds., *Trade in the Ancient Economy*. Berkeley: 16–26, 182–3.

(1993) "The 'Hoplite Reform' Revisited," *DHA* 1993: 47–61.

(1994) "The Nature and Standing of the Early Western Colonies," in G. R. Tsetskhladze and F. De Angelis, eds., *The Archaeology of Greek Colonisation: Essays Dedicated to Sir John Boardman*. Oxford: 1–10.

Souza, P. de (1995) "Greek Piracy," in A. Powell, ed., *The Greek World*. London and New York: 179–98.

(1998) "Towards Thalassocracy?," in N. Fisher and H. van Wees, eds., *Archaic Greece: New Approaches and New Evidence*. London and Swansea: 271–93.

(1999) *Piracy in the Graeco-Roman World*. Cambridge.

Stanley, P. V. (1980) "Two Thasian Wine Laws: A Reexamination," *AncW* 3: 88–93.

(1986) "The Function of Trade in Homeric Society," *MBAH* 5: 5–15.

(1990) "The Purpose of Loans in Ancient Athens: A Reexamination," *MBAH* 9: 57–73.

Starr, C. (1977) *The Economic and Social Growth of Early Greece*. New York.

(1982) "Economic and Social Conditions in the Greek World," in J. Boardman and N. G. L. Hammond, eds., *CAH*² III.1: 417–41.

Steffy, J. R. (1987) "The Kyrenia Ship: An Interim Report on Its Hull Construction," *AJA* 89: 71–101.

Stronk, J. P. (1992–3) "Greek Sailing Merchant-Ships *c*. 500–330 BC," *Talanta* 24–5: 117–40.

Stroud, R. S. (1974) "An Athenian Law on Silver Coinage," *Hesperia* 43: 157–88.

(1998) *The Athenian Grain-Tax Law of 374/3 B.C.* = *Hesperia Suppl*. 29. Princeton.

Sullivan, R. D. (1996) "Psammetichus I and the Foundation of Naukratis," in W. D. E. Coulson, *Ancient Naukratis* II: *The Survey at Naukratis and Environs Pt*. 1: *The Survey at Naukratis*. Oxford: 177–95.

Takabatake, S. (1988) "The Idea of *Xenos* in Classical Athens: Its Structure and Peculiarities," in T. Yuge and M. Doi, eds., *Forms of Control and Subordination in Antiquity*. Leiden: 449–55.

Tandy, D. W. (1997) *Warriors into Traders: The Power of the Market in Early Greece*. Berkeley.

Thompson, W. E. (1978) "The Athenian Investor," *RSC* 26: 403–23.

(1979) "A View of Athenian Banking," *MH* 36: 224–41.

(1982) "The Athenian Entrepreneur," *AC* 51: 53–85.

Tocqueville, A. de (1969) *Democracy in America*, ed. J. P. Mayer, trans. G. Lawrence. New York.

Tod, M. N. (1948) *Historical Inscriptions* II. Oxford.

Todd, S. C. (1993) *The Shape of Athenian Law*. Oxford.

Tracy, S. V. (1995) *Athenian Democracy in Transition: Attic Letter-Cutters of 340–290 B.C*. Berkeley.

Trevett, J. C. (1991) "The Date of [Demosthenes] 49: A Re-examination," *Phoenix* 45: 21–7.

(1992) *Apollodorus the Son of Pasion*. Oxford.

Tsetskhladze, G. R. (1994) "Greek Penetration of the Black Sea," in G. R. Tsetskhladze and F. De Angelis, eds., *The Archaeology of Greek Colonisation: Essays Dedicated to Sir John Boardman*. Oxford: 111–35.

Tuplin, C. (1986) "ΣΥΜΠΡΙΑΣΘΑΙ in Lysias 'Against the Corndealers'," *Hermes* 114: 495–8.

Vélissaropoulos, J. (1977) "Le monde de l'emporion," *DHA* 3: 61–5.

(1980) *Les nauclères Grecs: Recherches sur les institutions maritimes en Grèce et dans l'Orient hellénisé*. Geneva and Paris.

Vokotopoulou, I., and Christidis, A.-P. (1995) "A Cypriot Graffito on an SOS Amphora from Mende, Chalcidice," *Kadmos* 34: 5–12.

Walbank, M. B. (1978) *Athenian Proxenies of the Fifth Century B.C.* Toronto.

    (1980) "Greek Inscriptions from the Athenian Agora," *Hesperia* 49: 251–7.

    (1985) "Athens, Carthage and Tyre (*IG* ii² 342+)," *ZPE* 59: 107–11.

    (1987) "*IG* ii², 407 and *SEG* xxxii, 94. Honours for a Milesian Grain-Dealer," *ZPE* 67: 165–6.

    (1990) "Notes on Attic Decrees," *BSA* 85: 435–47.

Wallinga, H. (1964) "Nautika (1): The Unit of Capacity for Ancient Ships," *Mnemosyne* 17: 1–40.

Weber, M. (1976) *Wirtschaft und Gesellschaft*, 5th rev. ed., J. Winckelmann, ed. Tübingen.

    (1978) *Economy and Society: An Outline of Interpretive Sociology* I–II, trans. G. Roth and C. Wittich. Berkeley.

Weibe, R. H. (1967) *The Search for Order.* New York.

Westlake, H. D. (1948) "Athenian Food Supplies from Euboea," *CR* 62: 2–5.

Wheeler, E. L. (1992–3) Review of Pritchett (1991), *CJ* 88: 410–18.

Whitbread, I. K. (1995) *Greek Transport Amphorae: A Petrological and Archaeological Study.* Athens.

Whitby, M. (1998) "The Grain Trade of Athens in the Fourth Century BC," in H. Parkins and C. Smith, eds., *Trade, Traders and the Ancient City.* London and New York: 102–28.

Whitehead, D. (1977) *The Ideology of the Athenian Metic.* Cambridge.

    (1986) "The Ideology of the Athenian Metic: Some Pendants and a Reappraisal," *PCPhS* 32: 145–58.

Whittaker, C. R. (1978) "Carthaginian Imperialism in the Fifth and Fourth Centuries," in P. Garnsey and C. R. Whittaker, eds., *Imperialism in the Ancient World.* Cambridge: 59–90.

    (1990) "The Consumer City Revisited: The *Vicus* and the City," *JRA* 3:110 18.

    (1995) "Do Theories of the Ancient City Matter?," in T. Cornell and K. Lomas, eds., *Urban Society in Roman Italy.* New York: 9–26

Wickersham, J., and Verbrugghe, G., eds. and trans. (1973) *Greek Historical Documents: The Fourth Century B.C.* Toronto.

Wiedemann, T., ed. and trans. (1981) *Greek and Roman Slavery.* London.

Wilhelm, A. (1889) "Attische Psephismen," *Hermes* 24: 110–25.

Wilson, J.-P. (1997) "The Nature of Greek Overseas Settlements in the Archaic Period: *Emporion* or *apoikia*," in L. G. Mitchell and P. J. Rhodes, eds., *The Development of the Polis in Archaic Greece.* London and New York: 199–207.

Ziebarth, E. (1896) *Das Griechische Vereinswesen.* Stuttgart.

    (1929) *Beiträge zur Geschichte des Seeraubs und Seehandels im alten Griechenland.* Hamburg.

Index locorum

A LITERARY TEXTS

General index

NOTE: Citations of a place ("Megara"), its inhabitants ("Megarians"), or the adjective "Megarian" are all indexed below under the name of the place alone. Modern scholars are mentioned only where their views figure significantly in the text or notes. Ancient names appearing in the "Catalogue of *Emporoi* and *Nauklēroi*" (Appendix 4) are listed with their Catalogue number.